Landless Voices

A New Generation

The

Movimento dos Sem Terra

of Brazil

in

Song and Poetry

Edited by

Else R. P. Vieira

Translated by Bernard McGuirk

London

Spanish, Portuguese and Latin American Studies in the Humanities

Landless Voices: A New Generation
The Movimento dos Sem Terra of Brazil in Song and Poetry
Edited by Else R. P. Vieira
Translated by Bernard McGuirk

The rights of Else R. P. Vieira and Bernard McGuirk to be identified as authors in this work have been asserted by them in accordance with the Copyrights, Designs and Patents Act, 1988.

Individual essays and poems © the contributors and translators, 2020.

© SPLASH EDITIONS, 2020, an imprint of *Jetstone* Publishers Ltd.

Cover design by Francesca Pasciolla

ISBN 9781912399147

Dedicatória

A Sebastião Salgado. Seu compromisso com os oprimidos Sem Terra tem um existência continuada, nos alarmantes dias ora vividos, em seus projetos contra a crescente vulnerabilidade dos nativos da Amazônia.

Para os adolescentes das escolas dos assentamentos de reforma agrária Marcos Freire e Contestado, do Paraná, pelas promessas de um novo Brasil.

Para a Escola Estadual do Campo Iraci Salete Strosak e a Escola Estadual do Campo Contestado, oásis de lucidez na educação brasileira.

Para os diretores Rudison L. Ladislau e Samuel A. da Silva, pela destemida luta pelo respeito aos direitos humanos.

Para Sônia Schwendler, solidária na pesquisa e promoção da emancipação de gênero no Brasil.

Agradecimentos

A organizadora agradece ao Newton Trust e a British Academy pelo patrocínio ao Projeto 'Gender and Education in Brazil's Rural Areas' (2015-2018), à Faculdade de Educação e ao Núcleo de Estudos de Gênero da Universidade Federal do Paraná e à School of Modern Languages, Queen Mary University of London pela coparticipação no Projeto; às monitoras da Faculdade de Educação da Universidade Federal do Paraná e aos 70 professores das escolas secundárias do campo do estado do Paraná pela inestimável contribuição ao Projeto; a Bernard McGuirk pela tradução e a Francesca Pasciolla e Macdonald Daly pela assessoria técnica.

*

Dedication

To Sebastião Salgado. His commitment to the oppressed of the Sem Terra continues, in the alarming times of the present, in his projects combatting the growing vulnerability of the native peoples of Amazônia.

To the adolescents from the schools in the settlements of agrarian reform Marcos Freire and Contestado, in Paraná, for the promises of a new Brazil.

To the Iraci Salete Strosak Rural State School and the Contestado Rural State School, oasis of discernment in Brazilian Education.

To the headmasters Rudison l. Ladislau e Samuel A. da Silva, for the brave struggle for respect for human rights.

To Sônia Schwendler, for the joint trajectory in research and promotion of gender emancipation in Brazil.

Acknowledgments

The Editor wishes to acknowledge the Newton Trust and the British Academy for sponsoring the Project 'Gender and Education in Brazil's Rural Areas' (2015-2018), the School of Education and Nucleus of Gender Studies of the Federal University of Paraná and the School of Modern Languages, Queen Mary University of London for the co-participation in the Project; to the trainees of the School of Education of the Federal University of Paraná and the 70 teachers from the Rural State Schools in Paraná for their invaluable contribution to the Project; to Bernard McGuirk for the translation and to Francesca Pasciolla and Macdonald Daly for their editorial expertise.

Sumário

Ícones, símbolos e monumentos

Contents

A morte como horizonte de vida

A mulher sem-terra

Death as life's horizon

The landless woman

A luta pela terra: despossessão, viagens, ocupação, despejo

Acampamentos e resistência: as casas de lona preta

The struggle for land: dispossession, journeys, occupation, eviction

Encampments and resistance: the houses of black plastic

Assentamentos: o afago da terra

Diversidade de gênero: canções e poemas

Letras compostas por estudantes do ensino secundário

Settlements: the caress of the land

Gender diversity: lyrics and poems

Lyrics composed by secondary school students

Notas

Notes

Luta pela terra e educação: crianças empacotando os livros quando sua escola foi destruída pela polícia em agosto de 2020, no Quilombo do Campo do Meio, em Minas Gerais, produtor de café orgânico, onde se encontram 11 acampamentos dos Sem Terra.
Foto de Gean Gomes. Reprodução autorizada pelo Setor de Comunicação do MST.

Struggle for land and education: schoolchildren packing their books, when the school was destroyed by the police in August 2020, in the *quilombo* (former community of run-away slaves) Campo do Meio, in Minas Gerais, producer of organic coffee and home to 11 encampments of *Sem Terra* workers.
Photo by Gean Gomes. Reproduced with permission of the MST Communication Sector.

Free to think, free to sing:
A new generation of landless voices on gender diversity

Else R. P. Vieira

> Attention! Attention! It is a new era in Brazil:
> Girl is princess and wears pink and boy who is prince wears blue.

Damares Alves, Minister for Women, the Family and Human Rights, 2019

> From the beginning of creation, God made them male and female.

Mark 10: 6

> Unhappy, agonizing, out of the way […] I ask myself
> Why was I born wrong?

Anonymous Adolescent Student's Confession, 2015

Dressed in ceremonial white for her inauguration as the Minister for Women, the Family and Human Rights in Jair Bolsonaro's Presidency of Brazil (2019-2022), blatantly overlooking the full spectrum of colours of the rainbow flag, proudly did Damares Alves, a former Evangelical pastor and ardent defender of a Genesis ideology, reinforce a heteronormative gender script.[1] Her naïve use of a gender-colour coding associated with babies actually masks her anti-gender crusade, which disqualifies and pathologizes homosexuals and criminalizes struggles for gender equality: 'gays want to take the Bible out of circulation in Brazil', 'sex between women is an aberration comparable to sex with animals', 'homosexuals are sick' (in Maranhão Fº and De Franco, 2019: 315). The Minister added in the ceremony that 'the State is lay, but this Minister is terribly Christian' and a believer 'in God's designs', in addition to other statements that 'the time has come for the Church to rule the country' (in Maranhão Fº and De Franco, 2019: 313-15). Alves is but one of the religious fundamentalists and extreme right factions in Brazilian politics that saw in Bolsonaro their chance to ascend to power. The appointment of this 'terribly Christian' Minister is in fact the materialization of a

---

[1] In Brazilian usage, the Evangelical church subsumes Evangelical, Pentecostal and Neo-Pentecostal religious communities (Smith, 2019: 10).

growing theocratic direction and disregard for advances in human rights which culminated in Bolsonaro's election to the Presidency. Such ultra-conservative discourses, part and parcel of today's neo-conservative geopolitics, gained prominence in Brazil during the wave of protests which peaked on 20 June 2013, prior to the FIFA World Cup, and reverberate deeply to this day (Vazquez, 2019).[2]

Neo-conservative narratives around gender and sexuality have had a most conflictual coexistence with Brazil's LGBT discourses and liberal laws, some of the most progressive in South America. In further sharp contrast, in the same year of 2013, the country witnessed a watershed in the struggle of Brazilian homosexuals for full citizenship: same-sex marriage conducted by notaries was approved by the Supreme Court and the LGBT community could then benefit from a full panoply of rights (Sousa Filho, 2009). The pace of legal and cultural change accelerated with another momentous judiciary decision in 2016, the recognition of gay and lesbian couples' right to adopt a child by analogy with heterosexual unions characterized by stability, coexistence, and affection (Mello *et al.*, 2009). These advances also reflect a three-decade long political organization of Brazilian lesbian, gay and transgender activists.[3]

The secondary school student's lines above epitomize the youth's agonizing pain, torn between a legitimate homosexual orientation and religious fundamentalist discourses predicated on heterosexuality as the only natural form of sexual expression. The lines also

---

[2] The protests, initially against rises in bus fares prior to the mega-events of the 2014 FIFA World Cup and 2016 Olympic and Paralympic games, flared into dissatisfaction with Brazil's politics in 2013. However, the political force of the 'bancada evangélica' (Evangelical caucus), featuring members of the Assembly of God (a Pentecostal denomination), had already emerged in the November 1986 elections to the National Constituent Assembly (held 1987-88) (Smith, 2019: 16-17).
[3] Walter Benjamin scholar Žarko Cvejić (2019), *inter alia*, has drawn parallels between, on the one hand, today's economic and political crises and various social grievances giving rise to the extreme right-wing populism of Donald Trump in the USA and Jair Bolsonaro in Brazil, among others, and, on the other, the context of crises in the 1920s and 1930s, especially in Europe and North America, the latter giving rise to movements personalised by charismatic leaders, such as Mussolini and Hitler. A complicit media benefits the spread of the former's 'common sense' solutions, usually predicated on apparently inclusive but actually exclusionary notions of 'the people', such as Trump's legendary 'Build that wall!' (Cvejić, 2019: 385-87).

contextualize this introductory study's analysis of the emerging agency of adolescent students in the settlements of agrarian reform as they challenge the oppressive and exclusionary religious caucus in Congress as well as the truth regimes of a Genesis ideology which supports them. Generational dissensus particularly informs these students' materialist poetics and lyrics as they advance a progressive countryside gender agenda and promote the dignifying of those socially excluded by their gender orientation. They also seek to mitigate the pain of homosexuals victimized by homophobia.

The introductory study to the original 2007 edition of this volume, 'Music, Poetry and the Politicization of the Landless Identity' (Vieira, 2007), featured the constitution of the *cantadores* (poet-singers) as organic intellectuals and the mission of their art in the struggle for land in the formative years of the MST, Movement of the Rural Landless Workers (1984-2005). It brought out two major venues where the *sem-terra*'s cultural expressions are collectively produced and delivered, the marches and the cultural acts of the Movement called the *Mística*, and the ways these gatherings enhance solidarity and togetherness and dignify a culture the identity of which is defined by an absence, 'landlessness'. The important function of these versatile performers as mouthpieces and interpreters of oppressed people was stressed and so was their delivery of recited poems and lyrics in these major communal experiences, related to the historical role of oral performances for the transmission of culture in markedly illiterate groupings.

Sávio Bones (2003), drawing upon Antonio Gramsci, was the first to categorize the earlier generation of *cantadores* of the MST as 'organic intellectuals'. For the Italian political scientist, every social group organically creates for itself one or more levels of intellectuals who give it homogeneity and a consciousness of its own economic, social, and political field (Gramsci, 2000: 15). If organic intellectuals create a new formation within the traditional historic bloc, Bones's claim in relation to the original *cantadores* is that, to the extent that they challenge political and cultural submission, 'the poetry made by the men and women who carry a hoe' is an integral part of a 'counter-hegemonic movement, a sower of hope', heralding a new Brazil and a new world. The cultural production of organic intellectuals, as so strikingly stated, 'with hands calloused from poetry', is transformed into a means of resistance and struggle for land (Bones, 2003).

The present study advances the view that today's younger generation of dissenting voices from the settlements can be seen as organic intellectuals. Again in Gramscian parlance, their knowledge of the oppression of homosexuals derives from their particular countryside experience, whereas their attempts to act on reality through active participation in practical life are ultimately intended to change the course of history (Gramsci, 1971). Rising from a social class that does not normally produce publicly recognized intellectuals, these adolescents have been empowered by their close connection with a social movement, the MST, to exercise democratic action from below. These new landless voices also produce eloquent counter-hegemonic responses to growing obscurantism in Brasília, epicentre of escalating neo-conservative political power, amidst unrelenting attacks from extreme right-wingers in Executive and Legislative decision-making on homosexuals' freedom and LGBT achievements.

This updating addresses the organic intellectuals' agenda in another historical context, the exacerbated neo-conservative responses to the achievements of the struggle for the legalization of same sex relationships and cultural recognition of the legitimacy of gender diversity. It also shifts the focus to education and initially reviews the setbacks to the inherently progressive PNE (Plano Nacional de Educação/National Education Plan) through the intimidating intervention of the religious and ultra-conservative caucus in Congress. The review includes their obsessive invocation of a Genesis ideology and parallel belittling of what they derogatorily label a 'gender ideology'. It then concentrates on the secondary schools in the settlements of agrarian reform in Paraná as granaries for today's organic intellectuals. A further section will focus on the ways these newly constituted organic intellectuals, with a profound sense of history, have learned from the elder *cantadores* and picked up the baton against the gender oppression increasingly reinstated by neo-conservatism.

The analysis also addresses ways in which these new organic intellectuals have orchestrated the stored knowledge of national and international dissenting voices, across generations and races, in such as rock and rap, to promote one's autonomy over one's sexual orientation. An important focus is their intergenerational dialogue with the critical perspective of BRock (Brazilian Rock) of the 1980s, notably with the first post-dictatorship generation who grew up in

Brasília, created the bands Aborto Elétrico/Electric Abortion and Legião Urbana/Urban Legion, and expressly challenged the establishment's disrespect for and abuse of human rights.

The generation now featured shares a specific location, the settlements of agrarian reform, particularly the Contestado (in Lapa) and the Marcos Freire (in Rio Bonito do Iguaçu) settlements in Paraná. Even though youths in these two historical settlements are geographically distant, contemporaneity marks the period of their birth and a similarity of location in the agrarian reform settlements marks their childhood experiences, shaped by their parents' landmark struggle against Paraná's age-old land problems. It was in this southern state that Brazil's and Latin America's largest social movement, the MST, was formally established in January 1984. The state is home today to over three hundred settlements of agrarian reform and around twenty thousand settled families, equivalent to one hundred thousand settled individuals.[4] The politicized environment of these settlements, resulting from today's adolescents' parents' successful struggle for land and for education, has been a depository for emerging organic intellectuals. The two settlements were established in two non-productive *latifundia* respectively in 1998 and 2000, roughly around this generation's emergence. The similar phenomena that today's politicized and educated young generation has experienced in these settlements brought them a specific kind of consciousness and a conception of the aesthetic expressed in revolutionary terms.[5] Their agency as conveyed through a materialist poetics is also a legacy of the social role and the talent for political compositions and performances of those earlier organic intellectuals,

[4] Land problems have been long prominent in the state of Paraná. In the 1970s alone two and a half million people were expelled from about one hundred thousand small farms. This situation was aggravated in the early 1980s, with the flooding of rivers for the construction of powerplants; for example, 500 families lost their land for the building of the largest one, the Itaipu powerplant, to generate electricity for Paraguay and Brazil's industrialized states in the South. Landlessness, however, as a social category, dates back to the nineteenth century with the abolition of slavery and of the subsidized immigration of Europeans as farm hands without land ownership (see Fernandes, 2000).

[5] The conceptual framework proposed by Karl Mannheim's seminal 'The Problem of Generations' (1972), based on a common location in the historical and social process predisposing them to a certain characteristic mode of thought and experience (*Lagerung*), underlies this study of new landless voices.

the countryside *cantadores*.

This trajectory will also intersect with the ingenious strategies, deployed in this volume, of the translator of today's landless youth's materialist poetics and its profound sense of history. The main thrust of his strategy is functional equivalence, i.e., making the translation work in the target culture as the source text functions in the source culture, which may mean that, as André Lefevere would say, he will 'lay the old adage to rest once and for all', holding that translators 'have to be traitors' (1992: 13). As such, ever more faithful to their historical and cultural weave, the translator grafts British and American 1960s rock in English into the adolescents' lines. It may be the case that this free spirit is consistent with the landless youth's breaking of monological truth, inasmuch as his performative playfulness seeks to render the adolescents' texts meaningful to an English-speaking readership. He thus enhances the political role of translation in the creation of international platforms for oppositional groups.

The neo-conservative promotion of a 'Genesis ideology' and banning of a 'gender ideology' from education

The empty signifier 'gender ideology', according to José M. M. Faúndes, belittles the political agenda of the second wave of feminism and LGBT movements of the mid-1990s, whose progressive claims broadened the scope of expression of sexual practices, bodies and desires.[6] As a mobilizing tool against same-sex marriage, access to abortion and sexual education, it fosters moral panic and threatens women and LGBT by bundling together, under the same conceptual umbrella, feminism, LGBT movements, Marxism, global conspiracy and so on. As a discursive strategy of global neo-conservative activism, the label proposes that these movements' agendas are based on ideological constructions and promotes, instead, patriarchal and heteronormative positions by affirming that sex, gender identities and sexual desire are biological attributes (Faúndes, 2019: 406-9).

The defenders of a belligerent 'Genesis ideology' declared a holy war between, on the one hand, biology-based biblical conceptions of the sacred family and, on the other, sexual orientation-based readings of same-sex desire, believed to be a manifestation of demonic forces.

---

[6] Faúndes uses the acronym LGBTI. This chapter uses the best-known acronym LGBT interchangeably.

The former's biblical axiom, 'God created male and female', ties with hierarchical and binary sex-genders, the female born to be the auxiliary of the male, and a heteronormative view of parenthood, the heterosexual father and mother (Maranhão F° and De Franco, 2019: 317). It abominates homosexuals and transgendered people for going against the biblical prescriptive 'Be fruitful, and multiply'. It also targets academic studies and educational resources on gender equality.

The political-ideological-doctrinal movement of the extreme right and religious caucus in Congress, self-presented as the School Without Party Bill, fiercely attacked the progressive PNE whose discussions started in 2010 (Maranhão F° and De Franco, 2019). The argument of the supporters of the Bill, a prominent Brazilian offshoot of global neo-conservative activism, popularly referred to as 'the Gag Law', is that it would be encouraging 'gender ideology' in schools. The Bill bans any discussion of the theme of non-normative sexualities in schools, consolidates heteronormative gender roles and categories of desire, and sanctifies the family along traditional lines, thereby reinforcing intolerance and hatred towards homosexuality, with punitive consequences. Eduardo M. A. Maranhão F° and De Franco have surveyed statements by detractors of the initially progressive PNE: 'dialogues on gender and sexuality in the school environment would promote the end of the traditional Brazilian family' through 'child hyper-sexualization, paedophilia, rape, early pregnancy, abortion, stimulus to early homosexuality, mandatory use of restrooms for another sex-gender, transsexuality in childhood, zoophilia/bestialism and necrophilia' (2019: 313). The PNE was finally sanctioned in June 2014, only after its original progressive recommendations were excluded, as the result of the intense campaign via internet especially by ultra-conservative leaders.

The monothematic 'Genesis ideology' informs the Bill (Maranhão F° and De Franco, 2019) and cloaks the educational system in a mantle of neutrality through the interdiction of social critique. The 'Gag Law' implicitly legalizes parents' surveillance and encourages them to denounce progressive teachers who address such 'non-neutral' topics as gender and sexuality. Legal power particularly spills over into discussions of non-normative sexualities and sex education creating a climate of systematic intimidation of those Brazilian teachers blamed for promoting homosexuality.

Today's educated youths in the settlements of agrarian reform have raised counter-hegemonic voices against the Bill. They bring to the current gender agenda the legacy of the MST pedagogy. From its establishment, the MST has been particularly pro-active in constituting itself as a pedagogical subject (Caldart, 2003), including in its political agenda a tenacious struggle for the formal education of children, adolescents and countless illiterate adults in the encampments and settlements (Vieira, 2003). This pedagogy has been particularly ingenious in its work on the line between dehumanization and the rescue of a humanity nearly lost by thousands of people in their life and death struggle for land as a means of production. The educator Paulo Freire, in a statement in the I National Conference of Agrarian Reform Educators, is eloquent on this pedagogy as a way out of dehumanization and exclusion:

> The process of agrarian reform begins a new history, a new culture, a culture born of a process of transforming the world. For this very reason, it implies social transformations […], for example, the overcoming of a profoundly paternalist and fatalist culture in which the peasant disappeared […], as an almost totally excluded object […]. Through his re-incorporation into the process of production, he acquires a social position he did not previously have, a history he did not have […]. In truth, he discovers that fatalism no longer explains anything at all and that, having been able to transform the land, he is also capable of transforming history and culture. From out of that former fatalism, the peasant is reborn, inserted as a presence in history, no longer as an object, but as a subject of history. Now, this whole process involves the tasks of education (Freire, in Vieira 2003).

A decade and a half after the research that underpinned the website and related volume, *Landless Voices in Song and Poetry: The Movimento dos Sem Terra of Brazil*, it is timely to revisit and update the much-changed cultural context of the movement. No easy task, given the scope of social and, particularly, political changes that have intervened in both the form and content of the happily undiluted creativity of the poetic expressions revealed here for the first time. The stored political knowledge of the students and the liberating and transformative education in the settlements, it must be affirmed, would have remained latent were it not for the major educational intervention by the Newton-Trust funded project 'Gender and Education in Brazil's Rural Areas' (2015-18), convened by Else R. P. Vieira and Sônia F. Schwendler, who extend their thanks for the unique opportunity involved.

Starting with two pilot institutions, the Rural State Schools Iraci Salete Strozak and Contestado, respectively in the Marcos Freire and the Contestado settlements, the project pioneered the introduction of the ever-controversial and undeniably problematic issue of gender in the countryside educational settings of Paraná. Both schools are landmarks in the State of Paraná's history of the struggle for land and education. The first delivers education to 2,500 students in elementary, secondary, youth, adult, and special education in the State's largest concentration of settlements (Capitani, 2011); this school is also the base for 9 itinerant schools serving 67 encampments in the area. The Contestado settlement, located 70 kilometres from the capital, Curitiba, stands out for providing education from early childhood to graduation; it also hosts the first Latin American School of Agro-Ecology (Capitani, 2013).

The poems and lyrics of the new generation as analyzed here were composed initially by the students during the workshops on gender and sexuality in the pilot schools. Subsequently, two seminars, a second and calculatedly distinct dimension of the Newton-Trust project, each trained 70 countryside secondary school teachers (November 2016 and April 2017). The students' compositions were read out and invited the teachers' open discussion in the freedom afforded by the said seminars. Inspired by the enterprise of the students themselves, progressive teachers followed suit, solidarizing with the students. Vitally, the non-hierarchical pedagogy developed results from the realization that, through permanent action, nothing is unchangeable (Caldart, 2003). It is precisely via such agency that the adolescents bring into their performances and poems the spearheading of an emancipatory gender diversity agenda notably excluded from Brazil's originally progressive PNE.

Drag queen Priscilla Stefany: the transgender body politic in Paraná's agrarian reform settlements and encampments
Edenilson Prestes Mendes, alias drag queen Priscilla Stefany, epitomizes organic intellectualism produced in the schools of agrarian reform settlements in Paraná. He provides a model for politically

engaged activity produced by these schools, at the same time performing a marked role in affecting their institutional culture in terms of gender. As Gramsci would have it, he participates 'in a particular conception of the world, has a conscious line of [...] conduct, and therefore contributes to sustain a conception of the world or to modify it, that is, to bring into being new modes of thought' (1971: 9). The son of rural workers, he moved to the Marcos Freire settlement at the age of 15 and received his secondary education there. His unbroken trajectory in agrarian reform settlements also includes his work as a teacher in the Colégio Estadual do Campo Aprendendo com a Terra e com a Vida (meaningfully translated as Countryside State School Learning from the Land and from Life), in the Valmir Motta de Oliveira settlement, in the municipality of Cascavel, also in Paraná.

Mendes's pioneering gender-oriented activism includes a series of drag performances in the persona of Priscilla Stefany in the encampments and settlements of agrarian reform in Paraná and, by extension, in the Movement of the Landless Rural Workers. Her performances are followed by gender-awareness talks. Priscilla, as a subject embedded in the Landless culture, can be said to establish a point of agency, here understood, with an echo of Judith Butler (1999: 180-82), as a reflexive mediation between more conservative and restrictive frames of compulsory heterosexuality and other gender configurations and progressive gender discourses.[7] For Judith Lorber, 'in different cultures, times, and places, as long as there are clear-cut categories to transgress and send up, drag lives' (2009: xvi). Drag questions the man/woman binary and establishes more fluid gender and sexual meanings. As Taylor and Rupp emphasize, drawing upon Butler, drag queens accentuate the inherently performative nature of gender by making visible the social basis of femininity, masculinity and homosexuality (2004: 115).

The aesthetics of Mendes's self-staging and self-disclosure of a fluid sexuality weaves through this agency. Mendes recalls the way he articulated a personal sexuality through a first improvised drag act, thereafter Priscilla Stefany:

---

[7] The quotations in this study come from Mendes's talk after he wrapped up the first day of the Teacher-Training Seminar on Gender and Sexuality, performing a drag act as Priscilla Stefany. The seminar was held in Curitiba, in November 2016, as an initiative of the Project 'Gender and Education in Brazil's Rural Areas'.

The Movement of the Landless Rural Workers (MST) has always had homosexuals, including in its coordination, and we have all, in a way, been welcome, but we couldn't spell it out. There was a taboo. While living in the capital, Curitiba, and working in the Education Sector of the MST State Secretariat, I had an urge to speak out and to show that there are homosexuals in our rural settlements. In 2012 I was invited to recite a poem at the Workers' House at the Centre for Research and Support to Workers and Promotion of Transformation Agents in Curitiba [...] It was then that I took my friend's clothes and got dressed. I was 'mounted' [...] with thick, long black hair, big boots [...] When I got there, I dubbed an actress and spoke about prejudice. Priscilla Stefany was born.[8]

To name is to make exist, to re-name is to make exist in another identity. With transgressive humour, Priscilla talks of her mistake surrounding her process of renaming herself and recreating her theatrical personae. 'Stefany' alludes to Stephan Elliott, the first name of the director of the road movie *The Adventures of Priscilla, Queen of the Desert* (1994). 'Priscilla' is the name of a carnivalesque lavender-coloured bus which leaves streamers along the way as it cuts across the Australian bush country transporting a homosexual, a bisexual and a transgendered person to perform drag-show cabarets in remote hotels. The vehicle, playfully gendered into the feminine, subverts the national myth of heroic masculinity which, according to Anne Le Guellec-Minel (2017), the Australian outback has helped to forge.

---

[8] The acronym for the Centre is CEPAT. It was initially a joint initiative of the Jesuits and lay collaborators mostly from the Workers' Pastoral. Its premises, in a Jesuit Retreat, came to be called Workers' House; it offered training venues and accommodation for workers from the city and the countryside. In 2008 the premises were changed and the Workers' House, then under the Carmelites, was renamed Centre for the Promotion of Agents for Transformation (CEPAT). On the occasion of Priscilla's first performance the Centre was offering training on bread making for women from the settlements and encampments so that they could train others back in their communities. 'Mounted' (here) means fully dressed and made up as a woman.

I ended up christening myself Priscilla Stefany. I had not seen the film yet and it was later, when I got it as a gift, that I found out that this is actually the name of a bus – Priscilla, Queen of the Desert – that the members of a theatrical company got to transport the troupe to perform their drag-show cabaret in a hotel in the desert. But I like the name!

Priscilla also plays with the element of surprise surrounding her multiple personae:

'Who's coming today? Who is she? Where's the little face?' I say, Priscilla Stefany. 'Ah, but she only changes…' Yes, only the wigs and the clothes change, but the character that has life is always Priscilla Stefany […] blonde, brunette, short hair, long hair, mini skirt, maxi dress, but she is Priscilla Stefany.

'Drag plays with the forbidden – that is part of its appeal', and does so through its core elements: performance (it needs an audience to perceive the underlying joke that a man can be a woman or vice-versa) and parody, the latter based on an exaggerated gender display, then cut down as pretence to evoke laughter' (Lorber, 2004: xvi). However, not without moments of fear does she carry on her agency through drag performances and talks:

I am the one who does this work in the settlements and encampments […] When I was invited for a performance at the Peasant Resistance Encampment, I chose to dress up as Maleficent […] I made the horns, black clothes, black cloaks and all. I was scared to death… Imagine, it had to be in the bar, the only place that had a floor for me to wear very high heels. I didn't know that they had set up a security team, because they couldn't foresee the reaction of families in the encampments […] There is a risk that someone in the audience might not like it. And if I were stoned […] And suddenly, the lights were off, the sound started, and Maleficent enters exactly for the curse scene… Imagine those huge curved horns… I feared the structure of the bar. And then there was a gale, a gale so strong that the sides of Maleficent's cloak were blown like that. And then, suddenly, the curse stopped, and a song started. She is there alone, and I was dubbing the way she sings out her loneliness when someone stole her wings [...] I looked round and saw three guys dragging out another, a dark one. I thought, 'My God, and now?'. I continued but keeping an eye everywhere. The poor man was just drunk and said, 'My God, where did this horned demon come from?' This was what he was seeing, a tall, huge, horned creature, almost a metre long.

Through hyperbolic performances, Priscilla has been exploding the normative heterosexual binary and enabling conservative audiences in settlements and encampments to think about gender other than via biology. Her transgressive play with the forbidden has garnered positive responses in the encampment. Theatricality and humour made it more comfortable for a heteronormative audience to accept fluidity of gender and sexuality:

The children loved the performance because the character Maleficent had a tiny boy. A child came, I bent down, and he said: 'Maleficent doesn't wear pink shoes'. So I said: 'It's only you who knows, it's our secret'. The show was very well accepted. The ladies loved it because they had never watched a play. And now I introduce myself saying: 'I am Priscilla Stefany, she is a character. I consider myself an artist'. I take it to that side and so I start the discussion on sexuality.

Increasingly the Movement also acknowledged her multiple personae. Further than this, Edenilson/Priscilla were given empowering visibility and legitimacy in official ceremonies, a prelude to invitations for performances in other settlements:

On the tenth anniversary of the Programme Pedagogy of the Land in Paraná, in 2014, our training group was invited to the stage for a homage. I was transformed when I joined the procession. That corridor seemed like it would never end in my life... I was afraid of falling. Then they read out my name: Edenilson Prestes Mendes, Priscilla Stefany. I went ahead to receive the homage with the group. I now try to go to the encampments.

Priscilla solidarizes with and extends her agency to other excluded groups:

When I went back to the Iraci Salete Strosak Rural State School, in the Marcos Freire settlement, where I lived, I had a workshop during the day and the boys got in touch with me for an evening performance. They helped a lot in the organization, the deputy headmistress drove me there and her daughter did my make-up. Those giant skirts... and there are some boys who are emos, they wear black, black nails, black eyes, so I thought of them too because they may or may not be homosexuals, but it is a group that is also discriminated against. But if you talk to them, they are enlightened people, they are super-sensitive human beings, they create this shell in which to hide. So I dubbed a Night Dream song, which is an epic song, which is a kind of rock, but the background is lyrical.

Dress has always been a principal signifier of feminine identity and it was through sartorial desires and experiments with make-up that Priscilla defined her transgender identity. Here are her first intimations on the process of transformation and acceptance of the lack of coherence between sex, gender and desire as being her own sense of normality:

I designed my trousers, bought the material, told the seamstress to make them, nobody had the same. I wore black trousers with a sort of stripe on the sides. It was only me who had those trousers and woe to anyone who said I was a fag. I wasn't assumed to be, but my body screamed, I needed to show it, you know, I couldn't say I was, but through my body, my clothes, I was showing who and what I was [...] Because when I'm transformed, that's how I get out of Edenilson's more masculine body. Even though I would have a woman's body, I would never remove my penis. I'm not a transsexual. I don't consider myself in the wrong body, as some say, I love my body, I love myself as Edenilson, but I love myself a lot more when I'm Priscilla, and I have no problems with that. I permeate these two fields very calmly.

Conceiving of an individual's sexuality in terms of sexual orientation – made up of pleasures, sensations, fantasies, imaginations, erotic practices, etc. (Sousa Filho, 2009), not as the result of a rational act or a deliberate choice – is almost a consensus among experts today.

Priscilla's awareness-building in the settlements and encampments also involves enlightening the audience on gender-related misconceptions and misnomers. She creates empathy with the public as her theorization on sexual orientation, rather than the cliché of 'sexual preference', derives from her lived painful experiences in a context that makes the homosexual feel inferior and insulted:

> I came out in college. In a sexuality workshop, I screamed from the floor that I wouldn't accept the term 'sexual preference'. Who in their right mind would choose to be called an animal, an ox, a fruit, a 'viadinho'? Do you think that people in their right minds would choose this?[9]

Priscilla then addresses the boundaries between secrecy and disclosure, the gradual and very painful process of coming out and the resulting freedom from heteronormative constraints:

> Coming out of the closet [...] is a transition to be made, it is not at the first moment... It's a long, painful process... It is difficult to empower oneself and say, I am a homosexual and here I am. My name is such and I am from such a place. It's a process, and we have to respect this process as well. I came out to my family at the age of twenty-five. Everyone at a school where I used to teach knew, even the porter knew. We talked openly there, but at home nobody knew [...] But how painful the process is! As soon as I accepted myself, that I like myself the way I am, ninety percent of my homosexual's problems were over. Thereafter, it has been much easier to deal with the problems that arise. But until I reached that level of self-acceptance, of saying 'I like myself the way I am, I am that person, I don't need to be the he that society commands, or I am a she, a beautiful blonde.

The Genesis ideology resonates in Priscilla's several times stressed nuclear expression 'painful process'. The scholars Maranhão F⁰ and De Franco have drawn attention further to the theological basis for the abomination of homosexuals: 'Thou shalt not lie with a man as with

---

[9] 'Viadinho': the demeaning diminutive for the already pejorative colloquial word 'viado', meaning male homosexual.

a woman' (Leviticus, 22:18); 'The woman shall not wear that which pertaineth unto a man, neither shall a man put on a woman's garment' (Deuteronomy, 22:5), or 'the men also abandoned natural relations with women and were inflamed with lust for one another' (Romans, 1:26). Those who do not follow the biblical injunctions are doomed to rejection, silencing and annihilation. Edenilson/Priscilla talks of her suicidal response to the religious abomination:

> It's a very painful process to come out of the closet. I had a salon at home just for me [...] Wow, my hair was curly, down here, perfectly drawn curls. But since I fell into depression, I went bald on top. I always stress that, if I had come out at the age of fifteen, I would have a woman's body today. Of course, I went through the painful process of attempting suicide because I didn't accept myself. Then the church was sending me to hell. But when I'm like this, I love myself, and people who know me treat me well, at least in my presence.

Edenilson's/Priscilla's organic intellectualism in the settlements and encampments has been promoting inclusiveness and transforming the suffering homosexual from a sinful, abominated object of Genesis ideology into a political subject.

Setbacks to agency: asphyxiated Priscilla

Priscilla's politically liberating work towards the acceptance of transgendered inhabitants of the countryside, which started in 2012, suffered blows from the theocracy and ultra-conservatism which had been hatching in Brazilian politics and which formed the basis of Bolsonaro's eventual programme. Like one of the characters she had impersonated, Maleficent, she has a voice but could not sing. Asphyxiated Priscilla now advances a poetic response to neo-conservative activism. Her 2016 poem 'More oxygen for me' can be seen as an outcry against an overseeing prescriptive and prohibitive God looming increasingly high in Brazilian politics:

Bom se fosse fácil	It would be so nice
Alguém passar pela gente	If someone could just pass by
Sem nos julgar.	Without judging
Sem nos colocar dentro das caixas,	Without putting us in boxes,

| Dos padrões pré-estabelecidos | Patterns pre-conceived |
| Pela sociedade monocromática | By a black-and-white society[10] |

Priscilla's wish to recover the progressive 'multi-coloured mosaic of feminist and queer theologies' (Faúndes, 2019: 405) translates into a symbology that emphasizes bright colours, a centuries-old shorthand for homosexuality, and the Rainbow Pride flag. Initially designed as a symbol of hope and liberation for the 1978 San Francisco Gay Freedom Day celebration, from 1994 the flag has been planted in social consciousness as the symbol for LGBT recognition and pride. Jennifer M. Wolowic *et al.* (2017), in their study of the rainbow and pride semiotics, have stressed the several positive meanings now read into the flag. Not only has it evolved as a general symbol for social equality and individuality, but it has also constructed meanings of gender affiliation, feelings of comfort and accomplishment in oneself and ones' community, and a sense of global togetherness. A flag is a way of proclaiming visibility and Priscilla's poem reclaims access to what has now been obscured by the black and white 'which cover up the rainbow's colours,/Bright colours hidden by the smoke of prejudice'.

In the poem, growing transphobia in Brazil is emphatically compared to expanding lethal gases:

Assim como os CFC's, CO2, metano	Just as gasses, carbon, methane
Corroem a camada de ozônio	Corrode the ozone layer
Que protege toda a vida terrestre	That saves all life on earth
E toda a sua diversidade.	In its diversity.

The poem ends with an emphatic exhortation to life in all its diversity:

Viva!	Live!
Sinta!	Feel!
Brilhe!	Shine!
Grite todas as formas de amor,	Shout out all the forms of love,
Todas as formas de cor!	All the colours of the rainbow!

[10] This poem, as well as the subsequent ones by Roseli Lemonie and Ione Sereia, was composed during the Teacher-Training Seminar on Gender and Sexuality of November 2016, inspired by and in solidarity with the students.

*

'"Princes who wear blue and princesses, pink" does not consider a myriad of sensitivities and subjectivities that embroider people's gender and sexual and affective orientations with multi-coloured threads' (Maranhão Fº and De Franco, 2019: 321). An outcry against this oppressive binary comes from the educator Roseli Lemonie, from the Chico Mendes Rural State School, in Quedas do Iguaçu, Paraná. Lemonie expresses solidarity with a protean Edenilson by impersonating Priscilla and her transgender identity that forces the reader to think in a complex way about sex and gender. Lemonie disrupts the binary gender colour-coding, reinstated by neo-conservative activists: 'To wear blue's not for me/Pink, I think, is not my way'. She further adds an incongruous and intransigent 'black' in the fourth lines of the first and second stanzas, which draws attention to the disruption of Edenilson *cum* Priscilla's wider gamut of colours:

Branco,	White,
Rosa,	Pink,
Azul,	Blue,
Preto.	Black.
Criança,	Child,
Mulher,	Woman,
Homem,	Man,
Negro.	Black.

'Black' gains further emphasis as the colour of sorrow and fateful death for transgendered people in the third and fourth stanzas:

Cada um com sua cor	Each one with their colour
Cada um com seu jeito	Each one their own way
Mas tem cor que é dor	But there's colour that's sorrow
E a sua dor me condena	And sorrow kills me
Usar azul eu não quero	To wear blue's not for me
Rosa pra mim não combina.	Pink, I think, is not my way.
Usava o branco e o preto	I wore black and white
Viver assim era minha sina.	Life like that was my fate.

Lemonie challenges the religious extremists' abjection and belittling of homosexuals in equally Biblical terms. A queer theology, presumably deriving from Galatians 3: 28, reverberates in her concluding stanzas. Paul's position on gender matters may be problematic elsewhere, but is emancipatory in this specific verse: there is 'neither Jew nor Greek, neither slave nor free, nor male and female, for all of you are one in Christ Jesus' (Galatians 3: 28). Political, socio-cultural and gender/sexual aspects meet explicitly in the positive notes of this verse, indeed 'influential within the Christian church as a prominent, charter text, proclaiming gender equity' (Punt, 2010: 141). Lemonie's verse, in a similar vein, intersects with the Bible and sex/gender to promote equity and respect for homosexuals:

Igualdade, respeito	Equality, respect
Direito de ser quem sou.	The right to be who I am.
Usar a cor que eu quero	To use the colour I want
E ser por todos aceito.	And be accepted by them.
Venho clamar a você	I come to tell you
Que me desrespeita,	If you disrespect me,
Não aceita,	You don't accept me,
Posso ser sangue de seu sangue	I may be blood of your blood
Mas a igreja me rejeita.	But the church rejects me.
Fui o desvalorizado	I've been devalued
Homossexual, travesti.	Homosexual, transvestite.
Sou igual a você	I'm just like you
A morte, eu já senti.	Death, I've already felt.
Grito, clamo por respeito	I shout, cry out for respect
Que todos me aceitem assim.	Let all accept me as I am.
Eu sou ser humano,	I'm a human being,
Eu tenho sentimento.	I too have feeling.
Não sintam pena de mim.	Do not feel sorry for me.

Crying against the ideology of Genesis: 'Why was I born wrong?'
The title, 'Why was I born wrong?', encapsulates the sense of profound inadequacy of an oppressed lesbian youth coming to terms with her non-normative sexuality, perceived as pathological by ever-encroaching ultra-conservative discourses. The first-person narrative bespeaks the ritual of confession which permeates this secondary student's internalized mandate to articulate her sexual peculiarity

anonymously. The ritual of confession, an inheritance from Christianity, has in sexuality a privileged theme. Michel Foucault has elaborated on the paradoxes of this urge to confess sexuality, in that it liberates but also unleashes a power relationship:

> The confession is a ritual of discourse in which the speaking subject is also the subject of the statement; it is also a ritual which unfolds within a power relationship, for one does not confess without the presence (or virtual presence) of a partner who is not simply the interlocutor but the authority who requires the confession, prescribes and appreciates it, and intervenes in order to judge, punish, forgive, console, and reconcile; a ritual in which the truth is corroborated by the obstacles and resistances it has had to surmount in order to be formulated; and finally, a ritual in which the expression alone, independently of its external consequences, produces intrinsic modifications in the person who articulates it: it exonerates, redeems, and purifies him, it unburdens him of his wrongs, liberates him, and promises him salvation (Foucault, 1990: 61-62).

The student comes from a family where women by far outnumber men and whose biological sex displays a coherence between sex and the social scripts of gender: maternal love, gentle manners, playing with gender-specific toys enacting motherhood. The adolescent realized her gender is at odds with her sex:

Nasci numa família numerosa:	I was born into a big family:
Nove mulheres e dois homens.	Nine women, two men.
Família humilde, com muito	A humble family, lots of
amor maternal.	motherly love.
Fui crescendo, vendo, percebendo.	As I grew up, I felt
Eu era diferente, não era igual.	I was different, not the same.
Minhas irmãs, femininas, meigas.	My sisters, feminine, gentle.
Eu, robusta, desajeitada,	Me, sturdy, awkward,
Fora do normal.	Out of step.
Elas brincavam de bonecas e casinhas	They played little dolls' houses,
Eu era um piá infernal.	While I was an infernal boy.
O tempo foi passando e eu só	Time passed with me just
analisando.	thinking.
Estudei, brinquei, namorei, tudo	I studied, played, dated; all

xl

'normal'	'normal'
De repente percebi que eu era diferente.	Suddenly I realized I was different.
Aquela vida não era pra mim,	That life was not for me,
Não foi para isso que eu nasci.	That's not what I was born to be.

In the next three stanzas the student elaborates on the concept of normality and the ways she deviates from it. What is normal? It is a well-known fact that the concept of normality is socially and historically constituted. Roughly, her reading coalesces with what psychologists have summarized as the concept of normalcy in Brazilian society: to have a specific sex, to be heteronormative, to have emotional stability and lasting love, to have sexual and affective ties, to have a fulfilling sexual performance, to correspond to desirable aesthetic patterns, in due course to grow a family, to have intellectual potential for respected professions so as to perform well economically (Maia, 2009). The student voices out her sense of profound inadequacy relative to Brazil's social parameters of normality:

Infeliz, agoniada, fora do prumo.	Sad, in pain, out of the way.
Difícil aceitar, mas eu não era normal	Hard to accept I wasn't normal.
Restava pensar e pensar...	Thinking over and over again,
Restava pensar e pensar.	Ever shutting myself off.
Impossível acreditar;	It's impossible to believe,
No meio de oito irmãs	But amongst eight sisters
Eu me percebia desigual.	I saw myself as the odd one out.

Ainda hoje sofro, sonho, analiso	Still I suffer, dream, ponder
E ainda não encontrei a resposta.	And haven't an answer.
Só queria, do fundo do coração	I only wanted, in my heart,
Ter nascido, crescido,	To have been born, grown,
vivido, amado,	lived, loved,
Como uma mulher normal.	As a normal woman.

Anseios, desejos,	I long, desire,
encontros, desencontros,	date, disagree,
Um sonho desigual.	Unequal dreams.
Por mais que o tempo passe,	No matter how much time passes,
Eu vejo, leio, aprendo,	I see, I read, I learn,
Mas ainda não me aceito	But still don't accept myself as I,
Como uma pessoa normal.	As me, as a normal me.

Torn between a Genesis ideology and conflicting progressive ideas, and agonizing over her sense of non-belonging:

E essa é a pergunta	And here's
que eu mesma me faço:	what I ask myself,
Por que eu nasci errada?	Why was I born wrong?
Por mais que eu tente,	As hard as I try,
Eu não consigo ser o que sou,	I can't be what I am,
Fora do armário.	Out of the closet.

Can't or mustn't? Unable or inhibited by an increasingly intimidating ambience to articulate her condition? If confession also unfolds a power relationship, what is this external power both requiring the confession and stifling the youth? The 'Gag Law'? The correlating Genesis ideology embraced by the ultra-conservative crusade which limits the adolescent's enlightened understanding of her gender, sexuality and desire? The adolescent student unburdens her painful gender conflicts to the keen ear of the open-minded teacher Ione Sereia, from the Estrela do Oeste Rural State School, in Santa Maria do Oeste, Paraná. By lending an ear, the teacher, from an older generation than the student's, became receptive to the plight of the younger one, and turned herself into a political actor. Her agency, which subsumes casting the adolescent's confession in *cordel* form (string literature) and mediating its dissemination, brings to the world's ears the as yet unheard-of voice of this vulnerable and oppressed youth in gender terms.[11]

From a perspective supplementary to that of *The Ear of the Other*, Jacques Derrida, in *Circumfessions*, has blurred the distinction between the confessional genre and the autobiographical, claiming that every autobiography is a confession. The adolescent who articulated her sexuality and gender conflicts demanded the ear of the other to hear her words; the teacher lent her an ear and wrote the *cordel*'s narrative in the first person. The *autos* of the adolescent's autobiography may be thus transfigured into an otobiography. Derrida is resonant on the slippage from auto- to oto- in the very formulation of biographies:

---

[11] The *cordel*, originally sold in printed form in fairs to disseminate news, is also often read aloud or sung to a gathering of broadly illiterate listeners who, otherwise, would have limited access to information.

It is the ear of the other that signs. The ear of the other [...] constitutes the autos of my autobiography. When, much later, the other will have perceived with a keen-enough ear what I shall have addressed or destined to him or her, then my signature will have taken place. Here one may derive the political import of this structure and of this signature in which the addressee signs with his/her ear, an organ for perceiving difference. (Derrida, 1988: 51)

The 'otobiographical' *cordel* is particularly relevant in terms of agency. Christie McDonald, in the preface to Derrida's *The Ear of the Other*, suggests a certain complicity in otobiographies, understood as a 'contract for which an other signs off' and in that 'texts can only be understood when a reader allies with him and countersigns in his or her name, as one might validate a check or a document' (McDonald, 1985: ix). The teacher's complicit political agenda is thus clear: she confirms the student's experience and makes public, within an unfavourable Gag Law, the voice of one excluded from a sense of normality and predominant heteronormativity.

The translator, in turn, had already brought out the political dimension of the *cordel*. As far back as 2007, in his metalanguage as the translator of the poems and songs of the *Movimento dos Sem Terra*, he had stressed the challenge of confronting commitment and Brazil's revitalization of popular music as a vehicle for political activisms, as 'Brazil never ceases to explore and express its sensitivity to the [counter] ideological power of the protest song'. Sources, he added, have been, among others, international commercial brands. His choices now return to 'the prosodies – high and low – of Brazilian Portuguese and the broadsheet and *cordel* strains of popular imaginaries from across and beyond the nation' (McGuirk, 2007: xxi) to provide an international echo chamber to youth oppressed by the Genesis ideology.

The *cordel* is particularly relevant in political terms, given its social function in the countryside. Historically, the *cordel* creates an intimate relationship with rural communities as its singer fulfils the roles of a mouthpiece and interpreter of oppressed people, whose sorrows s/he expresses. The *cordel* has also been increasingly practiced by landless children and youth in the settlements where it has served as an educational tool as it ludically combines information and a number of mnemonic devices, including a regular rhyme scheme and a well marked rhythm. The teacher thus creates an experience that is, in one go, collective, political, and educational by giving the psychological space for this student with a non-normative sexuality to voice out her conflicts and anxieties. She also creates an echo chamber for others, equally inhibited by an unfavourable ethos, to open up.

Sereia's *cordel* is a polyphonic composition, in Mannheim's sense of absorbing the voices of at least two generations, the student's and her own. It challenges dominant voices, particularly the monological truth biases of the Genesis ideology. In addition, she exercises a woman's right to author(ize) herself, entering the realm of a poetic production traditionally reserved for the *cantador*, usually a man, given the historically itinerant nature of his work and the requirement of literacy, less frequent particularly among older rural women.

'Yellow Brasília' and the national symbols on the adolescent students' spotlight

Derrida has referred to the title as a chandelier which, from above, irradiates light on a text. The title 'Yellow Brasília' illuminates a reading of dissent from today's epicentre of neo-conservative power while, at the outset, it deconstructs the image of the city's iconic white architecture, evocative of dawn. The capital of Brazil and the national symbols are particularly targeted in this poem composed by secondary school students from the Iraci Salete Strosak Rural State School, Marcos Freire settlement, in 2016.

Yellow harmonizes with green, blue and white, making up the mythical and a-historical symbolism of the Brazilian flag. The four colours represent the country as nature, rather than politically: yellow stands for the country's natural wealth, green for its forests, blue for the perennial beauty of its starry sky, and white for order.[12] However, in isolation, as in the students' poem, the colour yellow, dissociated from the flag's *per se* controversial mythical thrust, becomes quite political, by virtue of its association in popular memory with whatever causes anger, such as betrayal. The illocutionary force of the ironical 'honourable country' below confirms Brasília's failure to uphold the principles of harmony represented by the national symbol and its blatant disrespect for its citizens:

---

[12] This inadequacy had already been raised by Zé Pinto, a *cantador* from the previous generation (reprinted in this volume).

Brasil, um país tão da honra,	Brazil, such an honourable country,
Não tem aceitação.	Will not accept,
Ninguém respeita os outros,	Will not respect others,
A diferença de todos.	Nor the difference in us all.

Queremos a igualdade,	We want equality,
Respeito na sociedade	Respect in society
E liberdade de expressão:	Freedom of expression:
Amar é a solução.	Loving's the answer.

| Lalalalalá. | Lalalalalá. |

The question mark in the title of another poem, 'Progress without change?', composed by the students from the same settlement, also in 2016, powerfully problematizes Brasília's neglect of the values celebrated by the national symbols. 'Progress' is a direct reference to the positivist intellectual bases of Brazilian politics between 1870 and 1910. According to Elías Palti (2018), positivism was conceived of in Brazil as an ideology of order in a moment of profound disarray and extreme popular unrest that culminated in a military revolution that dismantled the country's two pillars, monarchy and slavery. Positivism thus entered the symbolism of the Brazilian flag as the philosophy of the State at the time of the Proclamation of the Republic in 1889. The slogans encapsulated on the prominent central circle on the flag, 'Order and Progress', historically point to a new national beginning. For these adolescent students, however, history has fallen way behind such ideals. Equality is no longer a guiding principle in a context of homo- and trans-phobia. Progress has been halted:

É impossível progredir	It's impossible to progress
sem mudança	without change
E aqueles que não mudam	And those who don't change
suas mentes	their minds
Não podem mudar nada.	Change nothing at all.

The flag's star symbolism is the occasion for another contestation. These represent what was seen in the sky over Rio de Janeiro on the evening of 15 November 1889, the day of the Proclamation of the Republic. Individually, each star represents a state in the new republic. But the sense of unity conveyed by the constellations homogenizes individuals into a collective. Would there be only one sky in a continental-sized country? The acknowledgement of differences, the very core of LGBT advances worldwide, is emphasized via repetition of the refrain below, in the adolescents' reading of persisting disrespect in Brazil's history:

Nosso céu tem mais estrelas –	Our sky has more stars –
O meu, o seu, o céu de todos.	Mine, yours, the celestial sky of all,
Aliás, quantos céus existem?	Yes how many skies are there?
Quantos seres diferentes existem?	How many different beings?
Há céus e seres diferentes.	Different skies and beings, too.

The poem casts into readily assimilated and easily recited words the main political thrust of the MST pedagogy: to make history follow a different path. The aim of establishing a project that offers an alternative to all forms of exclusion finds fertile soil in the students' more recent gender agenda.

Landless Voices on the track of Brasília rock in the 1980s: 'Que cultura é esta?'
Repetition and allusion are important devices for social critique and persuasion among the *Sem Terra* (Vieira, 2007). Indeed, the title of a song, 'What culture is this?', emphatically repeated in the refrain, echoes a 1978 song, 'Que país é este?'/'What country is this?'. The 1978 rock song, composed by Renato Manfredini Junior, better known as Renato Russo, is paradigmatic of the politicized stream of Brazilian rock (BRock) and more specifically of Brasília rock. The intertext in the 2016 composition enables the appreciation of an important intergenerational transmission of historical experience.

'BRock', a contraction of Brazilian rock', refers to the specific genre that emerged in Brazil in the 1980s, noted for the engagement of its exponents with the country's social and political issues. Most of these exponents share a consciousness of belonging to one generation. They were born in the 1960s, that is, during the military dictatorship (1964-1985) 'in a social environment of repression and the gag'; the political opening of the 1980s strengthened civil society and, what with freedom of expression regained, new spaces for cultural and political performance enabled criticisms of the Brazilian establishment (Encarnação, 2018: 215). BRock was an urban development, originating simultaneously in Rio de Janeiro, São Paulo and, importantly for our purposes, Brasília.

Russo was a major exponent of BRock. He was born on 27 March 1960 in Rio de Janeiro, less than a month before the new capital of the country, Brasília, was inaugurated (21 April 1960). In 1973 his family moved to Brasília. Ana C. Lessa (2011) has explored the importance of city life as a BRock theme and how living in Brasília strongly influenced Russo's extremely political mind as well as his role in forming the band Aborto Elétrico in the late 1970s, the first band in the city to appropriate British and US punk (Lessa, 2011: 230). The name of the band is a direct reference to violence in Brasília; it is the baton that the police of the capital used to break up a manifestation at the university in 1968, which resulted in a young girl's miscarriage (Dapieve, 2006).

'Que país é este?'/'What country is this?' was first performed during parties in Brasília by Aborto Elétrico. This band, which broke up in 1982, was a forerunner of the Legião Urbana Band. The latter arrived in Brazil's musical scene during the country's flexibilization of the military rule and its first record was released in 1985, the year in which democracy was re-established. But the political role of Legião Urbana was undiminished with the crisis informing what was expected to be a new regime. 'Que país é este?' bitterly addresses corruption and the government's hypocrisy vis-à-vis the Brazilian Constitution. Russo would stress that, even though Congress was re-opened and elections were in place, civil and social rights were not respected, the natives' land rights were neglected and a blind eye was turned on the country's misery and violence (Lessa, 2011). 'What country is this?' is a particularly direct and straightforward song, with a simple and easily memorized structure. It has ever since been sung by multitudes to problematize Brazil's contradictions and deep-seated neglect of social problems. Lessa's challenge is eloquent: who were/are those 'runners' receiving the 'baton' from Russo? Are they singing about the same issues and with the same purposes? And to what effect? (2011: 267)

Students in the settlements of agrarian reform have picked up the baton from Russo. The intertext, 'What culture is this?', is repeated with increasing urgency in 'Prejudice: a huge problem', composed by students from the Contestado settlement. If 'What country is this?' has outlived the dictatorship during which it was composed and is ever meaningful in our days, it is because an unfinished past has returned in the present. This young generation of Brazilian organic

xlvii

intellectuals, also in a particularly direct and straightforward song, with a simple and easily memorized structure, problematizes Brazil's long-standing neglect of social problems. They have absorbed from Brasília-based revolutionary rock the energy to protest and adapted their discourse and musical genre to today's context of State-sanctioned homophobia:

Nas escolas, nas famílias,	In schools, in families,
Na sociedade e na vida,	In society, in life,
O preconceito é um problemão	Prejudice is a huge problem
Para o futuro da nação.	For the nation's future.
Que cultura é essa? (bis)	What culture is this? (repeat)
A cultura está errada,	A culture that's wrong
A de sermos diferentes:	That makes us different
Amor é normal,	'Cos love is normal,
Independente de se o sexo é igual.	Whether same-sex or not.
Que cultura é essa? (bis)	What culture is this? (repeat)

The song is a call to action. BRock's revolutionary ethos has been rekindled:

Os problemas têm solução	The huge problem may be solved
Se partirmos para a ação,	If we get out there for action,
Mas o Brasil vai evoluindo:	But Brazil is progress
Vamos fazer revolução	So why not start a revolution
Se acabarmos com o reconceito	Get rid of prejudice
E a discriminação.	End discrimination.
Que cultura é essa? (bis)	What culture is that? (repeat)
Preconceito? Aqui, não, meu irmão!	Prejudice? No, brother, not here, not now!

In the hope that 'Prejudice: a huge problem' will also be sung by multitudes…

Updating voices on intergenerational clashes: 'I'm leaving home'
A dialogue from a play produced by very young students of the 8th and 9th grades of primary education from the Contestado settlement emphasizes generational conflicts around gender orientation. The play was inspired by a previous workshop featuring homophobia – understood as general, psychological and social hostility to those who

supposedly feel desire for or have sex with individuals of their sex. The students debated Walcyr Carrasco's primetime soap opera *Amor à vida/Love for life* on explicit homophobia within a heterosexual family displaying a triumphant humiliation of the homosexual. The students particularly noted the father's contradiction, categorically reiterating his denial of prejudice, common among those who want to appear bereft of it, and yet voicing irrefutable intolerance.

In the students' play, the boundaries between secrecy and disclosure are blurred when the homosexual son confesses his homosexuality to his father. As above, the ritual of confession is liberating, but it unfolds a power relationship from the figure of authority, the father, who takes the confession. The father's exclusionary response is typically homophobic and heteronormative, beyond which he cannot conceive of any thinking. The students' progressive take further includes a corrective to the father's misuse of the word 'choice' for sexual orientation, which lies beyond one's will. Unconvinced, the father expels the son, but later reassesses his autocracy relative to the mother and an exclusionary bias and fetches the son back.

Son – Dad, I'm gay.
Father – What does that mean, boy?
Son – I like men not women.
Father – I didn't bring you up like this. You're a man, not a woman. To like a man?
Son – I know, dad, but nothing can change all that.
Father – But you already know, I do not accept that choice.
Son – That's got nothing to do with it, father, I really can like men, that won't change.
Father – You're not my son anymore. Get out of here! Forget that I'm your father.

Son – Easy, dad! You're angry. You don't know what you're saying. I'm leaving home, but when you accept it, come and get me. I forgive what you've said. I love you. I'm sorry for putting you through all this.

Mother – Where's my son? What have you done? You've not right to kick him out, he's your son.

Father – I've kicked him out 'cos he's turned gay. I won't accept it, I'll never accept it!

Mother – Where is our son?
Father – I'm sorry, I'm going after him.

'I'm leaving home' establishes a clear intertextual relationship with the Beatles' song 'She's Leaving Home', released in 1967. The intertext refers to the landmark historical experience of deep intergenerational conflicts in the context of the 1960s counterculture, particularly the youth's. For Vanessa P. Milani (2018), 'She's Leaving Home' specifically reflects the rise of feminist struggle in 1967, the year the Beatles released this song in their iconic album *Sgt. Pepper's Lonely Hearts Club Band*. 'She's Leaving Home' adopts a contrapuntal structure to enact a dramatic situation: the parents discover that their only daughter has run away from home, leaving only a note.

As Milani comments, the song alternates the parents' first person (interpreted by John Lennon) voicing with the third person (in Paul McCartney's voice) that narrates the events. It is as if the parents tried to justify themselves for the daughter's attitude or uttered a *mea culpa*, the mistake they made by not giving affection and attention to the daughter, only material comfort. McCartney's voice, on the other hand, explains the daughter's search for freedom and autonomy to live her own life. The daughter's attitude epitomizes the generational conflict of the mid 1960s, as young people sought a new way of life, different from that which their parents had had and denied consumerism as an end in itself. The woman becomes the protagonist of the songs, taking on prominent roles; the first-person plural (we) in the couple's speech breaks the hierarchy of man's views taking priority over women's. But the intergenerational conflict remains unresolved.

The intertext in the translation updates the said generational conflict in Brazil to today's gender diversity agenda. It makes the conflict meaningful to a British audience through allusion to the groundbreaking 1960s. With differences. The homosexual son becomes the protagonist taking up his role in the first person singular. The mother is not only a partner in the utterance; she challenges the father's autocracy and demands respect for her equal right in parental

1

decisions. The father does not indulge in *mea culpa* expressions but reconsiders his homophobia and goes after the son. The conflict is, ostensibly, resolved.

Interlocking rhythms across national frontiers: enhancing international solidarities

One of the seductions of translation is that it is 'the most intimate act of reading', posits the Indian post-colonial theorist, feminist and translator of Derrida into English, Gayatri Spivak (1993: 180). There are ways in which Bernard McGuirk's translation strategy empathizes with the countryside adolescents' contestation of cultural immutability and obscurantism. He once said: 'I am a free spirit, not a professional translator. I like to play with possibilities' (in Vieira, 2008: n.p.). The adolescents' profound sense of history poses challenges to the translator. How to render the cultural embedding of their compositions meaningful to an Anglo-Saxon audience? How to breed historical intimacy with the reader outside Brazil? How to re-site/re-cite the dense weave of Brazilian cultural memory and intertexts embedded in the adolescents' original? How to convey the Benjaminian sense of the resurfacing of an unfinished past that inhabits the youth's originals? At stake is not simply how the translation recasts Brazilian historical specificity but what potential impact it may have, in these cases, on the British or American sense of history and responses to cultural change. Can it also achieve what the prominent poet and translation theorist Haroldo de Campos (2007) had proposed for translation as a critical reading of one's own history?

Today's youths in the settlements have benefited from formal education and have had access to technology which has made the countryside less isolated. Whilst preserving countryside traditions, they have also opened up their horizons. Their intertexts bear witness to their engagement with various cultural productions nationally and internationally. It stands to reason that, for the immediacy of communication associated with lyrics and recited poems, McGuirk will dispense with what Spivak has referred to as useless footnotes in a translation mocking the discursive web of the original (1993). Neither will he bypass the Anglo-Saxon reader's aesthetic expectations with translational strategies such as amplification to clarify the composition's complex historicity and allusions to Brazilian culture. His rendering of the adolescents' experimentation with the language and weave of cultural texts confirms what Haroldo de Campos once said about his translation skills: 'He is most agile with the English language and pays very close attention to the poetic function' (in Vieira, 2008: n.p.). Performance is also as much a part of McGuirk's translational strategy as it is of his well-known critical register. Broadly speaking, his option has been to re-inscribe the adolescent students' poems and lyrics into the discourse of 1960s and 1970s British and American rock music, recognized as it has been and still is worldwide.

*

The poem 'The right to love and have fun', composed by very young students of the 8th and 9th grades of primary education from the Contestado settlement, while broadening the spectrum of conjugalities, expresses the need for greater recognition of homosexuals' right to public visibility, including that of their affections and leisure moments. In order to render in English the effect of immediacy intended by the adolescents, the translator absorbs and transforms an intertext from one of the best played rock lyrics in the 1960s, 'You've Lost That Lovin' Feelin'. It was composed by the husband-and-wife song writing team of Barry Mann and Cynthia Well and recorded in 1964 by the Righteous Brothers in Los Angeles. It subsequently consolidated its place in the world's repertoire through new recordings by such as Elvis Presley, Dionne Warwick, Roberta Flack, Joan Baez, among others.

O preconceito é grande,	Prejudice is huge,
Mas se pararmos pra pensar	But if we stop and sing
O quanto eles são felizes	They've got
com o amor que sentem	that lovin' feelin'
Mulheres com mulheres	Woman with woman
E homens com homens	And man with man
Têm também o direito de amar...	They also have the right
Dançar	To love... dancing.

The accompanying illustration, also produced by the adolescents from the Contestado settlement, picks up the thread: it displays two hearts, inside each of them is the nascent love of relaxed same sex couples. The 'lovin' feelin' graft from the English-speaking repertoire retains the musicality of the original in the translation. The intertext from a song informed by ideas of passion which, in general, produce positive responses in the listeners, builds on the adolescents' intended plea for positive recognition of homosexuals, whilst also updating the heteronormative original composition into a wider spectrum of sexualities. Further still, in order concisely to advance the adolescents' support for the cultural inclusiveness of same-sex couples, the translation changes 'lost' (the heart-breaking experience of a dying heterosexual passion) into the positive 'got' in new conjugalities.

*

The lyrics 'We're all human', also composed by the very young students of the 8th and 9th grades of primary education from the Contestado settlement, begin by interrogating the biblical notion of human perfection:

'Be perfect, therefore, as your heavenly Father is perfect' (Matthew, 5:48).

God's perfection – and of God alone –, the guideline in the Sermon on the Mount, implies that human beings will always fall short of perfection. The students' logical conclusion to a command that is incapable of being fully realized in this life is its reversal through the addition of a subversive line to the verse of Matthew:

Ninguém é perfeito,	Nobody's perfect,
Como ninguém é imperfeito.	No one's imperfect.

The biblical demonstration of human beings' inability to be perfect, as per Matthew above, has been understood by some as diminishing human agency (McCurry, 2007). The adolescents, however, demonstrate human autonomy to think beyond the heteronormative and hierarchical mould of the Genesis ideology ('And the rib that the Lord God had taken from the man he made into a woman and brought her to the man'). If all are equally human beings, and not necessarily perfect, they demand respect for those who fall outside the mould.

'Clay' takes up and carries further the students' point in the translation. This ingenious biblical intertext from Genesis in the translation ('And the Lord God formed man of the dust of the ground, and breathed into his nostrils the breath of life; and man became a living soul') emphasizes the adolescents' point on the sameness, not imperfection, of all human beings in this life:

Somos todos humanos,	We're all human,
Somos todos do mesmo jeito.	Made from the same clay.

Easily memorized rhymes in the original's exhortation to change as well as in the translation emphasize agency:

Vamos pensar diferente	Let's think in a different way.
Se quisermos que o mundo	If we want the world order
vá para frente.	to move with a sway.
Temos caráter,	We have our will,
sem preconceito;	so prejudice... no more;
Só queremos respeito.	Respect is what we're waiting for.

Changes in mind-set, such as same-sex marriages being increasingly legalized in the world, are unsettling. This is where the translation brings in the experience of the life-changing 1960s. The echo comes from Paul McCartney's 'Let it be' (1970) which talks of maternal wisdom bringing a note of strength and hope amidst troubled times. The soothing presence is that of his deceased mother Mary, an apparition in his dream, when he was going through an emotional turmoil. The religious homonym, 'Mother Mary', in turn, brings a sense of certitude and faith that things will get better in the future ('There will be an answer'). Rhymes, assonances and repetitions interlock sounds and histories in the consequently explicit McCartney-inflected translation:

Diversidade de gênero é legal,	Gender diversity's cool,
É ideal, é ideal.	Let be it, let it be.
Vamos pensar assim, assim, assim:	Let's think like this, like this:
Nem todo mundo é	There will be an answer
Igual a mim!	Just as there was for me!

(W)rapping up

Henry Louis Gates Jr., in his foreword to the Yale University Press 2010 *Anthology of Rap*, sums up some key points in this artistic performance which came out of the Bronx in the mid-1970s and extends a long-standing practice in the African American oral tradition: this art form born of young black and brown men and women who, sometimes engaging in political duels, found their voices in rhyme, and chanted a poetic discourse to the rhythm of the beat (Gates Jr., 2010).

In Brazil, the urban development of rap in the peripheries of the major cities 'has been associated with a new mood of social disaffection and militancy, especially, if not exclusively, among young working-class Afro-Brazilians [and] the collapse of what he

[George Yúdice] called the "consensual culture", the popularized confidence in a national project of social harmonization and racial democracy' (Treece, 2013: 178).[13] Urban rap has found a natural path into the *Sem Terra* adolescents' musical repertoire equally stamped by socio-political protest. It has also harmonized well with the *Sem Terra's* tradition of collective composition. What David Treece has mentioned in relation to Afro-Brazilian creativity, applies to Landless Voices, old and new, 'the ability to materialize the power of words in rhythmical structures [...] drawn from an historically accumulated store of knowledge' (2013: 190).

It is worth quoting in full the rap 'I'm like this for me', composed by the primary school students of the 8th and 9th grades from the Contestado settlement. Noteworthy is that the translation mimics the salient speech inflections from the original base of rap in American urban black youth and its stylized speech. There is an enchainment across stanzas of words that are almost the same but not quite (as Bhabha would have it). Sounds interlock through assonance. Alliteration and rhyme proliferate in the rhythmic assertion of one's right to change and of one's sexual orientation, as advocated in unison by the recently constituted new countryside organic intellectuals, and by their translator:

Homossexualidade:	Homosexuality:
Sou assim não pelos outros,	I'm like this not for others,
Mas por mim.	But for me.
O rap é legal;	Rap is cool;
Consigo assim,	I can be, you see,
Assim, assim.	Like that, like this.
Do meu corpo cuido eu,	Of my body I take care,
É o meu gosto quem decide sou eu.	My taste decides who's me.
Não teria preconceito	There'd be no prejudice
Se eu não fosse	If I weren't
Assim, assim, assim.	Like that, like this, like me.

---

[13] This collapse, Treece (2013) adds, was brought to a focus in 1992, the year of the mass street mobilization that led to the impeachment of President Fernando Collor de Mello and the massacre of hundreds of prisoners by military police in São Paulo's Carandiru jail.

This generation's political potentiality, inherent in the historical process of land struggle, in Mannheim's terms, was ready for a realization accelerated by the tempo of legal and cultural change. Maria Rita César's words sum up the revolutionary thrust of the poetics produced in and disseminated from Paraná's settlements of Agrarian Reform:

> The introduction of topics on gender equality and sexual diversity in Brazilian countryside high-schools [by those young students already promoting social struggle for land-ownership] opens the doors for subjective transformation and has a clear impact on the production of practices and discourses oriented towards gender equality and against discrimination of the LGBT population (César, 2018: n. p.).

The translator's dis-simulation of the body of Brazilian history, in turn, bears evidence that inside/outside are categories that organize references, but may be inadequate with regards to the struggle for gender emancipation, whether in the UK and the US sexual revolutions of the 1960s, or in today's context of the legalization of gender diversity. The translation's easily recognizable intertexts and easily memorized rhymes and assonances, while enabling a critical view of growing obscurantism in Brazil today, in solidarity, create worldwide listening posts for the counter-hegemonic agency of today's young Landless Voices promoting a progressive gender diversity agenda.

References

Bones, Sávio. *With hands calloused from poetry: The formation of the organic intellectuals by the MST.* **http://www.landlessvoices.org/ vieira/archive05.php?rd=WITHHAND546&ng=e&sc=3&th=4 2&se=0**.

Butler, Judith. *Gender Trouble: Tenth Anniversary Edition.* London: Routledge, 1999.

Caldart, Roseli Salete. 'Movimento Sem Terra: Lições de Pedagogia', *Currículo sem Fronteiras* 3, 1 (Jan/Jun 2003), 50-59.

Capitani, Raquieli. 'Assentamento desenvolve economia do município de Rio Bonito', in *Movimento dos Trabalhadores Rurais Sem Terra MST*, 2011. **http://www.mst.org.br/node/11623**.

Capitani, Raquieli. 'Assentamento Contestado desenvolve novo modelo de produção', in *Movimento dos Trabalhadores Rurais Sem Terra MST*, 2013. **http://www.mst.org.br/content/ assentamento-contestado-desenvolve-novo-modelo-de-rodu% C3%A7%C3% A3o.**

César, Maria Rita. Unpublished interview with Else Vieira and Sônia Schwendler, 2018.

Cvejić, Žarko. 'Blasting the Past: A Rereading of Walter Benjamin's *Theses on the Philosophy of History*', *Philosophy and Society* 30, 3 (2019), 321-46.

Dapieve, Arthur. *BRock: O Rock Brasileiro dos Anos 80*. São Paulo: Editora 34, 2005.

De Campos, Haroldo. 'On translation as creation and criticism', in Bernard McGuirk and Else R. P. Vieria (eds.), *Haroldo de Campos in Conversation*. London: Zoilus Press, 2007, 200-212.

Derrida, Jacques. *Otobiographies: The Teaching of Nietzsche and the Politics of the Proper Name*, trans. Avital Ronell. Lincoln: University of Nebraska Press, 1988.

Derrida, Jacques. *The Ear of the Other: Otobiography, Transference, Translation*, trans. Peggy Kamuf. New York: Schocken Books, 1985.

Derrida, Jacques. *Circumfessions*, trans. Geoffrey Bennington, Chicago: University of Chicago Press, 1993.

Encarnação, Paulo Gustavo da. '"Nasci em 62": algumas notas sobre uma breve história social de alguns roqueiros brasileiros dos anos 80', in José Adriano Fenerick (ed.), *Nas trilhas do rock: experimentalismo e mercado musical*. Goiânia: Kelps, 2018, 194-212.

Faúndes, José Manuel Morán. 'The geopolitics of moral panic: The influence of Argentinian neo-conservatism in the genesis of the discourse of "gender ideology"', *International Sociology* 34, 4 (2019), 402-17.

Foucault, Michel. *The History of Sexuality, Vol. I*, trans. Robert Hurley. New York: Vintage Books, 1990.

Freire, Paulo. 'Agrarian Reform and Education', in Else R. P. Vieira (ed.), *The Sights and Voices of Dispossession: The Fight for the Land and the Emerging Culture of the MST (The Movement of the Landless Rural Workers of Brazil)*, 2003. **http://www.landless-voices.org/vieira/archive-05.php?rd=INTERVIE409&ng=e&sc**

=3&th=41&se=0.

Gramsci, Antonio. *Selections from the Prison Notebooks of Antonio Gramsci*, ed. and trans. Quintin Hoare and Geoffrey Nowell Smith. New York: International Publishers, 1971.

Gates, Henry Louis, Jr. 'Foreword', in Adam Bradley *et al.* (eds.)*, The Anthology of Rap*. New Haven: Yale University Press, 2010, xxii-xxviii.

Lefevere, André. *Translation, Rewriting and the Manipulation of Literary Fame*. London: Routledge, 1992.

Le Guellec-Minel, Anne. 'Camping it out in the Never: Subverting Hegemonic Masculinity', in *The Adventures of Priscilla, Queen of the Desert* (Stephan Elliott, 1994)', *Revue LISA/LISA e-journal* XV, 1 (2017). **http://journals.openedition.org/lisa/9086; DOI: https://doi.org/10.4000/lisa.9086**.

Lessa, Ana C. *Brazil: 'Que país é esse?': Music and Power in Legião Urbana*. Unpublished Ph.D. thesis, University of Nottingham, 2011.

Lorber, Judith. 'Preface', *The Drag Queen Anthology: The Absolutely Fabulous but Flawlessly Customary World of Female Impersonators*. New York and London: Routledge, 2009, xv-xvi.

Maia, Ana Cláudia Bortolozzi, 'Sexualidade, Deficiência e Gênero: reflexões sobre padrões definidores de normalidade', in Rogério Diniz Junqueira (ed.), *Diversidade sexual na educação: problematizações sobre homofobia nas escolas*. Brasília: Edições UNESCO/MEC, 2009, 341-54.

Mannheim, Karl. 'The Problem of Generations', in Paul Kecskemeti (ed.), *Karl Mannheim: Essays*. London: Routledge, 1972, 276-322.

Maranhão Fº, Eduardo Meinberg de Albuquerque and Clarissa De Franco, '"Menino veste azul e menina, rosa" na Educação Domiciliar de Damares Alves: As ideologias de gênero e de gênesis da "ministra terrivelmente cristã" dos Direitos Humanos', *Revista Brasileira de História das Religiões* XI, 35 (Setembro/Dezembro 2019), 297-337.

McCurry, Jeffrey. '"Indeed You Will Even Have No Enemy": A Spirituality of Moral Vision in the *Didache*', *Spiritus* 7, 2 (2007), 193-202.

McDonald, Christie. 'Preface' to Jacques Derrida, *The Ear of the Other*. Lincoln: University of Nebraska Press, 1985, vii-x.

McGuirk, Bernard. 'Committing Translation or the Task of the Trans(at)l(antic)ator', in *Landless Voices in Song and Poetry by the Movimento dos Sem Terra of Brazil*. Compiled and annotated by Else R. P. Vieira; trans. Bernard McGuirk. Nottingham: Critical, Cultural and Communications Press, 2007, xxi-xxiv.

Mello, Luiz, Miriam Grossi and Anna Paula Uziel, 'A Escola e as Filhas de Lésbicas e Gays: reflexões sobre conjugalidade e parentalidade no Brasil', in Rogério Diniz Junqueira (ed.), *Diversidade sexual na educação: problematizações sobre homofobia nas escolas*. Brasília: Edições UNESCO/MEC, 2009, 159-82.

Milani, Vanessa Pinto. 'She's Leaving Home: o processo de feminilização nas canções dos Beatles, o movimento feminista e a contracultura', in José Adriano Fenerick (ed.), *Nas trilhas do rock: experimentalismo e mercado musical*. Goiânia: Kelps, 2018, 55-82.

Murphy, Michel K. 'The Politically Engaged Educational Developer as the "Organic Intellectual"', *New Directions in Teaching and Learning. Special Issue: Educational Development and Identity: Power, Position and the Profession* (2019), 75-84.

Palti, Elías José. 'Positivism, Revolution, and History in Brazil', in Johannes Feichtinger *et al.* (eds.), *The Worlds of Positivism: A Global Intellectual History, 1770-1930*. London: Palgrave Macmillan, 2018, 53-80.

Punt, Jeremy. 'Power and liminality, sex and gender, and GAL 3: 28: A postcolonial, queer reading of an influential text', *Neotestamentica*. 44, 1 (2010), 140-66.

Smith, Amy Erica. *Religion and Brazilian Democracy: Mobilizing the People of God*. Cambridge: Cambridge University Press, 2019.

Sousa Filho, Alípio. 'Teorias sobre a Gênese da Homossexualidade: ideologia, preconceito e fraude', in Rogério Diniz Junqueira (ed.), *Diversidade sexual na educação: problematizações sobre homofobia nas escolas*. Brasília: Edições UNESCO/MEC, 2009, 95-124.

Spivak, Gayatri. 'The Politics of Translation', in *Outside in the Teaching Machine*. London and New York: Routledge, 1993, 179-200.

Schwendler, Sônia F. and Else R. P. Vieira. *Landless Voices II: Gênero e Educação/Landless Voices II: Gender and Education*,

2018. **http://landless-voices2.org/**.

Underwood, Lisa and Steven P. Schacht (eds.). *The Drag Queen Anthology: The Absolutely Fabulous but Flawlessly Customary World of Female Impersonators*. London: Taylor and Francis, 2004.

Treece, David. *Brazilian Jive: From Samba to Bossa and Rap*. London: Reaktion Books, 2013.

Vazquez, Ana Carolina Brandão. 'Fascismo e O Conto da Aia: a misoginia como política de Estado', *Revista Katálysis* 22, 3, 597-606.

Vieira, Else R. P. (ed.) *The Sights and Voices of Dispossession: The Fight for the Land and the Emerging Culture of the MST (The Movement of the Landless Rural Workers of Brazil)*, 2003. **http://www.landless-voices.org/vieira/ index.php?ng=e**.

Vieira, Else R. P. 'Music, Poetry and the Politicization of the Landless Identity', in *Landless Voices in Song and Poetry by the Movimento dos Sem Terra of Brazil*. Compiled and annotated by Else R. P. Vieira; trans. Bernard McGuirk. Nottingham: Critical, Cultural and Communications Press, 2007, xxviii-lxix.

Vieira, Else R. P. 'Translating history and creating an international platform: Haroldo de Campos's "o anjo esquerdo da história"', in Maria Clara Castelões de Oliveira and Else R. P. Vieira (eds.), *Proceedings of the Symposium 'Tradução Literária e Adaptação: Tessituras Literárias, Intersemióticas e Histórico-Culturais'*. São Paulo: USP, 2008.

Wolowic, Jennifer M. *et al.*, 'Chasing the rainbow: lesbian, gay, bisexual, transgender and queer youth and pride semiotics'. *Culture, Health and Sexuality* 19, 5 (2017), 557-71.

Foreword to the 2007 edition of
Landless Voices in Song and Poetry

Else R. P. Vieira and Bernard McGuirk

This anthology brings together some of the countless songs and poems of the emerging militant culture of the MST – the Movement of the Landless Rural Workers of Brazil – officially set up in 1984, precisely at that moment when the social tragedy which still bedevils some four million families in Brazil was escalating. Landlessness festers in unhealed wounds of the nation's body politic. Five hundred years of landlessness can be traced back to successive papal bulls in the 15th and 16th centuries whereby territory yet to be discovered (but already inhabited by others) was donated to Portugal and Spain, ostensibly for the propagation of the Christian faith yet, no less, for exploitation by indissociable sovereign powers. The legacies of empire and the subsequent development policies adopted by successive regimes, notably, the military dictatorship of 1964 to 1985, encouraged multinational agribusiness, thereby aggravating the colonial condition of dispossession inherited through vast estates, Brazil's notorious latifundia. Two-thirds of the country's arable land is owned by fewer than three per cent of the population and by international conglomerates, resulting in an economy in which innumerable rural workers have been laid off, with very few, if any, compensatory social benefits.

Music, art and literature have long been sensitive to the vagaries and violence of the land problem in Brazil. Instance Glauber Rocha's *Cinema Novo* and Portinari's *Retirantes* portrait series. Important literary voices have also been heard speaking *for* the destitute, for example, Jorge Amado, Graciliano Ramos and João Cabral de Melo Neto. Music of the 1960s had a particularly important role in mobilizing the attention to the problem of populations national and international. Most recently, the world's gaze has been focussed on the plight of Brazil's dispossessed by Walter Salles and Fernando Meirelles through the blockbuster success of international cinema in films such as *Central Station* and *City of God*. But what of the expressions of the landless themselves? What do their own voices and sounds, poems and songs, tell us of the plight of those who go through the travails of landlessness and yet have had little or no access to any hearers at all?

Those dispossessed of land have also remained deprived of voice and of images. This anthology offers a public space, however minimal, for the expression of their anguish, their hopes and their commitment. Rosane de Souza, 14, and Francisco Macilom Nunes Aquino, 17, are also young voices who grew up with the MST and give us an insider's view. The militant poets who saw or assisted the Movement's being born and who give expression to this emerging culture are Ademar Bogo from Bahia, Ana Cláudia from Pernambuco, Aracy Cachoeira from Minas Gerais, Charles Trocate from Pará, Pedro Tierra from the centre-west of Brazil, and Zé Pinto from Minas Gerais and then Rondônia. Composers included in the anthology follow suit. The anthology also incorporates the expressions of today's intellectuals and artists who speak not quite *for* but *with* the landless people: Frei Betto, Chico Buarque, Haroldo de Campos, Paulo Freire, Antonio Candido and Oscar Niemeyer. The drawing of a ten-year old *sem-terra* from Pernambuco, Fábio Junior de Lima – a map of Brazil inside an open eye shedding three tears for those most wounded by its history: the native, the black and the female Brazilians – is but one of the illustrations in this book that render the *sem-terra*'s world visible to the reader.

The introductory statements in this first anthology, in book-form, of poems and songs produced by the *sem-terra* themselves, highlight different aspects of their expressions. Bernard McGuirk contextualizes some of the challenges faced by the translator, linguistic and cultural, in the context of poetry and song of commitment and solidarity. Else R. P. Vieira provides the background to the research; her essay analyses the major aesthetic and thematic tendencies of the music and poetry produced by this militant culture, whose first archive she compiled and organized according to categories elicited from their own voices, during her two-year field-work in Brazil (2001-2). She further explores the connections between these tendencies, the history of the Movement and the Brazilian cultural traditions, as well as the dialogue between the *sem*-terra and other dispossessed, or with those who express solidarity with them. Her claim is that a culture of opposition is not an island entire of itself – voices resonate, images are mirrored by others, elsewhere.

Committing Translation
or the
Task of the Trans(at)l(antic)ator

Bernard McGuirk

The translator of the poems and songs of the *Movimento dos Sem Terra* soon confronts commitment. The last few decades have witnessed the revitalizing of popular music as a vehicle for political activisms in Brazil. One obvious source has been the *música sertaneja* of land-deprived migrant workers, driven towards the cities and taking with them their country music, be it traditional or, more recently, influenced by the commercial brands of the southern cultures of the United States.

No less influential has been the *pagode* movement's samba-esque registering of the violent tensions of poverty in its hardly couched critiques of repressive regimes, military or otherwise. The performances echo, consciously or subliminally, the prosodies – high and low – of Brazilian Portuguese and the broadsheet and *cordel* strains of popular imaginaries from across and beyond the nation. Brazil never ceases to explore and express its sensitivity to the ideological power of the protest song.

At the time of writing, it was the centenary of the birth of the great Chilean poet Pablo Neruda. Inspiration of politically committed poetry and song for not a continent but a world, he was described by Federico García Lorca as being closer to blood than to ink. It was on such a note – often indissociable from tears or from wine – that the anguish and euphoria, the despair and hope that suffuse the texts I translated were approached and embraced. My locus of translation is, unavoidably and unapologetically, Anglophone; it is also, though tempered, European. As a critic and translator of, primarily, literatures in Portuguese, Spanish, French and Italian, I have exploited the availability of translation alternatives from those traditions as well as from any Brazil-specific contexts that have informed the choices made. Umberto Eco has written in his *Mouse or Rat? Translation as Negotiation*:

I frequently feel irritated when I read essays on the theory of translation that, even though brilliant and perceptive, do not provide enough examples. I think translation scholars should have had at least one of the following experiences during their life: translating, checking and editing translations, or being translated and working in close co-operation with their translators [...] Between the purely theoretical argument that, since languages are differently structured, translation is impossible, and the common-sensical acknowledgement that people, after all, do translate and understand each other, it seems to me that the idea of translation as a process of negotiation (between author and text, between author and readers, as well as between the structure of two languages and the encyclopaedias of two cultures) is the only one that matches experience. (36)

Let his words speak for me and the texts of the *MST* speak for themselves, to all.

The translations offered here do not demand any knowledge of national local lyrical forms or their echoes. However, it would be naïve to conceal or play down the impact of prominent Brazilian song-writers on the artistic production of the *MST*. For this reason, and reflecting the importance of such as Caetano Veloso, Gilberto Gil, Milton Nascimento and many others, the inclusion in this volume of my translation of songs by perhaps the most celebrated of them all, Chico Buarque de Hollanda, provides a telling counterpoint to the respective creations of the *MST* adherents themselves. My task therefore also involved not abandoning but suspending certain spontaneous choices of translation in favour of inter- and trans-action. The challenges were: differ, defer, never with indifference, always without deferance; address not only issues dear to the *MST*, primordial in this volume, but also the transactions, with and in the Movement, of Chico Buarque, Frei Betto and Haroldo de Campos and, thus, re-address previous tasks of the other – cultural inseparably from linguistic – translator(s).

These intra-cultural translators allow for the inter-action of Brazilians speaking and listening to Brazilians being listened and spoken to; in turn, they inspire that other, the trans(at)l(antic)ator whose sign/ature shuttles to and fro, ever seeking to perform intra-, but never faithful, ever faith-less, illusorily face-less, scorn-fully masking source, mourn-fully eschewing target, settling (lawlessly), for an ever extra- trans-mission of occupations, pre-occupations, needs, urgencies.

The Latin American protest-song explosions of the late 1950s and 1960s, of which Robert Pring-Mill reminds us in 1990, in *'Gracias a la vida': The Power and Poetry of Song*, have hardly left Brazil unaffected by the echoes, influences, hybridities and inter-texts of contemporary transculturations. He lists civil rights, the peace movement and the anti-Vietnam war demonstrations in the US; Italian Cantocronache; the Greece of Theodorakis; the Catalan Nova Cançó; the Portuguese Nova Canção; Irish songs of 'the troubles'; and Asian and African instances from the Philipines, East Timor and Mongolia, to Mozambique and Angola. Not least of the inter-texts of Brazilian protest song and poetry are the Cuban, Argentine and Chilean expressions which sprinkle the *MST* artists with inspirations taken from the archives of the Fidel Castro, Che Guevara and the *nueva canción* traditions.

If any one element of Pring-Mill's seminal analysis can be said to inform the texts of the *MST*, it is this evocation: 'Asked about his own songs (in 1973), the Uruguayan Daniel Vigliette said firmly that they were as much *de propuesta* as *de protesta*: designed not merely to protest but to propose – in other words not merely to "tear down fences" (quite literally so in Viglietti's own anti-*latifundista* "A desalambrar!") but also "to build bridges" and to be constructive' (10). Pring-Mill identifies three functions of such texts: to act in 'response to an immediate environment'; to be an 'instrument of political and social change'; to communicate a 'horizon of expectations' and 'presuppositions' (12). Yet he is quick to add a vital rider on cultural difference: 'the whole rhetoric of such poems and songs is very different from ours, partly because Spanish [here read Portuguese] handles issues more violently – more dramatically and emotionally – than English (sometimes in ways which we may find indecorous)' (14). He continues:

The messages of individual Latin American songs function within the framework of belief they foster and reinforce, in that extremely different social context. In countries where illiteracy is as high as it is in most of Latin America, where censorship and repression are so often at work, and where the official media are so rarely to be trusted, the message-bearing function of *poesía de compromiso* – sung or unsung – has an importance which it is not easy for a more literate academic audience to appreciate. Its messages perform a varied series of useful social functions […] all of which are doubly important in the context of predominantly oral cultures. Thus they serve both to report and to record events (interpreting them, naturally enough, from specific points of view, which will strike all those who disagree with them as prejudiced); they praise or lament heroes and denounce tyrants; they protest against abuses and propound solutions (whether these are viable or not); and they teach many kinds of practical lessons, which their listeners are encouraged to put into practice. (77)

Robert Pring-Mill would hardly have been surprised not to be granted the last word. He might also have smiled at the risky certainty, in respect not only of rhetoric but also of politics, of Perry Anderson: 'the symbolism of a former shoe-shine boy and street vendor achieving supreme power in the most unequal major society on earth speaks for itself […] A climate of popular expectation surrounds Lula that no President of the New Republic has ever enjoyed at the outset of his mandate. Hope of relief from the misery of the last years will not vanish overnight' (21). Nor – a mandate on – would the translated voices of the *Movimento dos Sem Terra*.

References

Anderson, Perry. *London Review of Books*, 12 December 2002.

Eco, Umberto. 'Of Mice and Men', *The Guardian Review*, 1 November 2003.

Pring-Mill, Robert. *'Gracias a la vida': The Power and Poetry of Song*. London: Department of Hispanic Studies, Queen Mary and Westfield College, 1990.

(Re)Searching the (*Sem*) *Terra*:
The Archive of the Poetry and Music of the MST

Else R. P. Vieira

Prior to 2003, the poetry and songs of the MST (Movement of the Landless Rural Workers of Brazil) were mostly unavailable to the public at large. The MST music was first recorded, in DVD form, outside the commercial circuit, after the *sem-terra*'s 1997 National March to Brasília; the circulation of the other four DVDs produced by late 2002 also remained internal to the Movement. Their poetry is mostly delivered orally; the few existing written records were on loose papers or in draft form in personal files. An overall lack of recognition and of cultural capital in which the *sem-terra* have been trapped hindered even more the dissemination of their expression.

A major initiative by the School of Modern Languages of the University of Nottingham opened new perspectives for the *sem-terra*'s expression nationally and internationally. A multi-disciplinary and multi-region umbrella research project into the cultural expressions emerging from landlessness *lato sensu* – the experience of the mass movement and re-settlement of peoples, devised by Professors Nick Hewitt and Bernard McGuirk – enabled me to direct a specific pilot project on the cultural expressions of the landless people in Brazil. As part of my activities as Senior Research Fellow in the Department of Hispanic and Latin American Studies of the University (2001-2002). Through intense field-work throughout Brazil, I searched for the primary sources, selected the material that was most representative of this militant culture, and compiled the first archive of their poetry, songs and respective lyrics of a scattered community of over 20,000,000 people – over one eighth of the country's total population – projecting it for the first time beyond the Movement (Vieira, 2003). Researchers from two other institutions were invited into this project, namely, Professor Bernardo Mançano Fernandes (UNESP-São Paulo), also the President of the Brazilian Association of Geographers, and Dr. Malcolm McNee, at the time a School Fellow in Luso-Brazilian Literary and Cultural Studies in the Department of Spanish and Portuguese at the University of Minnesota. Bridging the gap between the humanities and technology, this pilot project, with the assistance of the technology officer of the School of Modern Languages, John

Walsh, organized a database of the artefacts of the emerging culture of the MST across various media (paintings, film, literature, music, children's drawings and compositions, etc.). The second part of the database offers academic studies and reference material on the Movement and related topics, as well as statements and creative works by intellectuals and artists who express their solidarity with those dispossessed.[1]

Opening the School of Modern Language series, the bilingual archive *As Imagens e as Vozes da Despossessão: A Luta pela Terra e a Cultura Emergente do MST (Movimento dos Trabalhadores Rurais Sem-Terra do Brasil)/The Sights and Images of Dispossession: The Fight for the Land and the Emerging Culture of the MST* was launched in the House of Commons (Westminster) and in the World Social Forum (Porto Alegre, Brazil) in January 2003. The School provided more than an institutional niche for the research to be carried out. By housing the database, it has also offered a public space, nationally and internationally, for the *sem-terra* to express their anguish, their traumas, their hopes and their political platform. The material in this book, an expanded version of that published in the archive, is a further step towards breaking the chain of symbolic violence surrounding the expression of this group.

Crucial for the dissemination of both the poetry and the songs beyond Brazil was Bernard McGuirk's mastery of the various registers and regionalisms of Portuguese and his ability to convey in English the nuances and idiomatic expressions of this predominantly oral *sem-terra* culture. His poetic gift was also crucial for his rendering into English of their country rhythms, many of which bear traces of earlier forms inherited from Portugal. Particularly challenging are their characteristic metres and their creation of meaning through sound structure (discussed in the essay in this volume). The translations sound as natural as their texts in Portuguese. No use was made of what Gayatri Spivak condemns as 'useless footnotes' in a translation, which are 'an indication of absence of

---

[1] For a full description of the Project and of the database see Vieira, Else R. P. 'Enhancing Cultural Studies through a Web-Enabled Database: The Sights and Sounds of the Emerging Culture of the MST (The Movement of the Landless Rural Workers of Brazil)', *The International Journal of Technology, Knowledge and Society*, 2 (8), pp. 115-28.

intimacy' with the material and which additionally mock the dynamic intricacy of the textual fabric (1993: 184). The existing footnotes are my own intervention to provide contextual information. The translations themselves do not require footnotes, because McGuirk skilfully and almost imperceptibly uses strategies such as equivalence and compensation. Authenticity of expr-ession and fluency are the impressions imparted by the translations.

My direct work with the MST's poet-singers started with Zé Pinto, originally from the central state of Minas Gerais. The drastic cultural uprooting he experienced in his childhood, when his family had to migrate to the northern state of Rondônia (Amazon region), is recorded in his poetry and songs; he now lives in the sourthern state of Rio Grande do Sul. Close and intense contact with Aracy Cachoeira came next and brought another perspective, that of the north of Minas Gerais. Her extensive collection of photographs also adds life to her work with expropriated native tribes, to some landmark performances, as well as to her daughter's exemplary militant womanhood. These two poet-singers put me in contact with their counterparts in other regions of Brazil, namely, Ademar Bogo (a former seminarist, he is also a very productive articulator of the MST's agenda in essay form, now in the state of Bahia), Ana Cláudia (from Pernambuco, in the Northeast, a region riven by droughts and by the power of the land-owning aristrocacy since colonial times), and Charles Trocate (from the state of Pará in the Amazon, the stage of violent land conflicts, epitomized by the Eldorado de Carajás massacre of 1996). The survey of resources was complemented in the files of the MST in São Paulo.

These *cantadores* were key elements in making the MST culture tangible to me. The important insights I gained, in turn, enabled me to devise categories to organize their cultural artefacts in general. A major concern was to listen to the *sem-terra* and elicit categories from what they expressed rather than stifling the culture by the Procrustean use of categories alien to it. These categories were used to organize the poems and songs in this book and other artefacts of the MST's culture.

Music, Poetry and the Politicization
of the Landless Identity

Else R. P. Vieira

Collective action has become a central force and a common means of expressing political and cultural needs in twenty-first-century societies. In the vertiginous globalization of the world, power and decision making increasingly gravitate to transnational markets and bodies, a context in which to draw on collective identity is often the only way in which communities or groups can express their needs and choices (Jordan *et al.*, 2002: 5). It is in this light that we shall be examining the *Sem Terra*'s songs and poetry and the way they relate to the origins of the Movement and its shifting agenda across three decades. Their distinctive collective production and expression will also be seen to shift away from an era increasingly marked by individual enjoyment of art. The rehabilitation of country culture will be seen to be one of the hallmarks of their poetic and musical expression. The role of music and poetry in the constitution of a landless identity will be stressed, while the regional specificities of this national Movement will also be highlighted in terms of local history and culture.

Music, poetry, and the politicization of the landless identity

In the culture of the *Movimento dos Sem-Terra*, close links exist between music and poetry – both important collective experiences. Poetry or sung tunes are usually orally delivered during marches or during the cultural act of the Movement called the *Mística,* a secular equivalent to earlier forms of the religious gatherings from which the MST developed. The religious symbolism of their compositions aid these voices to express indignation against all forms of injustice.

In varying degrees, MST songs and recited poetry enhance togetherness and solidarity, express shared sentiments and the political views and values of a militant culture born out of landlessness. Yet this artistic production is more than the collective expression of a political culture which creates a mystique of integration. Poetry and music play a crucial role in authorizing and dignifying a culture born of extreme destitution. In the marches and the *Mística*, the *cantador,* for whom individual authorship or stardom can be lesser concerns, is an important force for social cohesion. The view of the poet-singer Zé Pinto, that the 'cantador passa uma energia', bears evidence to the power of music and of the poetic voice for the political construction of a collective identity.

Poetry and, in particular, music, were widely used during the 1997 National March (see below), but even then they will be seen to have remained mostly circumscribed within the Movement until their national and international dissemination in early 2003. Yet this March afforded the *sem-terra* unprecedented visibility. As pointed out by Maria da Glória Gohn, it brought the unthinkable to Brazilian homes, namely, that exclusion can become a social *locus*; through this March, landlessness established itself as the visible sign of an identity which, although constructed around an *absence*, could still be displayed through its icons and symbols. Still in her view, the greatest impact of the march was that it demonstrated the way in which that very lack, binding several excluded people together, can begin to be transformed into a positive symbol; the MST thus became a reference point, a banner for identities constructed in and on absence yet a model of the struggle against destitution. Such expressions, she concludes, seek to transform an identity negatively defined by a lack – *sem-terra* – into affirmative collective expressions of a 'we' (Gohn, 2000: 137).

The MST's marches and cultural acts bring together both the *sem-terra* and *Sem Terra*. The spelling shift signals the politicization of the landless identity. Zé Pinto draws attention to this crucial distinction in 'So I shall continue'. Lower-case and hyphenated *sem-terra* connotes a condition of dispossession, those rural workers who, in a Marxist sense, do not possess nor have access to the land as a means of production and subsistence. Crucially, landlessness means more than not having property: it also entails exclusion from any social benefits to be derived from territorial stability, such as education, health assistance and housing. Upper-case, non-hyphenated *Sem Terra* designates a political subject. *Sem Terra* relates to the continued militancy of the rural worker who has already received a plot of land but who remains a participant in the Movement and wants to be called *Sem Terra* in order to reaffirm his/her loyalty to the MST and his/her solidarity with the plight and struggle of those who have not yet received the same benefit.

Yet the landless identity cannot be essentialized by these polarities. The MST is better seen as a network of relatively diverse groups across the country sharing an identity defined by various forms of destitution and marginalization (such as roofless people, beggars, prostitutes). Their visibility and ability to survive require the establishment of such active solidarities which articulate, at a national level, a collective identity beyond landlessness. There are also those who constitute themselves as *Sem Terra* through identification. Such is the case of the poet Pedro Tierra. This distinguished politician, the son of *retirantes* from the North-East, uses a literary pseudonym (literally, Peter Land) which points to his identification with the *sem-terra* through the shared dramatic experience of being a poor and displaced peasant in Brazil.[1] His informal militancy with the MST has its roots in his participation, together with the the Movement's ideologue, João Pedro Stedile, in the CPT – *Pastoral Land Commission* – in whose experiences the MST has its genealogy.

What do these 'lives' recite and sing? What is distinctive about their poetry and songs? The mission of art and the role of the *cantador* (see below) is a major theme shared by these two major communal forms of the *sem-terra*'s artistic experience, but it finds a particularly fertile terrain in their poetry. Another striking feature shared by the MST's poetry and lyrics alike will be seen to be the definition of this militant culture's emblems and icons. Even though there are other shared areas, certain themes will also be seen to be more specific to one or of these two forms. Poetry tends to focus more on the *sem-terra*'s responses to impending death as part of their life's horizon. Expressions of profound grief follow massacres and the loss of companions. Of particular importance is their expression through poetry of their innermost feelings relating to the experience of exclusion. It is also mostly through poetry that the *sem-terra* establish networks of solidarity with other dispossessed segments.

Music remains their most widely used expression, partly because it has a marked role in the rural areas from which the *sem-terra* come and to which they aspire to return, partly because it is strongly emotive and thus likely to attract people to a shared project. Three themes are particularly eloquent in their music: the rehabilitation of rural traditions; education; and the relentless cycle of dispossession –

---

[1] Hamilton Pereira is his real name. He was agrarian secretary to the National Directorate of the PT/Workers' Party; in 1997 he was invited to direct Brasília's Department of Culture. He also contributed to the founding of unions for rural workers in many states throughout the country.

occupation – resistance in the encampments – eviction. Between 1997 and 2003, the Movement and/or its members produced five CDs in different parts of the country which reflect both regional specificities and the shifting agenda of the Movement throughout its history.

Three of the Movement's CDs will be featured in this study. One is the landmark *Arte em Movimento,* conceived during the momentous National Landless March to Brasília in 1997 and which plays a crucial role in defining the symbols of this militant culture's away from the official ones; it also renders explicit those Latin American icons and mentors who inspire their pedagogy of resistance. The second one is *Canções que abraçam sonhos* (1999), which includes the prize-winning songs of the *First Festival of Agrarian Reform* held in the state of Rio Grande do Sul and which reflects the ethos of the Movement in the more industrial south of the country, where it originated. The marked religious symbolism merges into the political in the songs about the marches and about the cavalry in the encampments. *Plantando Cirandas* (1999) is a collection of the songs which play an integral part in the Movement's important educational project.Their simple language is used as a memory aid, to disseminate knowledge, news and traditions, and to create a sense of the communal in which the values of solidarity and mutual aid underline a view of citizenship grounded on work and collective efforts. The children's hopes and aspirations are emphasized. The *cantadores'* poetics of natural life is used as a pedagogy of environmental awareness, as opposed to capitalist individualism and destructive greed. The two other CDs will be referred to in specific contexts. The *caipira* tradition will be highlighted as a form of contestation with reference to *Uma prosa sobre nós* (2001). *Um canto pela paz* (2001), recorded in Pará, the most violent state in terms of land problems, will be brought to bear with particular reference to the Eldorado de Carajás massacre in 1996.

The *Mística,* the *cantador* and the mission of art
The religious origins of the MST (notably the CPT, the *Comissão Pastoral da Terra*, further explain the predominance of music in the culture of the Movement. As in religious congregations, singing creates a sense of unity amongst millions of individuals, particularly in the case of those whose experiences of perpetual migration and fragmentation deprive them of the sense of security warranted by a

stable community. The *Místicas* forge a *Sem Terra* identity distinct from society at large. They have been described thus:

> A cultural and political act developed in various rituals, in which the *Sem Terra* express their readings of lived experiences through poetry, music, mime, painting, art in general. It is also a form of language of the unlettered who express, communicate, and interact in the building of the consciousness of the land struggle. (Mançano, quoted in 'Glossary', in Vieira, 2003)

The *Místicas* shift from the congregational to the communal. As pointed out, the communal production and enjoyment of music and poetry is a marked feature of MST culture which, in turn, sharply contrasts with the increasingly individual aesthetic experience of contemporary mainstream segments. Chanting is also a vital component of their marches, which are sometimes described as a motor moving a population towards an expected future of plenitude. The marches are a legacy of the religious origins of the Movement, namely the Catholic tradition of processions which socialize personal sacrifice and celebrate a collective identity. In their forward movement, marchers overcome obstacles to create a historic project of reconstruction. Famous historic marches of the oppressed are often consciously echoed, for instance Moses walking to the Promised Land, the Jews journeying through the wilderness from Egypt to Israel. The emphasis placed on the political clearly recalls the tradition set up by one of the MST's inspirations, Che Guevara, who created a trajectory leading away from a hostile history towards new horizons.

The *sem-terra* particularly maintain or revitalize the heritage of the narrative in verse originally used by the *cantador* in local fairs to disseminate news and stories. The *cantador* is associated with the oral heritage particularly of the rural North-East and North of Brazil: this versatile artist who writes verses and composes music would go around the rural areas singing, playing and telling stories in order to communicate news and events by word of mouth and in order to recount through verse the history and deeds of famous men in the region. His role of transmitter of culture is crucial in illiterate groupings and equally for integrating far-flung rural communities through the creation of a bedrock of shared knowledge. This artist also illustrates and casts the narrative in printed form, which is then called *cordel* (string literature). The *cordel* does not necessarily transform the collective experience into an individual one; as is the case in its original rural settings, the *cordel* is usually read aloud to a gathering of broadly illiterate listeners. The *cantador* is also a performer and the date of composition is usually the date of performance. Originally, the *cantador* was regarded as one predestined to be a mouthpiece and interpreter of oppressed people whose sorrows he expresses while bringing magic, joy and laughter.

The scholar Sávio Bones has described the MST's poets and singers as 'organic intellectuals', subscribing to the concept developed by the political scientist Antonio Gramsci. For this political thinker, every social group organically creates for itself one or more levels of intellectuals who give it homogeneity and the consciousness of its own economic, social and political functions (Gramsci, 2000: 15). If organic intellectuals create a new one within the traditional historic one, Bones' claim in relation to the MST poets is, to the extent that they challenge political and cultural submission, their production is an integral part of a 'counter-hegemonic movement, sower of hope, and herald of a new Brazil and a new world. The poetry made by the men and women who carry a hoe is transformed into a means of resistance and struggle' (Bones, 2003).

In the *Mística,* the *cantador* preserves the intimate relationship with the community as in the rural settings; his role is also crucial in activating the cultural memory of those distant from their roots. One difference is that the *cantador* is usually a man, given the itinerant nature of his work and the requirement of literacy, not common among rural women. Yet this gender dimension is diluted in the *Místicas,* to which women such as Aracy Cachoeira contribute both as composers of verse and as performers. Oral tradition explains some features of the poems and songs composed by the MST's *cantadores.* Rhythm, crucial to the oral transmission of cultures, combines with repetition and a characteristic syntax and metre as an aid to memory; at the same time, it enlivens the ritual. The lines of poetry and song usually hang together by sound and structure rather than by meaning alone. The *cantador* also explores the expressive potential of traditional verse forms, because poetry is meant to be effective communication in the sense of reaching the public in the most direct ways possible. The expression can be formulaic; concrete metaphors, associated with the life and work styles of rural communities, are common because they are easily recognizable and convey issues to the audience in a tangible way (notice, for example, how often they use 'sow' to represent the dissemination of knowledge or ideas, a metaphor which further carries clear religious and political undertones). Frequently used modes in the *Místicas* are the laments, anthems, poems of praise and commem-orative songs which register the history of the Movement. Amongst other examples of songs and poems of commemoration are 'Ao nosso Jornal', written on the tenth anniversary of the *Sem Terra* newspaper, and 'O sonho e o tempo', in celebration of the fifteenth anniversary of the MST.

With reference to the mission of art, the *sem-terra* poet-singers also subscribe to the long-standing tradition of the Latin American writer as a political revolutionary leader. In 'A arte de gerar'/'The Art of Sewing', the MST poet Ademar Bogo in fact establishes a literary lineage with the political militancy of such forerunners as Pablo Neruda, João Cabral de Melo Neto and D. Pedro Maria Casaldáliga. Denunciation and hope, as part of the continent's struggle for social justice and human rights, find an expression in these poets who, conceiving of art as a weapon responding to social and historical needs, endow it with a libertarian mission. Poets urge today's landless not to be mere passive recipients of a harsh destiny but agents in pursuit of a different fate. Rejecting silent resignation, the landless poets, unable to sow seeds, disseminate political resistance.

This militant culture's return to a materialist poetics and to ways of conceiving the aesthetic in revolutionary terms enables a parallel (not pursued here) with the so-called art of resistance and of national liberation struggles. Comparisons can also be made with the revolutionary literary canon in Latin America and, more specifically, for example, with the Nicaraguan Revolution's negotiation of Marxism and Christianity in its artistic project. Besides the communal nature of artistic experience and a shift-away from an attitude of individual resignation, a rhetoric of resistance in poetry and lyrics rereads history from the point of view of the destitute and constructs utopias on earth.

The congregational atmosphere, created by the singing and the reciting of poetry at MST gatherings, enhances the tone of exhortation to struggle. It further favours the socialization of sacrifice, as in Zé Pinto's 'E vamos indo'/'And off we go':

Cantaremos juntos,
Se sabemos que sozinhos
Não vamos chegar lá,
Nos daremos as mãos pelo caminho,
Se o cansaço nos alcançar
Na estrada, socializaremos o sacrifício.

[Then we shall sing together,/If we know we shan't arrive/If we stand alone,/Then we'll join hands as we go,/If tiredness affects us/On the way, we'll socialize the sacrifice].

Poetry is a calling in Aracy Cachoeira's writing which finds a place in social justice and whose voice unites the oppressed. Her 'Poesia' thus qualifies her for the role of mouthpiece for the destitute:

Quem tem alma de poeta,
Tem uma missão a cumprir,
Escrever tudo que sabe,
Com os outros repartir,
Este dom que Deus lhe deu,
Não guarde somente para ti.

[Whoever has a poet's soul,/Has a mission to unfold,/To write all he knows,/With others to share,/This God-given gift,/Don't keep it to yourself alone.]

The MST poets reject idealism in art. For example, Zé Pinto's 'Voei' imparts the view that the ultimate function of art is to mobilize and activate political consciousness. From his *cantador* father he inherited the mission to write and to disseminate engaged poetry:

Meu filho pegue a estrada […] Tem alguém te esperando […] Na esquina da esperança […] Cante um canto de revolta
E de vitória também
Porque cantar por cantar
Isso nunca lhe convém.

[Take to the road my son […]/For you there's someone waiting/On the corner of your hope […]/Sing a song of revolt/A song of victory, too/For to sing for singing's sake/Is never enough for you.]

Deep wounds in the body of history underscore today's bleak paradox: Brazil, the fifth largest country in the world (over three million square miles), is land-hungry; malnutrition is widespread among countless rural families for lack of a plot for them to farm and sustain themselves. Poetry is thus, ultimately, a tool for historical reconstruction. Believing in the transformative power of textual action, Zé Pinto further states in 'E vamos indo' that 'o que se canta também/Conta na construção da história' His more radical 'Poema de sangue' demands commitment while imparting the need for revolution through poetic form: there is beauty in the world, but we cannot forget the reality of hunger. The poet thus becomes a comrade whose mission makes a weapon of art. Struggle gives life to sounds in a context where political and revolutionary poetry is an injunction:

Hoje quando os ponteiros
Registrarem vinte e quatro horas
Mil crianças terão morrido de fome
Neste meu belo país
Da bola e do carnaval
Por isso, escrevo poema de sangue.

[Today when the hands of the clock/Mark another twenty-four hours/A thousand children will have died of hunger/In this my beautiful country/Of football and of carnival/That's why I write poems of blood.]

In the revolutionary rhetoric of Charles Trocate, from Pará, the writer's rebelliousness incites others to struggle. In 'O meu poema', he cultivates a style designed to move the readers and to affect their social and political consciousness. The originally red letters of the poem enact a revolutionary content; in fact, Trocate conveys a concept of art as the expression of nonconformism, 'meu poema é intransigente/É um poeta que alerta a farsa/Possui desobediência' ['My poem is intransigent/It's a poet alert to farce/He possesses disobedience']. In the also red-lettered 'O arame é uma peste', the barbed wire in the title highlights the land-struggle metaphor of the fence of the latifundium excluding the *sem-terra* from the means of production. As such he states that his poem is not apolitical:

Porque na minha mão vai
Uma bandeira
E as ferramentas de compor
Notas de justiça.
Porque seguro abertamente
A flor grávida de rebeldia!

[For in my hand flies/A flag/And I hold tools to compose/Notes of justice/For openly I clasp/The pregnant flower of rebellion!]

The poet's mission is to denounce but, ultimately, in so doing, he conveys a belief that the future contains the promise of happiness for the people. A didactic tone runs through the MST's poetry and music alike when the *cantador* initially condemns the capitalist project that devastates the forests, creates latifundia, throws the workers off the land and produces misery. Such is the case of 'Assim já ninguém chora mais' which denounces the farce of the owners of the unproductive latifundia who simply put a few head of cattle in the immense areas, an activity which neither produces food nor creates jobs. It also introduces the MST's platform against the landless going to the big urban centres only to end up in the slums and face unemployment and hunger. Greed backfires: a final note interrogates the capitalist as to how he is going to grass-feed his own children too. Again in a didactic note, the very popular track 'Floriô', also by Zé Pinto, points to the solution – Agrarian Reform – no matter how painful the roads to it can be. This song describes the happiness of the former *sem-terra* seeing the land flowering and producing after a long period of resistance and suffering under the grim conditions of the black plastic tents in the settlements, a period during which the persistent cry for agrarian reform was always heard.

The 1997 National March, the CD *Arte em Movimento* and the artistic constitution of a militant culture's symbols and icons
It was during the 1997 landless workers' National March to Brasília that the first CD, *Art in Movement*, was conceived. For two months, Brazil followed the daily progress of the three columns (strongly

suggestive of the momentous *Coluna Prestes*) coming from three different regions of the country, through TV coverage or in newspaper headlines. On 7 April 1997, a year after the notorious Eldorado de Carajás massacre, in the northern state of Pará, the three columns arrived in Brasília, the country's capital. With their red flags held aloft, the impressive presence of the congregation in the Square of the Three Powers in Brasília symbolically took over this space of established power. On the same day, delegations from 67 countries transformed the date into the International Day of Peasant Struggle and, importantly, as the result of the intense popular mobilization around the March, Agrarian Reform was put on the government's agenda and the MST became an interlocutor for the formulation of this project (Gohn, 2000: 136-41).

During the two-month march, a community of identification and solidarity was formed in a dynamic interaction between marchers in which art, particularly music, was vital. Zé Pinto's 'Order and Progress', evidence of the social and political power of music and the ways it can be a potent unifying force, became a symbol of that historic march. Zé Pinto was the exponent, in easy words and tunes, of what perhaps the landless felt and the march symbolized: the need for popular memory to be deconstructed, the need for some Brazilian slogans to be problematized, the need for a profound reconstruction to take place. The title of this song critically reproduces the slogan of the nineteenth century Republican flag of Brazil, created in a context of encroaching positivism from which a political programme of national construction was derived. The philosophical echo in the slogan is indeed from Auguste Comte's voicings that love is the principle, order is the basis and progress is the objective. The slogan, according to the designer of the flag, bore evidence to the aspiration of starting a country in true brotherhood, and in which order and progress were to be the guarantees of harmony to be demonstrated by history. Yet history has fallen way behind such ideals. Zé Pinto, evoking the *cantador*'s traditional role of mouthpiece for the oppressed, expresses the landless workers' perceived need to deconstruct the symbology of the flag and recast its slogan. Reality is a country in which, as pointed out by Frei Betto, eighteen million people live in slums or shanty towns, twenty-three million are abandoned children, eight million of whom live on the streets, sixty million people eat only once a day, one thousand children die from starvation each day and forty million are totally illiterate and therefore severely cut off from the exercise of citizenship.[2] So for Zé Pinto, 'order' now has to be understood as not starving, and progress as people's happiness and the return of the peasants to their rural roots. His song thus puts into readily assimilated and easily sung words the main political thrust of the MST: to make history, as in the march, follow a different path. The aim is to establish a project that offers an alternative to landlessness and other forms of exclusion.

Zé Pinto brings out a further inadequacy relating to the colours of the flag. Unlike that of other nations, the colours of the Brazilian flag do not carry a primarily political or historical symbolism; they create, rather, a mythical view of the country as nature (Chauí, 1994: 19-24). The green stands for the forests, the yellow for the natural wealth, the blue for the perennial beauty of the starry sky, and the white for order. Zé Pinto debunks this Edenic symbolism:

Queremos mais felicidade
no céu deste olhar cor de anil
No verde esperança sem fogo
bandeira que o povo assumiu.
Amarelo são os campos floridos
as faces agora rosadas
Se o branco da paz irradia
vitória das mãos calejadas

[For more happiness still/In the blue-washed gaze of our sky/Green of luke-warm hope/In the flag for so long waved./Yellow's for the fields in flower/For faces now so rosy/Will white glow ever peaceful/If won by calloused hands?]

Devotion to a flag implies a sense of responsibility to defend and uphold the ideals it represents. A change of flag usually signals a new regime. During the National March, the MST flag, an imagined symbol of a new Brazil, became increasingly visible. Against the apolitical nature-related symbolism of the Brazilian official flag, the MST's evokes the Communist USSR's hammer and sickle. It fosters another consciousness and further offers itself as an invitation to

---

[2] Statistics obtained from Frei Betto's *The Church and the Social Movements*, in 'Studies, Statements and References' (Vieira, 2003).

resist. The MST flag aims to be national in a different sense. The struggle for Agrarian Reform is to be nation-wide and carried out by entire families, as suggested by the man and woman in place of the stars. This noteworthy Marxist orientation becomes ever more evident in the predominant colour red in the banner with the tools of work, struggle and resistance, as well as in the MST's fundamental principle that eating is a right and not a privilege.

An anthem, like a flag, is a symbol of unity which condenses a cultural identity, prevalent ideology and shared history. It also has the important aim to set a group apart from others. As a musical expression played on ceremonial occasions, it unites a people around a common sentiment and reinforces an identity. The 'Anthem of the MST' had been composed in 1989 (two years after the raising of the flag) by the militant and former seminarist Ademar Bogo, but it was first recorded on the CD *Arte em Movimento*. The politically progressive conductor of the orchestra of the University of São Paulo (USP), Willy de Oliveira, also the son of peasants, was contacted to put the words of the Anthem to music; the challenge was welcomed and the conductor further brought the University choir into the recording (Mançano and Stedile, 1999: 134).[3] The anthem stands out in terms of expressing a political platform and an oppositional/militant identity. In its reconstructive project, bravery will unveil a new history; the key elements for this reconstruction are the hands of the workers, brotherhood and people's power. Recurrent body-related metaphors, such as 'strong arms that tear the ground' and 'let's fight fists-raised', are later consolidated into symbols of the Movement, associated with the rural workers' determination to struggle for their rights.

Art in Movement further records a revolutionary history and identifies communities of dissent and the deeds of inspiring revolutionaries with a past of popular struggle. The song '500 anos de resistência índia, negra, popular' explores the historical example of Zumbi, the leader of black slave resistance in the seventeenth century who for about sixteen years was in command of a community of approximately twenty thousand run-away slaves between the states of Pernambuco and Alagoas, the Palmares *quilombo*; Zumbi was killed

---

[3] The authors also mention the 'Anthem to the Flag of the MST', composed, upon request, by Pedro Tierra (133). This anthem can be heard in the clip of the film *Um homem, uma mulher, uma bandeira/A Man, a Woman and a Flag*, in Vieira, 2003.

by the Portuguese in 1695 when the *quilombo* was demolished. Also invoked is the historic resistance of Canudos in the Bahian Backlands (1893-97), involving thirty thousand people led by the mystic Antônio Conselheiro, as described in the classic *Os sertões* by Euclides da Cunha. The Canudos episode is seen as one of the high points of the poor peasants' struggle against repression, poverty, and hunger; it is also a paradigm for the collective system of ownership and production; from another perspective, it creates a pedagogy for massacres. Poetry complements this catalogue of inspiring leaders of resistance with Chico Mendes and Padre Josimo Tavares.

Another important reference for the construction of a pedagogy of revolutionary struggle in *Art in Movement* is Che Guevara (1928-67), who has become one of the icons in Latin America for his active part in the victorious Cuban Revolution. This historic leader provides not only the title for the song 'Companheiros de Guevara' but also the inspiration for those who march in pursuit of a utopian horizon. The poem 'O que pensaria Chê' immortalizes Che, not only as a picture on the wall, but as one whose ideals survive in the denunciation of empty plates, against which the poet incites comrades to struggle. Apart from those heroes already made sacred by official history, new, non-official ones are also created during the marches and the *Místicas*. Some are members of the MST, such as the youth who was forced by the police to repeat 'MST' and then tortured to death during the Eldorado de Carajás episode. He is remembered in the poem 'Oziel está presente'. The emergence of new martyrs is also the occasion for the documentation of official brutality and the pains endured by this community at the hands of the police and of the *jagunços* (hired killers), as will be seen later in the section 'Death as Life's Horizon'.

A photograph by the celebrated photographer Sebastião Salgado adorns the CD's impressive and powerful cover. It depicts a moment of victory for the peasants. After thousands of them, for months, had resisted hardships in an encampment on the lands of the Cuiabá plantation, a decree expropiating the latifundium on their behalf was finally issued.[4] Landless workers, men and women, with a look of determination rather than one of mere meek acceptance of the condemnation to live out an unjust fate, raise their machetes and

---

[4] In his caption to the photograph, here paraphrased, Salgado suggests that victory can perhaps be a misnomer for what has been achieved in reality is a simple act of justice (1998: 142).

scythes, representing their tools of work, but obviously also acting as powerful political symbols of struggle and resistance. The cover suggests that art has a transformational power and that music is more than an aesthetic expression: it is a libertarian project against oppression.

In this climate of intense mobilization, celebrated Brazilian artists creatively stood in solidarity with the *sem-terra* in the expression of indignation at the persistent attitude of impunity towards the criminals responsible for the previous year's massacre of the nineteen *sem-terra* in Eldorado de Carajás. A case in point is Salgado, who further produces the exhibition *Terra* which, to this day, has a great impact throughout the world; with a marked religious symbolism, his black and white photography depicts landlessness and the violent misery of Brazilian migrants; he donated the profits from the exhibition to the landless. The composer, singer and writer Chico Buarque de Hollanda, an exponent of the politically-committed strain of Brazilian Popular Music (MPB) who has had a career of unbroken success for over three decades, has recorded four songs for the occasion to accompany Salgado's book. The lyricism of his song 'Brejo da Cruz' takes the audience into the plight of children starving in the rural areas and the march towards the big town where migrants find only menial jobs, if they find any job at all; 'Fantasia' denounces that working on the land, pleasure, grace and happiness exist only as fantasy. In contrast, 'Assentamento' depicts the joy of countrymen leaving the urban centre and marching back to rural life in the settlements; 'Cio da terra' brings in the land as a caress and speaks of the miracle of abundant bread resulting from the cultivation of the land.

The internationally renowned poet and translator Haroldo de Campos uses harsh sounds and chopped syllables to express both solidarity with the landless and a sense of national shame and personal indignation at such impunity; his themes and images in 'o anjo esquerdo da história' revitalize the 1950s denouncements made by his predecessor João Cabral de Melo Neto whose funereal sounds in *Morte e vida severina* are a dramatic expression of the distorted cycles of a life ever presided-over by death. The solution he envisages is agrarian reform, and rescue will come not from neo-liberalism but from the Benjaminian left-winged angel of history.

Singing resistance: the encampments and the houses of black plastic and the CD *Canções que abraçam sonhos/Songs that Embrace Dreams*

> *Era uma casa muito engraçada*
> *Era de lona e não de tábua*
> *Esta casinha chama barraco*
> *Quem mora nela é quem não tem terra.*

These lines by the formerly *sem-terra* girl, Rosane de Souza, 14, in the epigraph, read in English as:

> There was a funny house
> Made of plastic, not of planks
> This little house they call a hut
> And in it live the landless.

They ironically echo the children's rhyme

> Era uma casa tão engraçada
> Não tinha teto, não tinha nada
> Ninguém podia entrar nela não
> Porque na casa não tinha chão
> Mas era feita com muito esmero
> Na Rua dos Bobos número 0.

[It was a funny house/It had no roof, it had nothing/No one could get in/Because the house had no floor/But it was built with great care/On Fools' Street number 0]

Repetition with a difference can be an important device for social critique. She craftily deconstructs the children's mockery inscribed in Brazilian popular memory: the house without a roof is not inconceivable; nor is the non-existence of a territorial basis (no floor) or of an address (Fools' Street number 0). Indeed, it is the harsh reality of a landless girl whose childhood experience is structured around provisionality. The effect of the re-contextualization of the song is that it points to the hardships of the encampments, their vulnerability, their total lack of comfort and, above all, the anguish of endless waiting under the shadow of constant intimidation. For this girl, the playfulness of childhood gives way to an early knowledge of struggle and an awareness of rights.

But the girl's parody also draws attention to the houses of black plastic as icons of an intensely political stage in the struggle for land. The encampments, as other politicized sites, are critical for those who have been silenced or marginalized. They mark out a shift from invisibility to reconfigured visibility, from non-existence to existence. Alternative spaces occupied by the *sem-terra* include non-productive latifundia but also their improvised houses of black plastic at the sides of the road. Miles of fragile sheeting – sprouting towns of sub-social conditions – become a spectacle to a world driving by. Such a geography of resistance is thematized in 'Pedacinho de chão': 'the black plastic along the roads is the mark of a search of conscience, of a challenge to the armed ones'.

The film *Raízes da Terra* (Vieira 2003), produced by the MST, highlights articles from the Brazilian Constitution that give rise to the understanding, on the part of the Landless, that it is legitimate to occupy non-productive latifundia because they do not fulfill the social function of the land as prescribed by law. This form of access to the land is thus a way of pressurizing the government to carry out agrarian reform. Images and various statements by the *sem-terra* in the film show the difficulties of life in the encampments as well as the vulnerability, constant threats and extreme discomfort faced by their inhabitants. The following dialogue from the film renders vivid the penury of the *sem-terra* in the encampments:

That's when the difficulties began, first as a lack of work, of food. Water was more or less two kilometres from the encampment, and had to be fetched by bucket. Very difficult, under a hot sun, you get back burnt to the marrow by the sun, in that heat, like fire! It was a long way away, difficult to get to, the town was 26 kilometers away and just to get the bus you had to walk 12 kilometres, passing through gunmen, so it was a very big hassle. There were 220 families without resources, without the means to live, with nothing. There I really experienced hunger. Hunger to make you weep, everyone like this and no solution. People ate cashews, they were in agony, they sucked sugar-cane, but there was no way people could put up with the hunger. Everyday people could not eat, sleep, the children didn't have the freedom to sleep with the men nagging us.

In a striking moment, the film shows a scene of eviction of the encamped landless and a confrontation with the police. A woman remarks on the power imbalance between the police and the *sem-terra*: 'on the day of eviction, they came on horseback, they brought dogs, everything imaginable to massacre us... There was a gunman'.

Many of the songs of the CD relate to the initial stages of the struggle for land: the journey, occupation and resistance. Such is the thrust of 'Chão e terra'/'Soil and land' which renders explicit the view of the encampment as a space of resistance: 'the black plastic along the roads is the mark of a search of conscience, of a challenge to the armed ones'. In general, the expression of political resistance in the settlements is wrought with religious symbolism associated with the Movement's genealogy in the Church. The ideologue Stedile has compared the experience of political resistance in an encampment to a Cavalry that at the same time creates a feeling of community and bonding (1999: 115)[5]. Pointedly, the song 'Tralhas de um acampado'/'A camp-dweller's junk' draws attention to poverty, namely the very reduced material world of the *Sem Terra* in the encampments that brings life down to the level of mere survival: some nails, a hammer, a small notebook, a pillow, a worn-out sheet, a mattress, a tilly lamp and a single-ring burner to make *mate*. The stark reality of social injustice and misery apparent in such subhuman conditions is counteracted by a spark of joy and fraternity: a guitar to make the comrades happy. Crucially, the religious intertext Calvary (nails, hammer) cannot be bypassed. By the same token, one is reminded of the Old Testament. Joshua and the sons of Israel camp for three days before crossing the River Jordan in pursuit of the promised land.

The creation of a pedagogy and icons of struggle and the tone of exhortation to struggle in the first CD thus give way to the voices of individuals expressing their sufferings and hopes in a greater variety of rhythms in the second CD, which includes the prize-winners of the *First Festival of Agrarian Reform* held in 1999 in the state of Rio Grande do Sul. The proximity to the Hispanic countries of the South

---

[5] Maria de Lourdes Beldi de Alcântara has drawn attention to the politicization of the religious discourse of the MST which has inspired me to pursue the analysis presented in this section.

may further account for the greater diversity of popular rhythms in this second CD: the slow *guaranias* characteristic of Paraguay and the tango, which originated in suburban Buenos Aires at the end of the nineteenth century, mix with Brazilian traditions and rhythms such as the open air serenade, the samba and the 'baião'.[6]

Many of the songs of the CD relate to the initial stages of the struggle for land: the journey, occupation and resistance. 'Procissão dos retirantes'/'The migrants' procession', the first track, strikes the keynote of the CD, signalling a shift away from the political spectacle of the national march to the centre of power in the first CD to the distress, agony and indignation voiced by the landless. The most striking motives on the CD *Canções que abraçam sonhos/Songs that Embrace Dreams* are families along the motorways fleeing from misery and joblessness – in movements against the current of a hostile history – and the harsh reality of the encampments. In fact, the first song voices out an open criticism of Brazil's contradictions: it has continental dimensions yet denies a space to those who want to work; it dooms to misery the landless people along the sides of the roads while fruitful land remains idle. 'Mãe Terra' personifies and genderizes the land as a woman to highlight that the earth is a benevolent mother who is asked to protect those in procession or forgive those struggling for a piece of land; the problem then is not physical but economic and social, and dispossession and exclusion breed pain, hunger and hatred.

'Pedacinhos de chão'/'Small pieces of land', another song on the CD, brings in scenes of the battered and fatigued landless along the motorways, foregrounding the swollen feet of those on pilgrimage towards an unpredictable future, only broken by the certainty that whatever the gain, it will 'be in the diminutive, a "pedacinho"'. Other voices join the chorus of those in physical suffering travelling away from exclusion and misery. 'Um naco de chão'/'A stretch of land' portrays an Indian thrown off his land; he had on his feet the dust of distances and on his face a look of distress; a broad smile of reanimation only opens on his face when, after many days of solitude and despair, his strength is failing when someone from the MST, out of brotherhood, gives him a 'chimarrão', the bitter tea typical of the south.

---

[6] The traditionally Brazilian 'baião' was originally a short musical text played during improvised 'desafios' – literally challenges – to allow time for the opponent to compose a reply; it later develops into a genre in its own right.

The landmark occupation of Encruzilhada do Natalino in 1981 by landless rural workers and, above all, the formalization of the MST in the state of Paraná in 1984 are defining moments in the struggle for the land in Brazil that bear evidence to the magnitude of the problem also in the South. Severino, the lonely crosser of the hardships of the Northeastern *sertão* backlands is now an anonymous crowd along the roads in the rural areas of the most prosperous region of Brazil. An echo of the migrants of the Northeast reverberates in the song 'Caminhoneiros', those who drive lorries, which recalls in difference the *paus-de-arara*, those trucks used for the transportation of the *retirantes* in long and inhumane travels from the Northeast to the South for as long as 20 days. Paradoxically, the *pau-de-arara*, a term frequently used in the southern states as a pejorative reference to those migrants from the Northeast, now describes the reality of lorries with the expropriated families lining up the roads in the very South. The eyes of the redundant peasant in 'Semeando a razão'/'Sowing reason' brighten up in revolt as he looks at the vast stretches of land and realizes that all this belongs to only one man. The collective and political dimensions of sowing are taken up in 'Cordão do povo em busca da terra'/'A ring of people in search of land', which, equating the greed of the Portuguese colonizers to that of the 'grileiros' or land-grabbers, calls out that the 'land is also ours', that is, it belongs to those who want to toil it with dignity. In 'A bandeira conduz o povo'/'The flag leads the people' there resonates the call to resistance of the first MST motto 'occupy and then resist'.

But away from the silent resignation of Severino, the wandering *Sem Terra* disseminates political resistance. The word becomes the seed in 'Semente palavra', a clear expression of the claim of a disenchanted man who, tired of waiting, wants his own 'land to grow'. 'Chão e terra'/'Soil and land' which renders explicit the view of the encampment as a space of resistance: 'the black plastic along the roads is the mark of a search of conscience, of a challenge to the armed ones'.

Again the religious glides into the political in 'Tributo ao trabalhador sem-terra'/'Tribute to the landless worker'. The song describes the physical sufferings and the distress of a man who experiences the intimidating closeness of death. From under the black plastic of the encampments, he bears witness to the assassination of a comrade. In anguish and revolt, he invites his remaining companions to share his opposition to social injustice and hatred towards the death-bringing latifundium by shouting the slogan 'Agrarian Reform is everybody's struggle'.

A shift-away from the Severinos of the South as well as from the merging of the political with religious symbolism in the expression of the landless emerges in the powerful gendered note of the tango 'Por honra e por amor'/'For honour and for love'. This song foregrounds the courage of a landless woman in an encampment who rejects the love of a man, probably a soldier who, as such, is associated with authoritarianism and the powers that repress 'her people' and the landless cause. The militant woman who leaves for Eldorado de Carajás, the site of the 1996 massacre which has become emblematic of the land struggle, is named Ana Sem Terra, one who repeats in difference the indomitable courage of her predecessor Ana Terra, an important historic reference in the conquest of land inside and outside the culture of the MST. In loneliness and pain, the abandoned man shares a lament with the melancholy tunes of his instrument, the bandoneon.[7]

The rehabilitation of country traditions, the empowerment of the 'caipira' culture and the CD *Uma prosa sobre nós*/*A chat about us*

Sister Teresa Cristina, a member of the Pastoral Land Commission, composed the *cordel* 'The narrative of the workers of the São João dos Carneiros farm', which presents the sequence of events that led to the expropriation and occupation as a form of access to land.[8] This took place in 1989, in Quixadá, in the northeastern state of Ceará, a region historically associated with great agrarian conflicts and constantly devastated by droughts. The last note struck by this *cordel* is one of the rural workers' great victory in the struggle for land.

Strikingly, the landless children and youth in the MST settlements often begin to practise or show a talent for the *cordel* at an early age. Equally, in this anthology, Francisco Macilom Nunes Aquino,

---

[7] For an in-depth analysis of the tango 'Por honra e por amor', in terms of the gender and class intersection in the struggle for land, of the establishment of a continental platform around deprivation through the appropriation of the musical expression of suburban Buenos Aires, and of the Sem Terra's transformation of Brazilian literary symbols to dignify the militant landless woman, see Vieira, 2005a.

[8] For an analysis of the process, see Bernardo Mançano's essay 'Occupation as a Form of Access to the Land', in 'Studies, Statements and References' (Vieira, 2003).

seventeen years old, also from the North-East, cannot tell his existence from that of the MST and as such narrates the Movement's history in the first person, absorbing it as his own life-story. Rosane de Souza, now settled in the southern state of Santa Catarina, narrates, also in this tradition, how the trajectory of struggle for land and against hunger and poverty developed in her a sense of dignity and self-worth as well as an awareness of her rights.

Another earlier tradition which they revitalize, particularly for children in the school setting, is the *ciranda*. Originating from Portugal, both a dance and a tune, the *cirandas* also combine the oral and the communal, again bringing back the collective dimension of music. In this performance, the children hold hands in a circle and the quatrains that they repeatedly sing invite a child to go to the centre of the ring and individually sing verses different from the refrain repeated by the chorus of the children around. The *cirandas* are particularly important in the education project of the Movement, insofar as didactic effectiveness depends on the principle of repetition combined with transformation.

The *sem-terra* also strive culturally to reconstruct and de-stigmatize elements of their earlier life that have become extinct or marginal in the metropolis. Crucial in all this process is the revitalization of the discourses and the cultural world of the *caipira* (bumpkin). This is a word of Tupi origin which is associated with the rural workers descending from the meeting of the Portuguese colonizers and the natives in the centrally-located states of Minas Gerais, Mato Grosso and Goiás; other regionally specific designations are *caboclo, jeca* and *sertanejo*. The *caipira* is usually perceived by city people as poorly educated, with rustic and awkward manners and outdated speech and customs; *caipira* speech retains many of the features of archaic Portuguese, the same holding true for their customs and traditions (Candido, 1993: 249). The *sem-terra*'s song 'Floriô', for example, confirms Antonio Candido's assertion; for the expression of 'blossomed', a native speaker of Portuguese today would use 'Floresceu', not 'Floriô'. This is a point made by Candido who also draws attention to the fact that this tradition underwent transformations because the Brazilian rural man is not a Portuguese in America but a combination of the Iberian with the native one. Candido, among others, reads this persistence of outdated customs as a sign of the *caipira*'s cultural and economic non-conformism; he or she refuses to yield to the pressures of fashion and of economic modernization, even at the cost of a life of penury. Thus, the return of the *sem-terra* to the modes of the *caipira* means not only rehabilitation of their rural origins but also the empowerment of a non-conformist culture.

The 'peculiar world' of cultural resistance of the Brazilian rural man', made up of the *desafio* (musical challenge), the bonfire on Saint John's day, the *Festa do Divino* (Celebrations of the Divine), the beliefs, and so on is what Candido further refers to (1993: 249). The composer Zé Pinto foregrounds others in *Uma prosa sobre nós/A chat about us*, a CD produced upon his initiative and based on his personal experiences which, however, is paradigmatic of today's *retirantes*/migrants in Brazil and their difficult uprooting. Some of their nostalgic songs rebuild in words and rhythms a place that has been lost, the moonlight serenade with the plaintive tunes of a viola in front of the girl's window being a case in point in the song 'Seresta'/'Serenade'. The Leopoldina train, introduced by the British in the interior of Minas Gerais, is addressed to take the guitar and the *caipira,* ill-adjusted in the big towns, back to the other serenaders in the south of Minas Gerais. Musical celebrations are remembered such as the one marking the end of the Saturday joint weeding, an occasion when the traditional *broas de fubá* (rustic corn-flower cake) are served; the festivity's religious procession on Sunday is further remembered in 'Só num foi pra nunca mais'/*'Only once was for never more'* The rigid code of honour of rural Brazil, another legacy from patriarchal Portuguese colonization, is foregrounded in 'Cantiga da moça roubada'/'The song of the stolen girl. The singing of the rooster outside at expected times is ominous. Gabriela has been 'stolen' so the father chases Manilim with a scythe, and has the wrong undone by taking both to the priest to be married, out of punishment.

'Lamentos e sonhos'/'Laments and dreams' focuses on another flow of the newly-spread *retirantes,* originally associated with those people of the arid *sertão* region in the Brazilian North-east who would pass through Minas, a central state in Brazil, on their way to São Paulo, because of the prolonged droughts. The song shows Minas now as a provider of migrants when it depicts a poor family, who have exhausted the attempts at farming there, on the back of a truck leaving for the unknown future in the distant north, which reflects the first land redistribution policies of the military government which prioritized the settlement of the Amazon area. The *mineiros* (literally miners), or people from Minas, are considered attached to their cultural traditions and loyal in their affective relationships and friendships. It is thus in sadness that the mother says farewell to the religious traditions of the state inherited from the colonial past, that the father looks for the last time at the coffee plantations and that the children, for whom everything is fun, still lamented the little canary that was wont to stay. In personal conversation with the composer, he reported the experience of fear of the family in the north, not only of the wild animals but mostly of the great violence associated with land issues in the Amazon. The coexistence of never-to-be-forgotten cultural traits and those arising from the new environment is suggested in the song in terms of the emergence of new speech patterns in rural Brazil: the regionalisms of the state of Minas, notably the *uai*, expressing surprise, astonishment, or wonder begins to mix with those of the north, like *cacai,* associated with the native culture, namely a bundle tied to one's back to carry food into the bush.

The revitalization of earlier cultural expressions parallels the presentation of rural life as an alternative to the uneven, disorderly and less than human progress of the big cities. 'So No One Cries Anymore' expresses the *sem-terra*'s fears of going to the city to face famine, unemployment and end up in the *favelas,* as has been the case with so many. These urban areas, which are increasingly associated with violence, are agglomerations of impoverished houses or huts built by people on low incomes (or no income at all), with extremely precarious living conditions and access, also generally lacking in minimum comfort, hygiene, privacy, and safety. The *sem-terra* also feels inadequate in the big cities, as portrayed by the song 'A Bumpkin in the São Paulo Metro'. The prohibition of simple everyday practices, such as lighting a fire, also triggers the *sem-terra*'s desire to revert in their migrant trajectory back toward the country. The moment of decision comes in the song 'Retorno ao campo'/'Return to the countryside' in which he apologizes to São Paulo and to his boss but he is going back, enough is enough of losing himself and his love in the underground.

The construction of a canon of exclusion: voicing a proletarian fraternity

The poetry of the *Sem Terra* is a 'class' poetry of a very special kind.

If one thinks of class in terms of the individual's position in the economic structure of society, the *sem-terra* are a classless people in that they are rural workers who have no access to the land as a means of production. If one understands the nation to be a form of solidarity which imparts a feeling of social belonging (Rucht and Neidhardt, 2002: 18), Brazil does not offer itself as a nation for all those socially and politically excluded. Paradoxically, exclusion creates other forms of groupings and another sense of collective identity. As the *sem-terra* construct 'networks of solidarity on the basis of deprivation' (Rucht amd Neidhardt, 2002: 22) with other '-less' segments of society (homeless, roofless, etc), they create an emotional and psychological space and, above all, politicize the conflict. The collective identity of the '-less' class, elaborated at length by Pedro Tierra in 'Pedagogia do aço'/'Pedagogy of steel', is visually indicated by the casting of the three times repeated 'excluded from the nation' in different lines; moreover, the lines that express diverse forms of exclusion are not printed level with the others, the graphic arrangement suggesting that they are pushed towards the margins of society. Social exclusion further entails an absent space for expression:

> Há uma nação de homens
>   excluídos da nação
> Há uma nação de homens
>   excluídos da vida
> Há uma nação de homens
>   calados,
>   excluídos de toda palavra.
> Há uma nação de homens
>   combatendo depois das cercas.
> Há uma nação de homens
>   sem rosto,
>   soterrados na lama,
>   sem nome
>   soterrados no silêncio

[There's a nation of men/excluded from the nation/There's a nation of men/excluded from life/There's a nation of men/muted,/excluded from each and every word./There's a nation of men/in combat beyond the fences./There's a nation of men/faceless,/buried deep in mud,/nameless,/in silence sunken.]

By grouping themselves with others from the proletariat, the dispossessed reinforce each other politically. Poetry thus becomes a space in which to condemn inhumanity and to draw up the geography of violence towards the excluded. Proletarian fraternity brings the Candelária massacre to full light. Outside this important Catholic church in the centre of Rio de Janeiro, to the indignation of many and to the shame of the country, eight street children were shot dead in July 1993. Other incidents related to the murder further accentuate the MST members' sense of injustice. They inevitably perceived the partiality of the justice system when a confessed criminal, amongst the Candelária assassins, was obtaining freedom while the MST leader Zé Rainha, evidently an innocent man, was being condemned. Candelária is thus today symbolic of the struggle against violence in the city and the country (see, for example, the lyrics 'Eldorado de Carajás' and 'Candelária').

In the originally green-lettered title 'A fala da terra'/'The earth speaks', Pedro Tierra casts the problem of the landless within the general problematic of the dispossessed and marginalized:

> A Liberdade da Terra não é assunto de lavradores.
> A Liberdade da Terra é assunto de todos quantos
> se alimentam dos frutos da Terra.
> Do que vive, sobrevive, de salário.
> Do que não tem casa. Do que só tem o viaduto.
> Dos que disputam com os ratos
> os restos das grandes cidades.
> Do que é impedido de ir à escola.
> Das meninas e meninos de rua.
> Das prostitutas. Dos ameaçados pelo Cólera.
> Dos que amargam o desemprego.

[The freedom of the land is not about workers./The freedom of the Land is about everyone who/Feeds on its fruit./About everyone who lives, survives, on wages,/About the homeless. About those who live under bridges./About those who dispute with the rats/The big cities' scraps./About those who can't go to school./About girls and boys of the street./About the prostitutes. About those threatened by cholera./About those embittered by unemployment.]

Poetry offers the main medium whereby a canon of exclusion is created. Aracy Cachoeira is the individual poet who perhaps contributes the most to the placing of the *sem-terra* within this broader horizon. Her trajectory is closely related to the problem of the natives. Some facts witnessed awoke in her a sense of indignation, for instance, when a native woman was found drowned and no explanation or enquiry was carried out even to clarify the case. An extreme form of repetition, her main device of persuasion towards the cause of the natives, is used in her 'Paz aos índios e ao mundo'/'Peace to the Indians and to the world', a geographical litany of the tribes that inhabit Brazil and the neighbouring countries. Special recognition of the Maxacali culture is demanded through poetic form: the name of this Indigenous group is the last to be mentioned and repeated four times; this group has serious problems because of low self-esteem and increasing loss of cultural references.

A poem that Cachoeira composed for the Aranãs has in fact become the anthem of the tribe. The Aranãs, a tribe of the Valley of the Jequitinhonha River, re-opened the question of Indian rights. With the help of the Pastoral Land Commission, they succeeded in recovering the land that had been lost to the farmers of the region. The poem was written on April 15, 2000, on the departure of the caravan from Belo Horizonte to take part in the Conference of Indigenous Peoples in Porto Seguro, in the state of Bahia. The context was that of the national commemorations of the Fifth Centenary of the Discovery of Brazil by the Portuguese in 1500 which triggered, amongst dispossessed segments, intense questionings and numerous protests against the Portuguese 'invasion' or colonization. For these, the event being celebrated marked the beginning of exclusion.

In a first-person confessional poem, Aracy Cachoeira assimilates the voice of Galdino Jesus dos Santos to describe his impotence in the face of unexpected death when, in the early hours of April 20 1997, having been sleeping at a bus-stop in W-3 South, Brasília, he woke up with his body in flames. This 44-year old native from the indigenous tribe Pataxó Hã-Hã-Hã was a councillor in his community, located in the south of Bahia. He had arrived in Brasília three days earlier, with a delegation of more than eight leaders of his people, for a series of meetings relating to the ownership rights of a property with an area of five farms located on native lands. Five upper middle-class men aged seventeen to nineteen had doused him with two litres of inflammable alcohol, setting fire to his clothes as a 'joke'. With burns on ninety-five per cent of his body, he died the next day. In the poem, Galdino is then portrayed ascending to Heaven and asking God to protect the Indians that are still alive. The Indigenous Missionary Council saw the jury's conviction of the defendants for homicide for base motives and cruelty to a defenceless victim as a recovery of hope for the ending of impunity.

Cachoeira also constructs a network of solidarity with the urban proletariat. In a poem written in 1988, as part of the unpublished collection *Poemas de São Paulo*, she examines the plight of another group of destitute, the *Sem Teto* (Roofless) beggars who live under the Chá Overpass in the centre of São Paulo and use cardboard boxes as improvised shelters or methods of gaining some privacy. The author found herself in that city one very cold night, when she saw a beggar breathe his last breath. For him, nothing more could be done. Moved by a deep feeling of solidarity, she interrupted her journey to write the requiem 'Debaixo do viaduto'/'Under the viaduct'.

Zé Pinto extends his solidarity to the street children. The assonance in the Portuguese title of his 'Rua e nua'/'Naked street' draws attention to the raw reality of street children as one made up of absences. They are deprived of a house, of affection (physical proximity is only to a rubbish dump), of a child's right to dream, of protection: the child knows of his impending death in the name of public security.

The expression of death as life's horizon: from the lyric to the revolutionary

The knives were sharpened, among the preparations for Santiago Nasar to be butchered on the grounds of false accusations of taking a girl's virginity. This everyone knew. Yet no one told him. Those familiar with Gabriel García Márquez will recognize those echoes of *Chronicle of a Death Foretold* which resonate in Pedro Tierra's title 'A morte anunciada de Josimo Tavares'. Josimo was a black priest, leader of the *posseiro* peasants (those who have possession of the land but not the the legal deeds of ownership), in the Bico do Papagaio region in Tocantins. This writer of militant poetry and active member of the Pastoral Land Commission was murdered in 1986, in the city of Imperatriz, Maranhão, by a gunman hired by the landowners. The gunman was the only one to be convicted. Pedro Tierra asks: 'who's the black boy/who defies limits'? Everyone knew of his death: the weapon, the fences of the latifundium, the old women who had been educated in pain, the Church. In his equally knowing sandals, Josimo goes on walking towards what is certain and inevitable: death. Here, while establishing a dialogue with the Latin America literary series on violence, Pedro Tierra also foretells the death of so many others.

Whereas the theme of impending death invites a more confessional tone for the expression of the *sem-terra*'s own sensibilities and feelings of loss, the concluding lines of some poems introduce a revolutionary rhetoric and a prophetic note on the determination to struggle on. The certainty of imminent death haunts the life of the *sem-terra* in Zé Pinto's 'Ligação do infinito'/'Phonecall from the infinite'. The brutal murder of the comrade Teixeirinha in his own encampment by military policemen of the State of Paraná triggers an exhortation to further struggle. In 'Cortejo'/'Cortege', Ana Cláudia, from the state of Pernambuco in the North-East, reports on the death of another comrade; his body is carried with the machete, his tool of work but also a symbolic invitation for continued struggle and resistance. The paronomasis in the Portuguese title of 'Luto(a)'/'Mourning combat' establishes the close connection between *luta* for land and *luto*. Ana Cláudia's mourning will not be a silent one, will not be covered in black but in the red, the colour of combat.

The related theme of massacres tends to bring in a note of indignation and revolt and does not always find its most expressive medium in confessional poetry. Massacres, in fact, are dealt with mostly on the CD *Um canto pela paz* produced in 2001 in Pará, it will be recalled, the most violent state in Brazil in terms of the land problem and nationally and internationally known for the Eldorado de Carajás massacre. The very title of the song 'Dezenove', composed by Ricardo Dias, draws attention to the collective dimension of death in this massacre. In the song 'A pedagogia dos aços'/'Pedagogy of steel', the lengthy enumeration of the names of the nineteen *sem-terra* killed overwhelms the listener with the extent of the tragedy. The historic register of violence through the *cordel* tradition, in 'Eldorado de Carajás', narrated by the survivors who witnessed the violence of stalking death, yet again reveals the clear numerical imbalance between the landless and the armed police. Another device used in these songs is the invocation of (in)famous massacres worldwide: in

'Chacina cyber', a comparison is established with Guernica. The world is reminded that the tragedy portrayed by Pablo Picasso is not different to that and others taking place in Brazil.

The Pará collection includes contributions by MST members but also creates a collective experience by giving voice to other oppressed groups and individuals in the area. Charles Trocate, also a poet, coordinated the production of the CD, which involved articulating the work of the composers and singers with a shared social project. The most noteworthy example of bringing together other social and political manifestations of the artisitic is the incorporation on the CD of MBGC (*Manos da Baixada de Grosso Calibre*, a group of slum-dwellers in Belém, in the state of Pará, who are integrated into the hip hop movement of the *favela*). The group attends all the MST events in the area even though they do not belong formally to the Movement. They composed and performed the song 'Eldorado dos Carajás' (track 12).

The wisdom of the woodland gods and the pedagogy of the revolutionary leaders

The CD *Canto pela Paz/A Song for Peace* (2002) reflects a social project to create new textual spaces to document, represent and reflect the needs, interests and visions of people in the Amazon area. The network of relatively diverse groups from the state of Para, in the Amazon area contributing to the CD are regional composers, singers, slum-dwellers, natives, peasants, former miners, professors and local institutions. This reflects their belief that destitution and human and ecological violence are not isolated phenomena but are shared by various segments in the region. Crucially, this broad horizon further subsumes the natives whose question of land rights establishes a link with the cause of the *sem-terra* of the region. The main thrust of the project is to give voice to those whose identity is defined by various forms of destitution and marginalization If socially isolated, those deprived do not directly perceive their condition as a common one (17). Music, as a symbolic form of solidarity, imparts feelings of belonging and helps to establish social identities in a rapidly changing environment. Networking through music thus enables them to externalize their problems, create an emotional and psychological space and, above all, politicize popular expression in the area.

The prominent motif of the disruption of nature, of life cycles and

c

of social organization by capitalists is depicted in the characteristically poetic and metaphoric language of the region. Charles Trocate foregrounds the specificity of expression: people in the Amazon area valorize melody and metaphor, struggles and utopias, which stands as a contrast to he more objective tone of the South of the country. In a predominantly oral culture, the mnemonic devices of music enable knowledge and the solutions for problems to be transmitted. The *cantadores* have a crucial role in perpetuating popular knowledge and presenting solutions embedded in the culture.

The fact that the initiative to produce the CD was taken by the poet and militant Trocate is further evidence that, beyond aesthetics, the MST is increasingly playing a key role as a dynamic oppositional force in Brazil and within global socio-economies. The denouncing of the cataclysmic effects of capitalism not only in terms of the destruction of the fauna and flora of the Amazon area but also on all areas of social life finds an expression on the CD. It also relates to the articulation of an array of regional composers and singers in a shared social project involving the poisoning of human beings; rural violence; the displacement of indigenous groups and the consequent loss of cultural roots; the growth of urban chaos resulting from migration from other provinces in Brazil as part of the project of colonization of the Amazon. Trocate's trajectory as an intellectual of the MST in the south of Pará has enabled him to draw upon a materialistic poetics to develop a rhetoric of resistance and a revolutionary aesthetics, and to explore, regionally and internationally, solidarity arising from exclusion and destitution.

An important institutional presence in this project of building social awareness is that of the City Council which further asked for the song Lamúrios/'Laments' (track 10) to be included on the CD even though its producer Ray Neves was from outside the region, because of the importance of the theme of poisoning by mercury used in mining in the region by such big companies such as Vale do Rio Doce. 'Bioretrospectiva'/'Bioretrospect', in turn, focuses on the deleterious effect of today's capitalism on the social tissue. This song relates to the discovery of gold and the consequent heavy migration between 1980 and 1991 to the state of Roraima This caused the population of 79,000 inhabitants in the region to escalate in one decade to 218,000, whereas the population of Ianomâmi natives in this area was drastically reduced. Indians were massacred, others fled to the slums in the capital of the state which mushroomed (Morissawa, 2001: 104). Iara, the water goddess, seeks protection for the 'children of the river disappearing'.

A major alliance is established between music and myth in the area. Nietzsche, in fact, has long recognized music as an art that not only reconciles one to life but that could also enhance it. Sound waves form intricate lines that create ordering patterns. By the same token, myth, man's earliest expressive mode, orders the everyday experiences of its hearers (or viewers). It communicates, in allegorical form, to members of a society a conceptual order and the social principles and attitudes determined by its history and institutions. Popular music in the Amazon area foregrounds such cultural importance of myth. The ancestral legends and beliefs cast into song are a means of conveying truths about nature, the social world, and human ethics. The mythical and the political are conjoined for the expression of the anger of the woodland gods in the song 'Deuses das matas'/'Woodland Gods' (track 7), by the local artist Eduardo Dias, who also made his studio available for the collective recording of the CD. In its wisdom, the choir of dissent made up by the Woodland Gods of the Amazon denounces the savage felling of trees in the region by the moto-serras. The composer of 'Deuses das matas'/'Woodland Gods', the local artist Eduardo Dias, exploits the sonority of the native's language and more specifically of the names of trees to enact the vertiginous felling of the ancient forest. All of the names of the trees have got five syllables, the stress rhythmically falling on the penultimate one (*maçaranduba, açaizeiro, macacaúba, samaumeira*); the strong penultimate syllable is followed by an unstressed one and by the monosyllable *cai/falls,* a shift from high to low that enacts the abrupt fall of the ancient and beautiful trees. *Samaumeira*: a tree with large trunk and attractive flowers. *Macacaúba*: a tree from the Amazon region, whose wood is used in expensive furniture. *Maçaranduba*: a tree native to Brazil, which has a red wood with a dark brown hue that is very useful in cabinet-making. *Açaizeiro*: the *açaí* palm tree, of great importance as food, is normally found on the banks of rivers and swampy lands of the Amazon region.

'We sing ... because our dead and our survivors want us to sing' is the quotation on the CD cover from the Uruguayan writer Mário Benedetti which ushers into the lyrics a tradition of struggle epitomized by Chico Mendes. The pluralized name, Expeditos, casts him as the representative of about seven hundred and twenty rural leaders murdered in the region since 1986. The death toll of Eldorado de Carajás notably conveys the violence associated with the land. Leaders, in unison, join the choir of Woodland Gods to say no to the devastation in the area. Some are named. The peasant leader Quintino Lira, murdered in 1984, by the landowners of the region, became legendary in the northeast of Pará for his escapes from the police. João Batista and Paulo Fonteles, both lawyers and representatives of the Communist Party of Brazil, and defenders of the working-class, were murdered, João Batista in front of his wife and children. Expedito Ribeiro de Souza, a poet, farmworker, and president of the Union of Rural Workers in the south and southeast of Pará, was the seventh person murdered at Rio Maria, which triggered the foundation, in 1991, by Father Ricardo Rezende, of the *Comitê Rio Maria* (Rio Maria Committee), an international solidarity network that aims at ending the murders of farmworkers and union-members by gunmen hired by large landowners in the south of Pará. The pluralized name, Expeditos, casts him as representative of a great number of rural leaders murdered in the region. Angelim refers to a more preterite history: at 21 years of age, he became the third Cabano President, on the occasion of which the Movement entered its most radical phase.

Nietzsche hears rhythm in the best of nature. Along these lines, the Amazon area, which valorizes melody and the metaphorical expression of reality, struggles and utopias, stands as a contrast to the more objective tone of the South of the country. Zeca Tocantins, an MST militant, focuses in 'Banzeiros'/'Ripples' (track 8) on the theme of economic violence in the south of the large state of Pará. His denouncing of brutal death, this time of those who opposed the capitalist model, draws jointly on the region's mythical imaginary and its bedrock of historical knowledge. This song is in fact a song from the 1970s, included on the CD because of its persisting relevance. It is the wind in the forest that strikes and conveys the note of political alert: spreading dry twigs, according to the region's mythology, brings bad omens. The sounds of history, warning the *Amazonenses* of catastrophe, also come from the forest. The bird Bem-te-vi spreads historical knowledge having been the witness to the killing of seventy Araguaia revolutionaries by an army of six thousand soldiers sent by the government in 1975, after they had resisted in the forest for two years (Mirossawa, 2001: 101). *Meninos do Araguaia*/the Araguaia children, refer to those youths who still looked like children when they fought in the homonymous guerilla war, which took place where what is now the state of Tocantins. In a country-house in the area, in 1969, a group of revolutionaries living on agriculture started to establish contact with the region's peasants in order to raise their political conscience as to the need for struggle against the *latifúndio*-owners and the dictatorial government.

The importance of nature for the definition of the regional identity and culture of the Amazon resurfaces in 'Do jeito que a gente é'/'The way we are' in which someone wakes up early in the morning, heads for the *igarapé* (a word of Tupi origin which refers to the small navigable rivers of the Amazon jungle), looks for *mururés* (vegetation of the rain forest) in the mirrors of the waters, gets a canoe and follows the ebb and flow of the waters in order to say what people are like.

The CD *Plantando Cirandas/Growing a ring o'roses*: music towards a critical education and environmental awareness

Amongst the themes distinctively associated with the *sem-terra* music, two are prominent: the rehabilitation of country culture and education. More than a theme, education is a fundamental component of the MST's project of social reintegration and dignification of the *sem-terra*. This further includes the organization of agricultural cooperation, technical and political formation and so on, after they gain access to the land. The MST Education Project has been recognized for promoting schooling in the historically neglected rural areas and has received important prizes and distinctions, including an award from UNICEF. There are one thousand primary schools in the settlements, in which two thousand teachers work with about fifty thousand children. The MST's literacy programme involves six hundred educators working with adults and adolescents.

Paulo Freire, author of the celebrated *Pedagogia do oprimido/Pedagogy of the oppressed,* has stated that, in the context of the *sem-terra*'s reinsertion into and as a subject of history through the conquest of land, the task of education is the exercise of citizenship and cutting the 'barbed wires' of ignorance (see Freire's interview in 'Studies, Statements and References', in Vieira, 2003). In its production of critical pedagogies, the MST's Education Project has greatly benefited from the theories developed by Freire, notably his major contribution towards the development of a critical education of the oppressed.

Music, a ludic way to teach, is recast as a critical and liberating pedagogy within the MST. This crucial mode of transmission of knowledge further reactivates the important function of oral memory in the rural experience of the landless learners. The CD *Plantando Cirandas* claims the rights of children to play, to dream and to be happy inasmuch as it focuses on the change from a '-less' condition to one of citizenship in the making with the conquest of land. The poet/composer Zé Pinto assimilates the identity of a child in order to express what it feels like to be young again after having experienced exclusion. Similarly, it expresses how life in an encampment transforms thosed who live there:

> Antes não éramos nada
> Pois sem saída ou chegada
> Éramos coisas jogadas
> Pelas pontes, viadutos
> E, vivendo assim um ser
> Não é possível ser nada.

> [Before we were nothing/Neither leaving nor arriving/We were a mere something/Over bridges under viaducts thrown/And, living like that, a being/Can be no one.]

The inseparability of literacy and a critical dimension, along Freire's lines, in the development of citizenship is highlighted in the song 'Pra soletrar a liberdade':

> Criança e adolescente numa educação
> decente pra um novo jeito de ser
> pra soletrar a liberdade na cartilha do ABC [...]
> Se o aprendizado for além do Be A Bá,
> todo menino vai poder ser cidadão.

> [for child and adolescent to have somehow/a decent education for a new way to be/to spell out freedom on the books of ABC/If apprentice-eship goes beyond the ABC/every child as a citizen can be free.]

'Vai, meninada'/'Go on kids', by Zé Pinto, stresses the manifold meaning of an educational project while relating it to the role of the *cantador*:

Numa ciranda de roda
vai a criançada
e a menina dos olhos desse caminhar
somos segredos da vida
numa flor desabrochar
numa flor desabrochar
Sementes de esperança no terra a brotar.
Quando crescer eu quero ser poeta
fazer poemas para liberdade
vou escrever em cada coração
uma canção para a felicidade
uma canção para a felicidade [...]
e aprender a ler nas entrelinhas
qual o segredo de saber amar.

[In a ring-a-ring o' roses go the kids/and today's march's favourite girl/we're the secrets of life/in a flower unfolding/in a flower unfolding/Seeds of hope/from the land in a twirl./When I grow up I want to be a poet/to write poems of freedom/I shall write on every heart/a song of happiness/a song of happiness [...]/and learn to read between the lines/the secret of how to love.]

In the process of identity reconstruction, school songs introduce and reinforce new values, such as the social benefits of *mutirão*, gender equality and sharing. This is the thrust of 'O trabalho gera vida'/'Work breeds life':

Minha escola construída
com a força do mutirão
trabalho gera vida no valor da união.
Com os meninos e as meninas
não tem discriminação
pra na hora da merenda
aprender partir o pão.

[My school was built/from the strength of teamwork/work breeds life from acting in union./Amongst the boys and girls/Discrimination's dead/when at break time/They learn to share their bread.]

Environmental awareness and resistance in the form of a poetics of natural life are also important in the agenda of the MST Education Project. 'A natureza que aprendi amar'/'Nature that I've learned to love' presents the earth as a mother to be loved. The child will not throw a stone at the bird, because it is 'a child of mother earth'. A binary structure codes good and bad in terms of the natives and rural workers in close interaction with nature and the region's history opposed to the exploitative outsider committed to selfish personal gains by any means and through the individual exploitation of the land. While the culture defines itself oppositionally, those inside tend to be favourably presented as socially progressive and committed to cultivating the land, whereas those outside are presented as destructive capitalists. Such dichotomies may be related to the oral narratives and the *cordel* used as part of the attempt to rehabilitate and dignify rural culture. These popular forms may also have been revitalized because of the effectiveness of their simple language as memory aids. In fact, the *cordel* has been particularly helpful in literacy programmes in informal settings: the illiterate buy the book and someone reads the text for them while they familiarize themselves with the codes of writing. Yet, in this respect, a further step might be the devising of a pedagogy to prepare the school children for negotiating their space outside their own environment

The voice of the other: the expression of plenitude in the settlement
It is worth noting that the musical and poetic production of the MST markedly revitalizes the role of the *cantador* as a mouthpiece for the oppressed. Over twenty songs in their overall production are about the period of struggle and the penuries in the encampments and in the houses of black plastic; eleven verbalize their hopes and dreams as a motor for struggle. Yet they do not seem to express their feelings relating to achievement. The settlement is referred to mainly as a future aspiration while they are in the period of struggle and of

resistance in the encampments. After land has been conquered and they are settled, they pointedly stress education as a reconstructive project. A similar panorama is seen in the poems, which in general thematize their icons of struggle and experience of exclusion, death and massacres. Zé Pinto, in 'Assim vou continuar'/'So I shall continue' is a clear expression of such teleological orientation:

Vamos ter cooperativa
Como tem noutros lugares
Construiremos escola para a meninada estudar
Também posto de saúde
Ter um posto telefônico
Energia, e a poesia de uma casa pra morar

[We'll soon have our co-operative/As others elsewhere do/We'll build a school for the kids to learn/Our own health centre/And a telephone, too./Electricity, and the poetry of a house to dwell in.]

Ana Cláudia, in her poem 'Nova cultura', brings out the desire for transformation rather than transformation as a concrete reality:

E a porta entreaberta
Do nosso querer
Fique livre e curiosa
Pra descobrir
Na cultura do povo,
Um novo jeito de ser.
PODER SER.

[And may the half-open door/Of our desire/Be free and eager/To discover,/In the culture of the people,/A new way of being.]

Her 'Conspiração'/'Conspiracy' stresses hope. She envisages a maternal and sweet earth welcoming those travellers:

Conspirem os oprimidos desta terra (…)
E a terra fértil, da esperança plantada
A terra-mãe agradecida
Nos fornece em seus braços
Doce guarita.

[Let the oppressed of this land conspire […]/And fertile land, planted in hope/Mother earth gratefully/Gives us, in her arms,/Sweet shelter.]

In 'Antes do sol se cobrir'/'Before the sun goes down', Zé Pinto projects the reaping of the fruits of solidarity sown during the journey towards the future:

Quero pedir a vocês que cuidem bem deste sonho […]
Pois quem caminha sozinho não sabe pra onde ir
Mas se vamos de mãos dadas na arte de replantar
Vamos descobrindo já: todo fruto que brotar
Tem que ser pra repartir

[I'm asking you to tend this dream […]/Who journeys alone never knows where to go/But if hand in hand we artfully resow/We learn and learn: every fruit that's borne/Is for all to share.]

It may be that, through years of penury and the immediate demands to struggle on, many *sem-terras* and *Sem Terras* have unlearned the ability to express joy. One of the songs by Zé Pinto falls outside this pattern. Its familiar rhythms and simple *caipira* language wrap the *sem-terra* in notes of joy. The singer and composer Chico Buarque de Hollanda joins in and, with lyricism, verbalizes the *sem-terra*'s transition to a new phase, that of the land already conquered and the start of a new life in the settlements. After years of struggle and inadequacy in the urban centres, the now *Sem Terra* leaves and 'unlives' that city and heads back towards the country:

Zanza daqui
Zanza pra acolá
Fim da feira, periferia afora
A cidade não mora mais em mim […]
Cansado de guerra
Morro de bem
Com a minha terra

[Ramble here/Ramble there/End of fair, beyond the city's rim/The city dwells no more in me […]/Weary of war/I die at one/With my land.]

'Caressing the land', Chico Buarque's metaphor in 'Cio da Terra', expresses, within the context of the *Sem Terra* who returns to the country, the long-craved for re-establishment of contact with the telluric. Religious and amorous images combine to express this epiphany. The earth is a woman, sexually and maternally: a woman to be fondled, a woman who wants her desires to be explored, a woman who responds to caresses; a woman as a protective and nurturing mother who reveals the cycles of fertility. Man and the land-as-woman want to be one and share vital energies with the now upper-case *Sem Terra*. The seed is planted in the womb of this woman in rut. The moment is right, wheat abounds. The biblical miracle of the multiplication of bread repeats itself. The *sem-terra* is now bread-full. From Utopia to the reality of the settlements, albeit for a few, the moment is one of plenitude.

References

Alcântara, Loudes Beldi. 'The Landless Movement: an analysis of the religious discourse', in *CESNUR, the Center for Studies on New Religions.* **http://www.cesnur.org/2001/london2001/alcantara. htm**

Andrade, Mário de. *Dicionário Musical Brasileiro.* Belo Horizonte: Itatiaia; Brasília, DF: Ministério da Cultura; São Paulo: Instituto de Estudos Brasileiros da Universidade de São Paulo: Editora Universidade de São Paulo, 1989.

Bones, Sávio. 'With hands calloused from poetry: the formation of organic intellectuals by the MST', in 'Studies, Statements and References', in Else R. P. Vieira (ed.), *As Imagens e as Vozes da Despossessão: A Luta pela Terra e a Cultura Emergente do MST (Movimento dos Trabalhadores Rurais Sem-Terra do Brasil)/The Sights and Images of Dispossession: The Fight for the Land and the Emerging Culture of the MST*, 2003 (**www.landless-voices.org**).

Candido, Antonio. 'Caipiradas', *Recortes*. São Paulo: Companhia das Letras, 1993.

Chauí, Marilena. 'Raízes teológicas do populismo no Brasil: teocracia dos dominantes, messianismo dos dominados', in Dagnino, Evelina (ed*.*). *Anos 90: Política e sociedade no Brasil*. São Paulo: Editora Brasiliense, 1994.

Enciclopédia da Música Popular Brasileira Popular, Erudita e

Folclórica. 2.ed. São Paulo: Art Editora: Publifolha, 1998.

Fernandes, Bernardo Mançano. 'Occupation as a form of access to the land', in Else R. P. Vieira (ed.), *As Imagens e as Vozes da Despossessão: A Luta pela Terra e a Cultura Emergente do MST (Movimento dos Trabalhadores Rurais Sem-Terra do Brasil)/The Sights and Images of Dispossession: The Fight for the Land and the Emerging Culture of the MST*, 2003 (**www.landless-voices.org**).

Fernandes, Bernardo Mançano and João Pedro Stedile. *Brava Gente: a trajetória do MST e a luta pela terra no Brasil*. São Paulo: Editora Fundação Perseu Abramo, 1999.

Frei Betto. 'The Church and the Social Movements', in Else R. P. Vieira (ed.), *As Imagens e as Vozes da Despossessão: A Luta pela Terra e a Cultura Emergente do MST (Movimento dos Trabalhadores Rurais Sem-Terra do Brasil)/The Sights and Images of Dispossession: The Fight for the Land and the Emerging Culture of the MST*, 2003 (**www.landless-voices.org**).

'A bandeira', in *Sobre o Brasil*. Houston: Consulado-Geral do Brasil em Houston. **http://www.brazilhouston.org/noframepor/bandeira.htm**

Gohn, Maria da Glória. *Mídia, terceiro setor e MST: impacto sobre o futuro das cidades e do campo*. Petrópolis: Vozes, 2000.

Gramsci, Antonio. *Cadernos de Cárcere, Volume 2*. Edição de Carlos Nelson Coutinho com Marco Aurélio Nogueira e Luiz Sérgio Henriques; tradução de Carlos Nelson Coutinho. Rio de Janeiro: Editora Civilização Brasileira, 2000.

Jordan, Tim *et al*. 'Social Movement Studies: Opening Statement', *Social Movement Studies* 1, 1 (2002), 5-6.

Leite, Márcia Pereira. 'The *favelas* of Rio de Janeiro in Brazilian Cinema (1950 to 2000)', in Else R. P. Vieira (ed.), *City of God in Several Voices: Brazilian Social Cinema as Action*. Nottingham: Critical, Cultural and Communications Press, 2005.

Raízes da Terra/Roots of the Land. Film produced by the MST of São Paulo. Clip available in 'Film', in Else R. P. Vieira (ed.), *As Imagens e as Vozes da Despossessão: A Luta pela Terra e a Cultura Emergente do MST (Movimento dos Trabalhadores Rurais Sem-Terra do Brasil)/The Sights and Images of Dispossession: The Fight for the Land and the Emerging Culture of the MST*, 2003 (**www.landless-voices.org**).

Rucht, Dieter and Friedhelm Neidhardt. 'Towards a "Movement Society"? or the possibilities of institutionalizing social movements', *Social Movement Studies* 1. 1 (2002), 7-30.

Salgado, Sebastião. *Terra: Struggle of the Landless.* , trans. Clifford Landers. London: Phaidon Press, 1998.

Spivak, Gayatri Chakravorty. *Outside in the Teaching Machine.* London: Routledge, 1993.

Um homem, uma mulher, uma bandeira/A Man, a Woman and a Flag. Film produced by the MST of São Paulo. Clip available in 'Film', in Else R. P. Vieira (ed.), *As Imagens e as Vozes da Despossessão: A Luta pela Terra e a Cultura Emergente do MST (Movimento dos Trabalhadores Rurais Sem-Terra do Brasil)/The Sights and Images of Dispossession: The Fight for the Land and the Emerging Culture of the MST,* 2003 (**www.landless-voices.org**).

Vieira, Else R. P. (ed.). *As Imagens e as Vozes da Despossessão: A Luta pela Terra e a Cultura Emergente do MST (Movimento dos Trabalhadores Rurais Sem-Terra do Brasil)/The Sights and Images of Dispossession: The Fight for the Land and the Emerging Culture of the MST,* 2003 (**www.landless-voices.org**).

Vieira, Else R. P. 'Sem Terra/Desterrados: The Music of Dissent of the MST in Dialogue with the Tango Culture', *Image and Narrative* 1,10 (2005a). **http://www.imageandnarrative.be/worldmusica/elserpvieira.htm**

Vieira, Else R. P. (ed.). *City of God in Several Voices: Brazilian Social Cinema as Action.* Nottingham: Critical, Cultural and Communications Press, 2005b.

Manifestação pública Brasília, 1990
Foto de Bernardo Mançano Fernandes. MST Formação e territorialização. São
Paulo: Editora Hucitec, 1996 Reprodução autorizada.

March in Brasilia, 1990.
Photo by Bernardo Mançano Fernandes, reproduced in *MST: Formação e
territorialização*, São Paulo: Editora Hucitec, 1996. Reproduced by permission.

Ícones, símbolos e monumentos

Icons, symbols and monuments

A bandeira do MST

Pedro Tierra

Com as mãos
de plantar e colher
com as mesmas mãos
de romper as cercas do mundo[1]
Te tecemos

Desafiando os ventos
sobre nossas cabeças
Te levantamos

Bandeira da terra,
Bandeira da luta,
Bandeira da vida,
Bandeira da liberdade!

Sinal de liberdade!
a que juramos:
não nascerá sobre tuas sombras
um mundo de opressores.

Sinal de terra
Conquistada!
Sinal da luta
e da esperança
sinal da vida
multiplicada

E quando a terra retornar
Aos filhos da terra
repousará sobre os ombros,
dos meninos livres
que nos sucederão!

The flag of the MST

Pedro Tierra

With the hands
That plant and reap
With the same hands
That fences break[1]
We weave you

Challenging the winds
Above our heads
We raise you

Flag of land,
Flag of strife,
Flag of life,
Flag of freedom!

Sign of freedom!
To which we swear:
Oppressors' worlds
O'er your shadows won't be born.

Sign of land
Conquered!
Sign of the fight
And of hope
Sign of life
Multiplied

And when the land returns
To the sons and daughters of the land
It will rest on the shoulders
Of children free
To succeed us!

Ao nosso jornal

Ademar Bogo

Não és grande, não importa. [2]
Importa tua identidade.
Tu não circulas de graça
Importa que atinjas a massa
no campo e na cidade.
Já tens dez anos, bom tempo!
De todo esse Movimento
tu tens tudo registrado.
Não podia ser o contrário
não tens dia nem horário,
'fala' até sem ser chamado!
E ao lembrar de tua infância
pequeno, sem elegância
que recordações tu trazes.
Mas esta é tua memória!
Certeza. Só tem história
que com luta a história faz!
Se o futuro te intimida
que nada! És novo ainda!
Vamos… o sonho fazer.
É assim mesmo. Longa estrada
mas que seria da jangada
sem água pra se mover.

E o que seria de nós
se tu não fosses a voz
que anuncia o amanhecer!
Nossas saudações sinceras
toda a luta pela terra,
te homenageia aos clamores.
A terra é irmã. o amanhã
pertence a nós, trabalhadores.

4

To our newspaper

Ademar Bogo

You are not big, that doesn't matter. [2]
What's great is your identity.
Free, you do not circulate,
What matters is you reach the masses
In country and in city.
Now you're ten years old, so long!
Everything about this Movement
written down you have it all.
Otherwise it couldn't be
for you have neither day nor hour,
'speak out' even if not called upon!
Remembering your infancy,
inelegant, so small,
what reminiscence I recall.
But your memory is this!
Certainty. For history is
For those who fight, a history to make!
If the future intimidates,
Say no! You are still young!
Move on… your dreams awake.
The way ahead is long, for sure,
but what would become of the boat
with no water on which to float?

And what would become of us all
if you were not the call
that announces the dawn!
Our sincerest salutations,
the whole struggle for the land
with raised voice to you pays homage.
The land is a sister. Tomorrow
belongs to us, the workers. [2]

O que pensaria Chê?

Zé Pinto

Na parede um retrato do 'Chê'
Na velha cadeira preguiçosa de fios
Azuis cor do céu
Um raro descanso.
véu da noite começa a cobrir
E na penumbra do cansaço
A viagem inicia.
Num país de ilusões tão profundas
E de pratos tão rasos,
De dimensão continental
E nem um taco de terra pra tantos,
De riquezas tão esnobes
E salários tão baixos.
Quando numa curva do trajeto
Surge, de repente, uma pergunta,
'Disso tudo, o que pensaria "Chê"?
Se não fosse hoje
Apenas um quadro na parede?'
Antes que o viajante desperte,
que sabemos na certa
É que amanhã descobrirá
Que para os que sonham,
Nunca foi 'Chê' apenas
Um quadro na parede.

What would Che think?

Zé Pinto

A picture of 'Che' is on the wall
In a lazy old chair worn out, thread-bare,
Midst sky-blue hues only now he risks
A rest so rare.
As veil of night quick falls
From its weary dusk
To our march he calls.
In a country of illusions plenty
And plates as empty
As a continent grand,
Yet, for so many, not a scrap of land,
With riches snobbish
And wages low.
When, suddenly, a question,
At a bend in the road,
Is raised: 'What would "Che" think of this?…
If he weren't today
But a face on the wall?'
Before the marcher wakes,
We know for sure
Tomorrow will show
For those who dream
'Che' was never
Just a face on the wall.

300 anos de Zumbi

Zé Pinto

A invasão chegou de barco
Nesta América Latina
Veio riscado da Europa
Este plano de chacina
Vinham em nome da civilização
Empunhando a espada
E uma cruz na outra mão.

Aqui encontraram vida
Aqui implantaram morte
Aqui encontraram flores
Aqui implantaram fogo
Aqui encontraram ouro
Aqui implantaram roubo.

E com batismo de sangue
Aqui implantaram crença
Eram as aves de rapina
Em louvor ao Deus Clemente
Nos pelourinhos da morte
Tanto sangue derramado
Pra mão-de-obra barata
Índio e negro escravizados.
Caçados como animais
Filhos arrancados dos pais
Se o negro não tinha alma
negro não era gente
Se negro não era gente
Era então mercadoria
Mas foi no pranto do desencanto
Que o negro aprendeu cantar;
Mas foi na penumbra da senzala
Que o negro aprendeu sambar;
Mas foi na raça da negritude
Que o negro aprendeu lutar.

300 years of Zumbi

Zé Pinto

Here in Latin America
Invasion by boat began
Came scripted from Europe
As genocide plan
In the name of civilisation they land
With the sword in one fist
And a cross in the other hand.

Here they found life
Here they sowed death
Here they found flowers
Here they sowed fire
Here they found gold
Here they sowed theft.

In baptisms of blood
Here they sowed belief
Swooped as birds of prey
In praise of a Clement God
So much blood was spilled
In the stocks of death
To gain cheap labour
Indian and black enslaved.
Hunted like beasts
Children from their parents snatched
If the black had no soul
The black was not with human matched
And if he had no soul
Then he was mere merchandise
But it was disillusion's lament
That the black man learned to sing;
T'was in the slave quarters' penumbra
That the black man learned to samba;
T'was in negritude's light
That the black man learned to fight.

São três histórias
Neste grande continente
Uma bem antes dos invasores chegarem
E a segunda cinco séculos de invasão
E a resistência índia, negra, popular.

E a terceira é que vamos construindo
Pra destruirmos a raiz de todo mal.

O grito negro de ZUMBI
Vem dos Palmares
Em novos tempos
Pra romper a tempestade
Já com trezentos anos que se passaram
Ainda se ouve o eco
Liberdade, liberdade, liberdade!

In this great continent
There are but three tales
One from before the invaders came
The second five centuries more of invasion
And resistance, of Indian, Black and the people.

The third is the one we are still constructing
To destroy the root of all evil.

The black cry of ZUMBI
Comes from Palmares
To break the storm
In new eras
Three hundred years on
Still the echo is one
Freedom, freedom, freedom!

A caminho de Canudos

Zé Pinto

Pra onde vais conselheiro
Nessa peleja medonha
Construindo a decisão
De rasgar campos desertos
De ternura e plantação

De conduzir sua gente
A pegar arma e semente
E combater um dragão
Valente como o demônio
Maldito como a ganância
Que aprendeu roubar do povo
Direito de ter pão

Batalhões de maltrapilhos
Sonhadores, povo ordeiro
Nos trilhos, sangue e pólvora
Pela ação indecorosa,
Do exército brasileiro

Mas a caneta escreveu, mesmo entre os estampidos,
Pois quem luta por justiça
Dificilmente é vencido
Soldados embasbacados e oficiais perdidos
Mas embebido em vingança, o dragão urrou de raiva

Muito mais metralhadoras
Muito mais tanques de guerra
E o povo tombou por terra como quem vira fumaça
Mas dentro de suas mãos, mulheres e homens caídos
Sementes de liberdade quase no último suspiro
Deixaram cair na terra,
E vão brotando na gente
Igual a um pé de milho

On the road to Canudos

Zé Pinto

Conselheiro where are you going
In your frightful chore
Deciding
To tear up fields bereft
Of plantation tender

Your people to lead
To take up arms and seed
And to fight a dragon
As brave as the demon
As cursed as the gain
That taught to rob people
Of their right to bread

Battalions of the ragged
Dreamers, orderly,
On the trail, blood and gun-powder
'Cos of the indecorous deed
Of the Brazilian army

Yet, even amidst the gunfire, the pencil scored,
For whoever fights for justice
Is vanquished at great cost
Soldiers baffled and officers lost
But imbibed with vengeance, the dragon wrathful roared

Many more machine-guns
Many more tanks
And the people fell to ground as if turned to smoke
But in their hands, women and men, fallen
Seeds of freedom near their last gasp
Dropped into earth,
Sprout on in us all
Like a stalk of corn

Assim já nínguém chora mais

Zé Pinto

Sabemos que o capitalista
diz não ser preciso
ter Reforma Agrária
Seu projeto traz miséria
Milhões de sem-terra
jogados na estrada
com medo de ir pra cidade
enfrentar favela[3]
fome e desemprego
Saída nessa situação
é segurar as mãos
de outros companheiros.

E assim já ninguém
chora mais
ninguém tira o pão
de ninguém
chão onde pisava o boi[4]
é feijão e arroz,
capim já não convém.

Compadre junte ao Movimento[5]
Convide a comadre
e a criançada
Porque a terra só pertence
a quem traz nas mãos
os calos da enxada
Se somos contra o latifúndio
da Mãe Natureza
Somos aliados
E viva a vitória no chão
Sem a concentração
dos latifundiários.

So no one cries anymore

Zé Pinto

The capitalist, we know,
says there's no need
for Agrarian Reform
Yet his project brings misery
Millions of landless
on the road are thrown
in fear of going to the city
to face *favelas*[3]
famine and no job
The way out of this plight
is to join hands
with our comrades.

And so no one
cries any more
no one from anyone
takes bread
the ground where once the oxen trod[4]
is beans and rice,
fodder will no longer suffice.

Brother join the Movement[5]
Invite the sister
and the children too
For the land belongs only
to those whose hands
show callous of the hoe
If we're against the latifundium
Of Mother Nature
we are allies
And long live victory on the land
With so few
landlords.

Seguimos ocupando terra
derrubando cercas[6]
conquistando o chão
Que chore o latifundiário
pra sorrir os filhos
de quem colhe o pão
E a luta por Reforma Agrária
a gente até pára
se tiver, enfim
coragem a burguesia agrária
de ensinar seus filhos a comer capim.

Occupying land we go
knocking down the fences[6]
conquering the ground
Let the landowner weep
For the child of whoever harvests bread
To smile
And the fight for Agrarian Reform
we'd even halt
if the agrarian bourgeoisie
had got the guts
to teach its kids to feed on fodder.

Ordem e progresso

Zé Pinto

Este é o nosso País
esta é a nossa bandeira
é por amor a esta Pátria-Brasil
que a gente segue em fileira.

Queremos mais felicidade
no céu deste olhar cor de anil
No verde esperança sem fogo
bandeira que o povo assumiu.
Amarelo são os campos floridos
as faces agora rosadas
Se o branco da paz irradia
vitória das mãos calejadas.

Queremos que abrace esta terra
por ela quem sente paixão
quem põe com carinho a
semente pra alimentar a Nação
A ordem é ninguém passar fome
Progresso é o povo feliz[7]
A Reforma Agrária é a volta
do agricultor à raiz.

Order and progress

Zé Pinto

For this our country
This our flag
For love of fatherland Brazil
We march in file

For more happiness still.
In the blue-washed gaze of our sky
Green of luke-warm hope
In the flag for so long waved.
Yellow's for the fields in flower
For faces now so rosy
Will white glow ever peaceful
If won by calloused hands?

So let this land embrace
Whoever feels its passion
Whoever sows with tenderness
The seed to feed the Nation
Order says let no one starve
Progress proclaims a people happy[7]
Agrarian Reform returns
The workers to their roots.

Hino do Movimento Sem Terra

Ademar Bogo

Vem, teçamos a nossa liberdade
braços fortes que rasgam o chão
sob a sombra de nossa valentia
desfraldemos a nossa rebeldia
e plantemos nesta terra como irmãos!

Vem, lutemos punho erguido
nossa força nos leva a edificar
nossa pátria livre e forte
construída pelo poder popular.

Braço erguido, ditemos nossa história
sufocando com força os opressores
hasteemos a bandeira colorida
despertemos esta pátria adormecida
amanhã pertence a nós trabalhadores!

Nossa força resgatada pela chama
da esperança no triunfo que virá
forjaremos desta luta com certeza
pátria livre operária camponesa
nossa estrela enfim triunfará!

Anthem of the Sem Terra

Ademar Bogo

Come, let's weave our freedom
strong arms that tear the ground
in the shade of gallantry
let's unfurl our rebelry
and in this land let's plant as brothers!

Come, let's fight fist-raised
our strength leads us to build
our homeland new and strong
erected on the people's power.

Arms raised, let's tell our history
with strength our oppressors smother and
let's raise the coloured flag
let's wake this sleeping motherland
for us the workers will tomorrow stand!

Our strength once rescued by the flame
of hope in triumph yet to come
from this fight we'll forge for sure
a peasant homeland free for workers
in the end will shine our star!

As vozes de um monumento

Else R. P. Vieira

As formas livres deste monumento (v. p. 24), com dez metros de altura, projetado pelo renomado arquiteto Oscar Niemeyer, em tributo às vítimas da violência no campo no Paraná, falam por ele e por um dos temas de sua arte, a busca de uma utopia estética para a resolução dos problemas sociais, segundo D. K. Underwood.

O monumento está situado próximo à capital do estado do Paraná, no quilômetro 108 da rodovia BR 277. Este estado protagoniza, de várias formas, os problemas da terra no Brasil, a exemplo do desalojamento de 12.000 famílias quando da construção da Hidrelétrica Binacional de Itaipu, na sua fronteira com o Paraguai. Significativamente, o Paraná foi o palco do *I Encontro Nacional do Movimento dos Trabalhadores Rurais Sem Terra* de 21 a 24 de janeiro de 1984, quando o MST se formalizou como movimento nacional.

Cravado no local onde foi morto o líder camponês Antônio Tavares Pereira, o Monumento constitui um marco de mais um episódio de violência no campo no Brasil. Mas ele não faz ressoar os gritos dos que sob ele jazem nem os lamentos das Viúvas da Terra que em 2 de maio de 2001 fizeram sua inauguração oficial. A arte de Niemeyer no Monumento transcende os limites da realidade. Suas linhas apontam para um mundo novo, sem fronteiras, onde, espera-se, pela ação política e pelo trabalho, as mudanças sociais se concretizarão e melhores condições de existência se realizarão.

Assim se expressa sobre o Monumento o poeta e secretário executivo da Comissão Pastoral da Terra do Paraná, Gerson de Oliveira:

[...] o braço erguido de camponês, lavrado no concreto branco, parece empurrar o monumento para o alto, para a liberdade, na força revolucionária que esses homens e mulheres carregam. O camponês é o próprio monumento. Uma coisa só. A foice – proibida – ferramenta do trabalho e símbolo de uma luta, está definitivamente na mão do trabalhador [...]. [Niemeyer] devolveu ao homem a dignidade de seu trabalho. É assim que, na curva da história, o sem-terra e o arquiteto têm um encontro para a eternidade.

Voices of a Monument

Else R. P. Vieira

The free forms of this monument (see p. 24), ten metres in height, designed by the renowned architect Oscar Niemeyer, in tribute to the victims of violence in rural Paraná, speak for him and for one of the main themes of his art, the search for an aesthetic utopia for the solution of social problems, according to D. K. Underwood.

The monument is situated close to the capital of the state of Paraná, at kilometre 108 on highway BR277. The state of Paraná is symptomatic, in many ways, of the land problems in Brazil, instance the eviction of 12,000 families at the time of the building of the Binational Hydroelectric dam of Itaipu, on the frontier with Paraguay. Significantly, Paraná was the venue of *The First National Assembly of the Rural Landless Workers' Movement*, from 21 to 24 January 1984, when the MST was formally established as a national movement.

Sited at the exact spot where the peasant leader Antônio Tavares Pereira was killed, the monument marks yet one more violent episode in rural Brazil but it does not resound with the cries of those that lie beneath it nor with the laments of the Widows of the Land who, on 2 May 2001, officiated at its inauguration. Niemeyer's art in the Monument surpasses the limits of realism. Its lines point to a new world, without frontiers, where, it is hoped, through political action and through work, social changes will be brought about and better conditions for living will be achieved.

The poet and executive secretary of the Pastoral Land Commission of Paraná, Gerson de Oliveria, writes of the Monument as follows:

> [...] the raised arm of the peasant, worked in white concrete, seems to push the monument upwards, towards liberty, with the revolutionary force borne by these men and women. The peasant is the monument itself. One thing only. The scythe – outlawed – work-tool and symbol of struggle, is definitively in the hand of the worker [...]. [Niemeyer] handed to the man the dignity of his work. So it is that, on the curve of history, the landless and the architect are conjoined for eternity.

23

Monumento Antônio Tavares Pereira, com dez metros de altura, projetado por Oscar Niemeyer em tributo às vítimas da violência no Paraná.
Foto de Carlos Carvalho, Arquivos do MST de São Paulo. Reprodução autorizada.

Monument Antônio Tavares Pereira, 10 metres high, designed by Oscar Niemeyer as a tribute to the victims of land violence in the state of Paraná.
Photo by Carlos Carvalho, MST Archives São Paulo. Reproduced by permission.

Missão da arte

Mission of art

O anjo esquerdo da história

Haroldo de Campos

os sem-terra afinal
estão assentados na
pleniposse da terra:
de sem-terra passaram a
com-terra: ei-los
enterrados
desterrados de seu sopro
de vida
aterrados
terrorizados
terra que à terra
torna
pleniposseiros terra-
tenentes de uma
vala (bala) comum:
pelo avesso afinal
entranhados no
lato ventre do
latifúndio
que de im-
produtivo re-
velou-se assim u-
bérrimo: gerando pingue
messe de
sangue vermelhoso
lavradores sem
lavra ei-
los: afinal con-
vertidos em larvas
em mortuá-
rios despojos:

The angel on the left of history

Haroldo de Campos

the landless at last
are settled in
full possession of the land:
from landless to
landed: here they're
interred
their life's breath
unearthly
earthed
terrified
earth which onto earth
returns
land-holders pleni-
potentiary of a (single
bullet) common grave:
outside in at last
holed deep into
the broad-bellied
acres of the latifundio-
land once barren
so sudden-
ly shown to be most f-
ecund: udder-spawning profit
crop of
reddening blood
un-laboured
labour: here they're
larvaed at
last
on mortal
remains:

ataúdes lavrados
na escassa madeira
(matéria)
de si mesmos: a bala assassina
atocaiou-os
mortiassentados
sitibundos
decúbito-abatidos pre-
destinatários de uma
agra (magra)
re(dis)(forme) forma
– fome – a-
grária: ei-
los gregária
comunidade de meeiros
do nada:
enver-
gonhada a-
goniada
avexada
– envergoncorroída de
imo-abrasivo re-
morso –
a pátria
(como ufanar-se da?)
apátrida
pranteia os seus des-
possuídos párias –
pátria parricida:
que talvez só afinal a
espada flamejante
do anjo torto da his-
tória cha-
mejando a contravento e
afogueando os
agrossicários sócios desse
fúnebre sodalício onde a
morte-marechala comanda uma
torva milícia de janízaros-ja-
gunços:

coffins laboured
from the scanty timber
(timbre)
of themselves: the assassin bullet
stalks them
thirst-squatting
death-settlers
decumbents cut down pre-
destined for a
meagre (earth) acre a-
grarian
– famine –
re (de)(formed) form
here they are: gregarious
commune share-cropping
nothingness:
shame-
faced in
agony
vexed
– shamecorroded by
inmost abrasive re-
morse –
landless
('how shall we extol thee?')
homeland
laments its dis-
possessed pariahs –
parricide patria
for maybe only at last the
fiery sword
of the crooked angel of history flam-
ing against the wind and
burning the
agrokilltural cronies of that
sombre sodality where
field-marshal death commands a
grim militia of janissary-gun-
men:

somente o anjo esquerdo
da história escovada a
contrapelo com sua
multigirante espada po-
derá (quem dera!) um dia
convocar do ror
nebuloso dos dias vin-
douros o dia
afinal sobreveniente do
justo
ajuste de
contas[8]

only the angel on the left
of a history groomed against
the grain shall manage with its
multiswirling sword
(if only!) one day to
convoke from the nebulous
mass of days to
come the at last
overriding day of the
just
adjustment of
accounts[8]

Voei

Zé Pinto

Um dia um homem me disse:
Meu filho pegue a estrada
Ponha o sonho na sacola
Vá embora, vá embora
Sei que a lua aqui na roça
É banhada de beleza
Só que mais bela é a certeza
Que tem na outra estação.
Tem alguém te esperando
Na esquina da esperança
Eu sei, vai ficar partido
meu pobre coração.
Sei também que tua mãe
Vai soluçar de tristeza
Mais vai dizer com certeza:
Eu vou rezar por você.
Cante um canto de revolta
E de vitória também
Porque cantar por cantar
Isso nunca lhe convém.

I flew

Zé Pinto

One day a man to me did say:
Take to the road my son
Put your dreams in your knapsack
Go away, go away
I know that here on the plot the moon
Is bathed in beauty
Though lovelier still is the certainty
Of the season yet to come.
For you there's someone waiting
On the corner of your hope
I know my poor heart
Will be broken.
Your mother, I know, too,
Will sob with sadness
But she'll say for sure:
I'll pray for you.
Sing a song of revolt
A song of victory, too
For to sing for singing's sake
Is never enough for you.

Poema de sangue

Zé Pinto

Hoje quando os ponteiros
Registrarem vinte e quatro horas
Mil crianças terão morrido de fome
Neste meu belo país
Da bola e do carnaval
Por isso, escrevo poema de sangue.

Muitos guerreiros da dignidade,
Da igualdade
E dos novos valores
Abandonaram as trincheiras
Ou apontam saídas por uma terceira via
Tentando ignorar os gemidos
Mendigos da miséria
Por isso, escrevo poemas de sangue.

Onde estão os poetas que escreviam pelas ruas?
Que recitavam pra lua?
Que dedilhavam as violas?
Pra ver brotar a semente numa semente de roda.
Não adianta negar:
A televisão ditou e muitos obedeceram.
A ilusão agenciou
E quem na onda requebrou
Não pôde ser seresteiro.
Pois descobriram ligeiro
Que a ignorância de um povo
Sempre rende mais dinheiro
Por isso, escrevo poemas de sangue.

Mas se as ervas daninhas
Não conseguem nunca
Dominar toda a plantação,
Há muitas árvores
Que ainda estão produzindo bons frutos.
Pois é desses frutos que alimentaremos
É dessas sementes que replantaremos
Mas eu lhes afirmo
Que ainda é preciso
Por isso, escrevo poemas de sangue.

Poem of blood

Zé Pinto

Today when the hands of the clock
Mark another twenty-four hours
A thousand children will have died of hunger
In this my beautiful country
Of football and of carnival
That's why I write poems of blood.

Many warriors of dignity,
Equality,
New values
Abandoned the trenches
Or point to solutions through a third way
Trying to ignore the begging
Moans of misery
That's why I write poems of blood.

Where are the poets who wrote in the street?
Who recited to the moon?
Who plucked the guitars?
To see seed sprout on a seed-wheel.
There's no use denying it:
Television dictated and many obeyed.
Illusion was the agent
And whoever wallowed in those waves
Couldn't be a serenader.
For soon they were sure
A people kept in ignorance
Always pays more
That's why I write poems of blood.

But if the weed
Can never succeed
In taking over the plantation,
There are many trees still
Bearing good fruit
And it's from that fruit that we'll feed
And it's from that seed we'll replant
But I tell you again
That there's still a need
That's why I write poems of blood.

O arame é uma peste!

Charles Trocate

As entranhas da terra,
Cansadas de serem violadas
Pelo discurso
Pelo vácuo dos arames,
Estão abertas!

E lá sangra
grito dos despossuídos

E a mão camponesa acena
Sua hora!
arado irá vingar-lhes
Revirar seu manto
E o crepúsculo da vida...

Tudo planto
Porque o caos envergonha os cios
Porque defronte a minha frente
Está o arame
Cometendo
assassinato!
E milhões de cifras rondando impunes

Tudo planto
Porque o poema não é apolítico
Porque na minha mão vai
Uma bandeira
E as ferramentas de compor
Notas de justiça...
Porque seguro abertamente
A flor grávida de rebeldia!

Barbed wire is a plague!

Charles Trocate

The land's womb,
Weary of being
Raped by talk
By the void of barbed wire,
Is open!

Bleeding from it comes
The cry of the dispossessed

And the hand of the peasant signals
It's time!
The plough will avenge them
Turning its blanket
And life's twilight…

I plant everything
For chaos shames the land's desire
For right in front of me
Stands barbed wire
Committing
Murder!
And tons of money circulate unpunished

I plant everything
For the poem isn't apolitical
For in my hand flies
A flag
And I hold tools to compose
Notes of justice…
For openly I clasp
The pregnant flower of rebellion!

O meu poema

Charles Trocate

A Eli

meu poema não se cala
É cotidiano…
É um punhal, é isso mesmo
Uma necessidade.
Intenso, antecipa e, ora dirão…
É um estilo
Sem esconderijo

meu poema
Decreta existência, aqui, ali.
Possui infâncias,
É uma flor, é isso mesmo
Uma morada;
Ignora a ordem
pressuposto
veredicto da ignorância

meu poema é intransigente
É um poeta que alerta a farsa…
Possui desobediência, é isso mesmo
Um coração.
Não finge, não foge.
É de arribação
Está aos vivos hoje, é justo de intenção.

My poem

Charles Trocate

To Eli

My poem is not silent
It's daily…
It's a knife, it's even
A necessity.
Intense, it anticipates and, now they'll say…
It's a style
With no hiding place

My poem
Decrees existence, here, there.
Possessing childhoods,
It's a flower, it's even
A home;
It knows no order
No assumption
No verdict of ignorance

My poem is intransigent
It's a poet alert to farce…
It possesses disobedience, it's even
A heart.
It doesn't feign, it doesn't flee.
It's birds migrating
It's for those alive today, it's bent on justice.

Poesia

Aracy Cachoeira

Poesia é um pedaço da gente
Rabiscada num papel,
É a voz do coração,
Que soa com gosto de mel.
Muitas vezes é uma mágoa,
Mostrada sem perceber,
Retalhos da nossa mente,
Que teimam em aparecer.
Qualquer poesia é uma parte,
Da alma de um poeta,
Pedindo para ser entendida,
Buscando a estrada correta.
Poesia é um pouco de paz,
É um pouco de emoção,
É tristeza, é alegria,
Que invade o coração.
Quem tem alma de poeta,
Tem uma missão a cumprir,
Escrever tudo que sabe,
Com os outros repartir,
Este dom que Deus lhe deu,
Não guarde somente para ti.

Poetry

Aracy Cachoeira

Poetry's a bit of all of us
Scribbled on a scrap of paper,
It's the voice of the heart,
Resounding with a taste of honey.
Very often it's a wound,
Shown uncomprehending,
Rags of our mind,
Fearful of being seen.
Any poetry is a part,
Of the soul of a poet,
Asking to be understood,
Looking for the right road.
Poetry's a little peace,
A little emotion,
It's sadness, it's joy,
Invading the heart.
Whoever has a poet's soul,
Has a mission to unfold,
To write all he knows,
With others to share,
This God-given gift,
Don't keep it to yourself alone.

A arte de gerar

Ademar Bogo

A poesia é o suspiro apaixonado que sai naturalmente como o hálito perfumado da boca daqueles que teimam levar o corpo através de passos firmes, para construir o futuro por onde passarão as futuras gerações. Deixaremos como herança aos que ainda vão nascer, para que sintam através do coração, o perfume de cada passo dado como cicatrizes abertas no tempo de cada existência. Somente produz poesia quem sabe sentir e herdar as poesias já produzidas pela vida da natureza e da humanidade. É o coração quem alerta o caminhante dizendo que:

> Há uma flor desabrochando
> há uma árvore dormindo
> há uma montanha gritando.
> há nuvens e arco-íris
> há ternura e paixão
> há fome, gente morrendo
> há dor dentro da canção.
> há lábio aberto sorrindo
> há povos em procissão
> há guerras no tempo indo
> há luar cá no sertão.[9]
> há seresteiros cantando
> há casais de bicho amando
> há sonhos no coração...

A poesia é como o mar, que transforma sua prepotência em humildade, prostrando-se aos pés das montanhas, a esperar que a água doce da serra venha lhe matar a sede. O mar não destrói a montanha, porque sabe que não teria mais onde encostar a cabeça na hora que quisesse descançar do balanço das ondas. Assim como a poesia preserva a Vida para que esta se deixe alimentar por ela.

A beleza, cansada foi embora, descansar nos acampamentos dos Sem Terra, à espera de que a terra devolva-lhes o espaço para deixar nascer sementes de beleza e sensibilidade, para germinar um, futuro de paz e solidariedade.

The art of sowing

Ademar Bogo

Poetry is the passionate sigh that springs as naturally as perfumed breath from the mouth of those that dare to bear their bodies firmly striding, to build the future where coming generations will walk in turn. As our legacy to those to be born, we shall leave for them to know in their hearts the perfume of each step we have taken like open scars in every lifetime. Only whoever knows how to feel and to inherit poetry already produced by nature and humanity can produce poetry at all. And it is the heart alerts the marcher by saying:

> a flower is blooming
> a tree is sleeping
> a mountain is shouting.
> there are cloud and rainbow
> there are tenderness and passion
> there are hunger, people dying
> there is sorrow in the song.
> there are open lips smiling
> there are people on the march
> there are wars in these times
> there's moonlight here in the *sertão*.[9]
> there are serenaders singing
> there are animals coupling
> there are dreams in the heart...

Poetry is like the sea, which turns its power to humility, laying itself at the foot of the mountains, hoping that the sweet water of the hills will come to slake its thirst. The sea does not destroy the mountain, for it knows it would have nowhere to lay its head whenever it wanted to rest from the endless lapping of the waves. So, like poetry, it preserves life so that life can be fed by it.

Beauty, tired, slipped away, to rest in the encampments of the *Sem Terra*, waiting for the land to give back space for seeds of beauty to sprout with sensitivity, to sow a future of peace and solidarity.

Neruda,[10] Drummond,[11] João Cabral,[12] Marighella,[13] Casaldáliga....[14] renascem na sombra das lonas pretas e se transformam em sonhos naqueles que aprenderam a amar a vida, olhando para um ponto imaginário do horizonte utópico, onde descansa a hora da chegada.

Nós estamos aqui. Nós queremos sonhar e mostrar as belezas que há nos labirintos de nossa existência.

Um dia entenderemos as flores, quando elas nos dirão que, só pode produzir perfume quem não teve medo de se deixar florescer.

Neruda,[10] Drummond,[11] João Cabral,[12] Marighella,[13] Casaldáliga...[14] are born again in the shade of black plastic, transformed into dreams of those who learned to love life, staring at an imaginary point of the utopian horizon, where rests the hour of their arrival.

We are here. We want to dream and to show what beauties lurk in the labyrinths of our being.

One day we shall understand the flowers, when they tell us that only those that don't fear flowering can give off a perfume.

A fala da terra

Pedro Tierra

A Liberdade da Terra não é assunto de lavradores.
A Liberdade da Terra é assunto de todos quantos
se alimentam dos frutos da Terra.
Do que vive, sobrevive, de salário.
Do que não tem casa. Do que só tem o viaduto.
Dos que disputam com os ratos
os restos das grandes cidades.
Do que é impedido de ir à escola.
Das meninas e meninos de rua.
Das prostitutas. Dos ameaçados pelo Cólera.
Dos que amargam o desemprego.
Dos que recusam a morte do sonho.

A Liberdade da Terra e a paz no campo têm nome:
Reforma Agrária.
Hoje viemos cantar no coração da cidade.
Para que ela ouça nossas canções e cante.
E reacenda nesta noite a estrela de cada um.
E ensine aos organizadores da morte
e ensine aos assalariados da morte
que um povo não se mata
como não se mata o mar
sonho não se mata
como não se mata o mar
a alegria não se mata
como não se mata o mar
a esperança não se mata
como não se mata o mar
e sua dança.

The earth speaks

Pedro Tierra

The freedom of the land is not about workers.
The freedom of the Land is about everyone who
Feeds on its fruit.
About everyone who lives, survives, on wages.
About the homeless. About those who live under bridges.
About those who dispute with the rats
The big cities' scraps.
About those who can't go to school.
About girls and boys of the street.
About the prostitutes. About those threatened by cholera.
About those embittered by unemployment.
About those who refuse the death of dream.

Freedom of the Land and peace in the fields have a name:
Agrarian Reform.
Today we've come to the city's heart to sing.
For the city to hear our songs and to sing.
And to light up again tonight the star of everyone.
And to teach the organisers of death
and to teach the wage earners of death
that a people can't be killed
just as the sea can't be killed
dreams can't be killed
just as the sea can't be killed
joy can't be killed
just as the sea can't be killed
hope can't be killed
just as the sea can't be killed
nor its dance.

Coração Brasil

Zé Pinto

Meu patrão eu não vim te pedir,
Vim cobrar o que é meu por direito
Nas estradas que já percorri
Vi retrato de sonhos desfeitos
Vi criança pedindo comida
E o emprego uma rara ilusão

Mas agora a paciência minguô
E aqui tô que tô seu doutor
E não tô só não

Esperar só as graças de Deus
Já não dá , Já não dá, Já não dá
E farinha com água demais seu doutor
Pra apenas alguns, caviar

Viola de encanto, de canto e de pranto
Não quer mais apenas chorar
Viola de intriga, de estrada e poesia
Viola caipira
Insiste em me acompanhar

Meu patrão eu não vim te pedir
Vim cobrar o que é meu por direito
Nas estradas que já percorri
Vi retratos de sonhos desfeitos
Vi favela engasgada de fome
E o campo sem ter plantação
Mas agora paciência minguó
E aqui tó que tó seu doutor
E não tó só não

Esperar só as graças de Deus…

meu nome é José Brasileiro
meu pai é Joaquim do Brasil
Minha mãe é Maria Nação
Nunca vi coração pra ser tão varonil

Brazil heart

Zé Pinto

I haven't come to ask you boss,
I've come to take what's mine by right
On the roads I wandered
I saw the portrait of undone dreams
I saw the children beg for food
Employment as a rare illusion

But patience now has waned
And here I am, sir, yes, I'm here
And not alone, sir, no, oh no

To await only the grace of God, sir,
Is now not on, not on, not on
It's flour and water that suffice, sir,
Caviar is but for some

Guitar of enchantment, of song and lament
No longer wants only to weep
Guitar of intrigue, of poetry and the road
Country-bumpkin guitar
Insists it will accompany me

I haven't come to ask you, boss
I've come to take what's mine by right
On the roads I've wandered
I saw the portraits of undone dreams
I saw shanties stifled with hunger
And the fields unplanted
But patience now has waned
And here I am, sir, yes, I'm here
And not alone, sir, no, oh no

To await only the grace of God, sir…

My name is José Brasileiro
My father is Joaquim do Brasil
My mother is Maria Nação
I've never seen a heart so manly

Crianças despejadas, durante a aula, na Fazenda São Domingos. Sandovalina, São Paulo, 1995.
Foto de Bernardo Mançano Fernandes, in *MST: Formação e territorialização*, São Paulo: Editora Hucitec, 1996. Reprodução autorizada.

Children evicted during classes on the São Domingos Farm. Sandovalina, state of São Paulo, 1995.
Photo by Bernardo Mançano Fernandes, in *MST: Formação e territorialização*, São Paulo: Editora Hucitec, 1996. Reproduced by permission.

Cânone da exclusão

Canon of exclusion

Brejo da Cruz

Chico Buarque de Hollanda[15]

A novidade
Que tem no brejo da cruz
É a criançada
Se alimentar de luz
Alucinados
Meninos ficando azuis
E desencarnando
Lá no brejo da cruz
Eletrizados
Cruzam os céus do Brasil
Na rodoviária
Assumem formas mil
Uns vendem fumo
Tem uns que viram Jesus
Muito sanfoneiro cego
Tocando Blues
Uns têm saudades
E dançam maracatus
Uns atiram pedras
Outros passeiam nus
Mas há milhões desses seres
Que se disfarçam tão bem
Que ninguém pergunta
De onde essa gente vem
São jardineiros
Guardas noturnos, casais
São passageiros
Bombeiros, babás
Já nem se lembram
Que existe um brejo da cruz
Que eram crianças
E que comiam luz
São faxineiros
Balançam nas construções
São bilheteiros
Baleiros e garçons

Marshland Cross

Chico Buarque de Hollanda[15]

The news
At Marshland Cross
Is that the urchins
Feed on light
Hallucinating
Children turning blue
Dying
There at Marshland Cross
Electrified
They cross Brazilian skies
In the bus-station
Taking on a thousand shapes
Some sell smokes
Others think that they are Jesus
Many blind play hurdy-gurdy
Playing Blues
Some miss home
While dancing to the band's old tunes
Some throw stones
Others wander naked
But there are millions of these folk
Who disguise themselves so well
That no one asks
Where they come from
They are gardeners
Night-guards, couples
They are passengers
Plumbers, nannies
They don't remember any more
That there is a Marshland Cross
That they were children
And that they once ate light
They are janitors
They dangle from building-sites
They are ticket-sellers
Sweet-vendors and waiters

Já nem se lembram
Que existe um brejo da cruz
Que eram crianças
E que comiam luz.

They don't even remember
That there is a Marshland Cross
That they were children
And that they once ate light.

Debaixo do viaduto

Aracy Cachoeira

Com fome e frio, sobre um pedaço de papelão,[16] o pobre velho estende a mão trêmula, desamparada.
Mão cansada, que já não agüenta e aos poucos se abandona vazia.
Agora somente o olhar perdido, decepcionado, sofrido, buscando compreensão.
Olhar tristonho de quem ansioso espera de alguém um gesto de amor.
Assim as horas se passam, enquanto uma esmola espera, suas forças vão se acabando, seu íntimo se desespera.
Num último esforço possível, apalpa o estilangado[17] seco, pega o cobertor enfumaçado, e na mais dramática cena, agarrado aos trapos suspira, enquanto calmo e sereno, o último sopro de vida, lentamente se expira.
Mas não haverá choro, não haverá velório, nem luto, é apenas mais um mendigo que morre, debaixo do viaduto.[18]

Under the viaduct

Aracy Cachoeira

With hunger, cold, on a cardboard scrap, [16] the poor old man outstretches his
shaking, helpless hand.
Tired hand, that can take no more and soon gives up, empty.
Now only the vacant stare, deceived, suffering, seeking
understanding.
So sad an anxious stare from one awaiting, from someone, a gesture of love.
So the hours pass, he waits and waits for alms, his strength ebbing away, as
inside he despairs.
In a last possible effort, he touches the dry tatters, [17] he tugs the grimy
blanket, and in the most dramatic scene, clinging onto his rags he sighs, now
calm and serene, the last breath of his life, as slowly he expires.
But there'll be no tears, there'll be no vigil, nor mourning, it's just one more
beggar dying, under the viaduct. [18]

Rua e nua

Aracy Cachoeira

Menino travesso de idéias santas, distorcidas,
Visitante do lixo companheiro,
Uma olhada ligeira no berço sujo
Onde voltará a dormir pela madrugada
Se alguém não o fizer dormir para sempre.
Em nome da segurança
De quem não pode correr risco.
Menino de sonhos castrados,
Parido na rua,
Por uma realidade, crua e nua,
De moral, ternura e justiça!

Naked street

Aracy Cachoeira

Ragamuffin riddled with sainted, twisted thoughts,
Visiting your friend the rubbish dump,
With fleeting glance at dirty cradle
Where you'll slip to sleep at dawn,
If you're not put first to sleep forever
In the name of a security
Of those who can't take risks.
Boy of dreams castrated,
Spawned in the street,
Out of a reality naked and raw,
Out of morality, a tender and just law!

Galdino no céu

Aracy Cachoeira

A fumaça subiu, lá no céu ela parou, junto com ela, Galdino,[19]
Para Deus se apresentou,
Dizendo Senhor meu Deus, a terra que a mim deixou veio gente covarde
E de lá me expulsou.
Quando fui reagir, fogo em mim tocou, na capital do país
Meu corpo em chama ficou.

É fogo, é suicídio, doença, miséria e dor,
Pataxó, Maxacali, Ianomâmi, Kaiowá,
Ticuna, Guajajara, Guarani, Xacriabá.[20]
Ninguém escapa da saga,
dos malvados lá da terra,
nossa gente é de paz,
não quer mais saber de guerra.

Socorro, Senhor meu Deus,
aos índios que ali restaram
Socorro, socorro eu peço.
Se a coisa não melhorar
na virada do milênio
nenhum índio vai restar.

A fumaça subiu lá no céu ela parou…
Junto com ela Galdino…

Galdino in heaven

Aracy Cachoeira

The smoke rose up, 'til in the sky it stopped, and with it, Galdino,[19]
He introduced himself to God,
Saying Lord my God, to the land that left me came the cowards
that threw me off.
When I went to react, I was touched by fire, in the country's capital
my body went up in flames.

It's fire, it's suicide, illness, poverty, sorrow,
Pataxó, Maxacali, Ianomâmi, Kaiowá,
Ticuna, Guajajara, Guarani, Xacriabá.[20]
Not one escapes the saga,
Of the evil-doers down on earth,
Our people are peaceful,
We want to hear of war no more.

Help, Lord my God,
The Indians left down there
Help, help I pray.
If things get no better
At the turn of the millennium
No Indians will be left.

The smoke rose up, 'til in the sky it stopped…
And with it Galdino…

Quinhentos anos de farça

Aracy Cachoeira

Um clarão no céu, fogos a pipocar.
Um clamor na mata, índio a lamentar.
Branco comemorando o que acha que descobriu.
Indio lamentando o que o branco destruiu.
Champanhe estourando, os ricos se fartando à mesa,
Na floresta o índio chora a perda da natureza.
Quinhentos anos[21] de ganância, descaso e perseguição
Com os primeiros habitantes desta rica e famosa nação.
Quinhentos anos de farsa, massacre e violência.
Quinhentos anos de luta em busca da sobrevivência.
Quinhentos anos de fé, esperança e resistência.
É o índio brasileiro, provando sua existência.

Five hundred years of farce

Aracy Cachoeira

A clearing in the sky, fireworks a-fizzing.
A clamour in the brushwood, an Indian lamenting.
The Whiteman commemorates what he thinks he discovered.
The Indian laments what the Whiteman destroyed.
Champagne corks a-popping, the rich at table getting fat,
In the forest the Indian is weeping at the loss of nature.
Five hundred years[21] of plunder, abandon and persecution,
Before the first inhabitants of this rich and famous nation.
Five hundred years of farce, of massacre and violence.
Five hundred years of struggle for survival.
Five hundred years of faith, of hope and resistance.
That's the Brazilian Indian, proving his existence.

Aranã quer terra

Aracy Cachoeira

Aranã busca seu povo[22]
Aranã busca seu chão
Aranã tem sua raiz
Cultura, sua tradição

Aranã quer terra
Aranã quer terra
Aranã quer terra
Aranã quer terra

Se ajunta Aranã, se ajunta
No Vale Jequitinhonha[23]
Se ajunta Aranã
Acaba com esta vergonha

Aranã quer terra

Aranã busca seu povo
Perdido pelas Gerais
Aranã quer sua terra
Não agüenta sofrer mais.

Aranã wants land

Aracy Cachoeira

Aranã wants his people [22]
Aranã wants his ground
Aranã wants his roots
His culture, his tradition

Aranã wants land
Aranã wants land
Aranã wants land
Aranã wants land

Aranã's joining up, joining up
In the valley of Jequitinhonha[23]
Aranã's joining up
He's had enough of this shame

Aranã wants earth

Aranã wants his people
Lost across Minas Gerais
Aranã wants his land
He can't bear suffering any more.

Paz aos índios e ao mundo

Aracy Cachoeira

Paz para Naruane-Nauê,
Pankararu, Nandewa,
Assurini, Moyoruna, Bacajá.

Paz para Crenak, Caxixó, Pancararé,
Kirirí, Gavião, Xavante, Ofoié,
Tixção, Cinta Larga, Waurá, Tembé.

Paz para Terena, Kaiabi, Xacriabá,
Sateré-maué, Xucuru, Kaxinawá.
Paz para Guató, Guarani, Wapixana,
Pataxó, Ram Ran Raê, Ianomani, Kaiowá.

Paz para Ticuna, Guajajara, Makuxi,
Kaiangang, Camba e Maxacali.

Maxacali, Maxacali,
Maxacali, paz ao mundo,
Paz a ti.

Peace be to the Indians and to the world

Aracy Cachoeira

Peace to Naruane-Nauê,
Pankararu, Nandewa,
Assurini, Moyoruna, Bacajá.

Peace to Crenak, Caxixó, Pancararé,
Kirirí, Gavião, Xavante, Ofoié,
Tixção, Cinta Larga, Waurá, Tembé.

Peace to Terena, Kaiabi, Xacriabá,
Sateré-maué, Xucuru, Kaxinawá.
Peace to Guató, Guarani, Wapixana,
Pataxó, Ram Ran Raê, Ianomani, Kaiowá.

Peace to Ticuna, Guajajara, Makuxi,
Kaiangang, Camba and Maxacali.

Maxacali, Maxacali,
Maxacali, peace to the world,
Peace to thee.

A pedagogia dos aços

Pedro Tierra

Candelária,
Carandiru,
Corumbiara,
Eldorado dos Carajás…

A pedagogia dos aços
golpeia no corpo
essa atroz geografia…

Há cem anos Canudos,
Contestado,
Caldeirão…

A pedagogia dos aços
golpeia no corpo
essa atroz geografia…

Há uma nação de homens
            excluídos da nação
Há uma nação de homens
            excluídos da vida
Há uma nação de homens
            calados,
            excluídos de toda palavra.
Há uma nação de homens
            combatendo depois das cercas.
Há uma nação de homens
            sem rosto,
            soterrados na lama,
            sem nome
            soterrados no silêncio

Eles rondam o arame
das cercas
alumiados pela fogueira
dos acampamentos.

Pedagogy of steel

Pedro Tierra

Candelária,
Carandiru,
Corumbiara,
Eldorado dos Carajás…

Pedagogy of steel
Beats the body
Atrocious geography…

One hundred years ago Canudos,
Constestado
Caldeirão…

Pedagogy of steel
Beats the body
Atrocious geography…

There's a nation of men
        excluded from the nation
There's a nation of men
        excluded from life
There's a nation of men
            muted,
            excluded from each and every word.
There's a nation of men
            in combat beyond the fences.
There's a nation of men
            faceless,
            buried deep in mud,
            nameless,
            in silence sunken.

They prowl the wire
of the fences' barbs,
faces aglow in the fire
of their camps.

Eles rondam o muro das leis
e ataram no peito
urna bomba que pulsa:
sonho da terra livre.

sonho vale uma vida?
Não sei. Mas aprendi
da escassa vida que gastei:
a morte não sonha.

A vida vale um sonho?
A vida vale tão pouco
do lado de fora da cerca...

A terra vale um sonho?
A terra vale infinitas
reservas de crueldade,
do lado de dentro da cerca.

Hoje, o silêncio pesa
como os olhos de uma criança
depois da fuzilaria.

Candelária,
Carandiru,
Corumbiara,
Eldorado dos Carajás não cabem
na frágil vasilha das palavras...

Se calarmos,
as pedras gritarão...

They prowl the walls of the law,
and pressed to their breast
is a ticking bomb:
dream of a land set free.

Is that dream worth a life?
I don't know.
But from this life scant and spent,
I've learned that in death there's no dream.

Is life worth a dream?
Life's worth so little
Outside the fence...

Is the land worth a dream?
The land's worth endless
stocks of cruelty,
inside the fence.

Silence weighs heavy today,
like the eyes of a child
after the shooting.

Candelária,
Carandiru,
Corumbiara,
Eldorado dos Carajás, won't fit
In the fragile vase of words...

If we stay silent,
The stones will scream...

Candelária

Protásio Prates – Tuca

Quando a bala bate o sino • bate mais do que o metal
quanta dor nesse menino • que confiou na catedral
Recostou-se pra fugir • da solidão do seu destino
quem diria que seria • teu sono eterno, menino.

Candelária, Candelária • Por quem dobram teus badalos
seria pelos que clamam • ou talvez pelos que calam
Na miséria desse povo • quem decide é o fuzil
Que vergonha, Candelária • és a estampa do Brasil
Que vergonha, Candelária • és a estampa do Brasil.

Quando o chumbo pesa muito • na consciência de quem tem
vão ao mundo esses clamores • que nos chegam do além
Dá-me gana devolver • o mesmo chumbo também
pois justiça só existe • quando o caso lhe convém.

Quem deixou a meninada • pelas ruas solta ao léu
trancou Cristo entre paredes • e fechou a porta do céu
que eu faço, o que tu fazes • Com essa bestialidade
se o modelo que corrompe • vem da própria autoridade.

Candelária

Protásio Prates – Tuca

When the bullet strikes the bell • it strikes more than metal
So much pain in that boy • who trusted in the cathedral
He took refuge • from his lonely destiny
Who could tell what would be • your eternal dream, my boy.

Candelária, Candelária • for whom do your bells toll
Would it be for those who clamour • or perhaps for those still silent
In the misery of the people • what decides is the rifle
How shameful Candelária • you're the emblem of Brazil
How shameful Candelária • you're the emblem of Brazil.

When the lead weighs heavy • on the conscience of whoever has one
Out to the world go the screams • which come to us now from afar
It makes me want to send them back • the lead too
for justice only exists • for convenience's sake.

Whoever left the kids • running loose in aimless streets
Locked up Christ within the walls • and shut the gate of heaven
What do I do, what do you do • with the bestial
Model that corrupts • when it comes from authority itself

Enterro das vítimas do massacre de Eldorado de Carajás, estado do Pará.
Foto de João Ripper, Arquivos do MST, São Paulo. Reprodução autorizada.

Burial of the victims of the Eldorado de Carajás massacre, in the state of Pará.
Photo by João Ripper, MST Archives, São Paulo. Reproduced by permission.

A morte como horizonte de vida

Death as life's horizon

Receita para matar um sem-terra

Frei Betto

Tome um agricultor
Desplantado de sua terra,
Desfolhe-o de seus direitos,
Misture-o à poeira da estrada
E deixe-o secar ao sol.
Deposite-o, em seguida,
No fundo do descaso público.
Adicione a injúria da baderna.
Derrame o pote de horror ao pobre
Até obter a consistência do terror.
Acrescente uma dose de mau presságio
E salpique, com a mão do ágio,
Denunciosas fatias de pedágio.
Deixe repousar no silêncio
A ganância grileira,
As áreas devolutas,
A saga assassina
De quem semeia guerras
Para amealhar terras.
Ferva a mentira
No caldeirão oficial
Até adquirir densidade
Em rede nacional.
Sirva à repressão
Impunemente
Na bandeja do latifúndio.

Recipe for killing the landless

Frei Betto

Take a rural worker
Unplanted from his land,
Strip the leaves of his rights,
Mix him up with road dust
And lay him in the sun to dry.
Drop him, in an instant,
In the common pit of discard.
Stir in the slur of riot.
Spill the pot of horror on the poor
'Til the mix is thick with terror.
Add a dash of ill-omen
And sprinkle, speculating,
Threatening strips of toll-charge.
Leave to set in silence
Grileiro-grabber land-greed,
Lands left fallow,
Assassin saga
Of war-sowers
Land-hoarders.
Boil down the lies
In official cauldrons
'Til density's settled
In a national network.
Serve up repression
With impunity
On the latifundium's estately tray.

A morte anunciada de Josimo Tavares

Pedro Tierra

Há um dizer antigo
entre os homens da raça dos rios:
a morte quando se anuncia,
devora a sombra do corpo
e inventa a luz da solidão.

Você se afastou sob o sol.
Era 14 de abril.
Busquei-lhe a sombra
sobre o chão da rua
e não havia sombra.

Ainda busquei tocá-lo.
Falamos da vida
e da morte.

(A arma que me matará,
Já está na oficina...)
É você sorria manso,
desde a defendida
solidão dos místicos.
Falamos da luta
e da necessidade de prosseguir
(os tecelões da morte
forçam os teares,
arrematam os fios
do tecido que te cobrirá...).

Incendiaram nossas casas.
Destruíram plantações.
Saquearam celeiros.
Derrubaram cocais.
Envenenaram as águas.

Invadiram povoados.
Torturaram nossos pais.
Arrancaram as orelhas dos mortos.
Atiraram nos rios corpos mutilados.
Derrubaram a cruz que erguemos,
sinal aceso da nossa memória.

Josimo Tavares's death foretold

Pedro Tierra

There's an old saying
Amongst the river peoples:
Death foretold
Devours the body's shadow
And invents the light of solitude.

You departed in the sun.
On the 14th of April.
I sought your shadow
In the street
And no shadow was to be seen.

I still sought to touch you.
We spoke of life
And we spoke of death.

(The weapon that will kill me,
Is already in the workshop...)
And gently you smiled,
From the firm-defended
Solitude of mystics.
We spoke of strength
And the need to go on
(For the weavers of death
Force the looms ever on,
Finishing threads
Of the cloth that will cover you...).

They set fire to our houses.
They destroyed plantations.
They sacked our granaries.
They overturned coconut groves.
They poisoned the waters.

They invaded villages.
They tortured our mothers and fathers.
They ripped the ears from our dead.
They threw mutilated corpses into the rivers.
They knocked down the cross we raised,
Flaring signal of our memory.

Cortaram a língua dos nossos irmãos,
Violaram nossas filhas.
Assassinaram inválidos.
Queimaram crianças de colo,
Cercaram a sangue e fogo
a terra que trabalhamos.
Quem emprestará a voz
ao idioma do perdão
e protegerá com súplicas
riso dos assassinos?

Aniquilaram a raiz da esperança.
Esgotou-se o tempo de tolerar
e desatou-se a hora da vingança:
primitivo nome da justiça.

Todos sabiam dessa morte.
A cerca do latifúndio [24]
sabia.
Os pistoleiros, os assalariados da morte,
a polícia fardada e paisana, o GETAT,[25]
os garimpeiros, os bêbados, as prostitutas,
as professorinhas, as beatas,
as crianças brincando no areal da rua
sabiam.

Os homens da terra, os posseiros, os saqueados,
as mulheres alfabetizadas pela dor
e pela espera
sabiam.

prefeito, o juiz, o delegado, a UDR,
os fazendeiros, os crápulas
sabiam.

As mãos dos assassinos
poliam as armas.

A igreja sabia
e esperava...

They cut out the tongues of our brothers,
They raped our daughters.
They murdered invalids.
They burned children in their mothers' laps,
They laid siege with blood and fire
to the land that we worked.
Who will lend voice
to the language of pardon
protecting with beseeching
the laughter of assassins?

They annihilated the roots of hope.
The time of tolerance is gone
and the time for vengeance is come:
in the primitive name of justice.

Everyone knew of this death.
The fence of the latifundia [24]
knew too.
The gunmen, salaried agents of death,
the uniformed country police, the GETAT,[25]
the prospectors, drunkards, prostitutes,
young women teachers, old women of the Church,
the children playing in the sandy street
knew too.

The men of the land, the *posseiros*, the pillaged,
the women educated through pain
and through waiting
knew too.

The prefect, the judge, the delegate, the UDR,
the landowners, the debauched
knew too.

Assassin hands
polished their guns.

The church knew
and waited...

A haste orgulhosa do babaçu
sabia.
E dobrava as palmas num lamento
e multiplicava a ciência dessa morte,

>   os passarinhos, o relógio dos templos
>   mastigando o comboio das horas
>   e não se deteve, a água dos rios
>   não se deteve, fluindo irremediável
>   a hora dessa morte.

A pedra dos caminhos
sabia
e permaneceu muda,
O vento sabia
e anunciava seu gemido todavia
indecifrável.

Tuas sandálias sabiam
e continuaram a caminhar.

Eu, que nasci voltado à alegria
e vivo a contar o rosário interminável
dos mortos
>   não fiz o verso,
>   espada de fúria,
>   que cindisse em dois
>   comboio das horas
>   e descarrilasse o tempo de tua morte.

Você sabia.
E sorria
apenas.
Como quem se lava
para chegar vestido
de algodão
e transparência
à hora da solidão.

Quem é esse menino negro
que desafia limites?

The proud spear of the babassu-palm
knew
And bent its fronds in a lament
and multiplied the knowledge of that death,

> the little birds, the church clocks
> chewing on hours in convoy
> didn't stop, and the river water
> didn't stop, flowing irremediable
> at the hour of the death.

The stone on the roads
knew
and remained silent,
The wind knew
and announced its groan still
indecipherable.

Your sandals knew
and kept on walking.

I who was born joyful
and lived counting the interminable rosary
of the dead
> I did not write the verse,
> sword of fury,
> that might split in two
> the convoy of hours
> derailing the time of your death.

You knew.
And smiled
a little.
Like someone who washes
in order to arrive dressed
in cotton
and transparency
at the time of solitude.

Who's the black boy
who defies limits?

Apenas um homem.

Sandálias surradas.
Paciência e indignação.
Riso alvo.
Mel noturno.
Sonho irrecusável.

Lutou contra cercas.[26]
Todas as cercas.
As cercas do medo.
As cercas do ódio.
As cercas da terra.
As cercas da fome.
As cercas do corpo.
As cercas do latifúndio.

Trago na palma da mão
um punhado da terra que te cobriu.
Está fresca.
É morena, mas ainda não é livre
como querias.

Sei aqui dentro
que não queres apenas lágrimas.
Tua terra sobre a mesa
me diz com seu silêncio agudo
Meu sangue se levantará
como um rio acorrentado
e romperá as cercas do mundo.

Um rio de sangues convocados
atravessará tua camisa
e ela será bandeira
sobre a cabeça dos rebelados.

Hardly a man.

Worn-out sandals.
Patience and indignation.
Pure smile.
Night-time honey.
Undeniable dream.

He fought against fences.[26]
Fences all.
Fences of fear.
Fences of hate.
Fences of earth.
Fences of famine.
Fences of the body.
Fences of the latifundium.

I bring in the palm of my hand
a fistful of earth that covered you.
It's still fresh.
It's dark but still not free
as you wanted it to be.

I know inside
that you don't just want tears.
Your earth on the table
tells me in its sharp silence:
my blood will rise
as a river torrent
breaking open all the world's fences.

A river's blood of others called
shall flow across your shirt
and it will be the banner
held above the heads of rebels.

Cortejo

Ana Cláudia

Olhas o corpo que passa
Com tua foice na mão
Com tua enxada nas costas
Olhas e voltas pro chão
Este chão que produzes
Que é teu meio de vida
Sendo a tua perdição.

Olhas sem compreender
Comentas sem entender
Quem matou aquele irmão
Irmão na sina e na saga
Um nó no peito de trava
Quem deu cabo àquela vida
Que só a vida buscava?

Se não abrires teus olhos
Se não tiveres a terra
Se não entrares na guerra
Começada por outras mãos
Tu serás sem duvidar
Mais um que a morte sugou
Olhando a vida passar.

Cortege

Ana Cláudia

You look upon the corpse that passes by
With your sickle in hand
With your hoe o'er your shoulder
You look and return to the ground
The ground that you furrow
As your means of life
Being your loss.

You look without comprehending
You ask without understanding,
Who killed that brother,
Brother in our fight and in our fate
With a lump in the throat, tight-chested,
Who brought an end to that life
That only life sought?

If you won't open your eyes
If you won't take the lands
If you won't join the war
Begun by other hands
You will be without doubt
Just another sucked in by death
Watching life pass by.

Ligação do infinito

Zé Pinto

Alô, aqui é Teixeirinha,[27]
Estou ligando pra dizer
Que daqui tô com vocês,
Já não importa a hora
E nem tão pouco o mês
Pois agora sou um anjo
Sem trombetas e sem asas
Mas tão bem politizado
Pois ajudei a levar o fardo
Da resistência e da dor,
Também muito desespero
Senti diante do fato
Numa execução sumária
Que me pesa sobre os ombros
Mas pouco antes do tombo
Já quando perdia a fala
Senti no fundo d'alma
Uma voz que insistia
Por Joãos e por Marias:
'Avante Reforma Agrária'
Aí vai um grande abraço
Aos companheiros Sem Terra
E a tantos que acreditam
E se juntam nessa guerra,
Pois se na roda da história
Não pode haver marcha a ré
Apelo diretamente ao meu filho e à mulher
Que caminharam comigo
Em glórias e sofrimento
Se junte aos acampamentos
Deste país de milhões
Que marcham em romaria
Rumo ao novo em construção.
E no dia da vitória,
Que todos se dêem as mãos
Pra gritar com liberdade
Que a luta não foi em vão.

Phone call from the infinite

Zé Pinto

Hello, this is Teixeirinha,[27]
I'm calling to say
That from here I'm still with you,
Now the hour doesn't matter
Nor the month
For now I'm an angel
Without trumpets or wings
But so politicised
Since I helped take up the burden
Of resistance and of sorrow,
Much despair too
I felt at the fact
Of a summary execution
Hanging heavy on my shoulders
But a little before I fell
As I was losing speech
I felt deep in my soul
A voice insisting
For each João and each Maria:
'Onward Agrarian Reform'
Here's an embrace
For my *Sem Terra* comrades
And for those who believe
And join in this war,
For if on the wheel of History
There can be no marching back
I appeal directly to my son and wife
Who walked with me
In glory and in suffering
Join up with the camps
Of this country of millions
Who march in procession
On the way to constructing anew
And on the day of victory
Let all hands join together
As they shout in freedom
The fight was not in vain.

Luto(a)

Ana Cláudia

Meu luto não será calado
Nem resignado
Será alto e forte
Rebelde e fino

E também não será preto
Será vermelho e combativo
Nascedor de todos os que tombaram.
Meu luto não fica em casa
Porque meu lugar é o mundo

Meu luto tem 500 anos[28]
E fica mais velho

Quando ao começo do dia
Volto meu olhar para a história
Sonho com novas borboletas
E flores margaridas.

Mourning combat

Ana Cláudia

My mourning will not be muted
Nor will it be resigned
It will be tall and strong
Rebellious and fine

Nor will it be dark
It will be red and in combat
Born from all that have fallen.
My mourning doesn't stay indoors
For my place is out there in the world

My mourning is 500 years old[28]
And is older yet

When at daybreak
I cast my eye back over history
When I dream anew of butterflies
And of marguerites.

Mobilização e protesto das mulheres Sem Terra, em 8 de março de 2001, no centro de São Paulo.
Foto de Maísa Mendonça. Reproduzida com a permissão do MST São Paulo.

Landless Women's mobilization and protest, on March 8th 2001, in the centre of São Paulo.
Photo by Maísa Mendonça. Reproduced with the permission of the MST São Paulo.

A mulher Sem-Terra

The Landless Woman

É tempo de colher

Ademar Bogo

Há momentos na história
Em que todas as vitórias
Parecem fugir da gente
Mas vence quem não desanima
E busca em sua auto-estima
A força pra ser persistente.

Regando o deserto da consciência
Um novo ser nasceu,
É hora de ir em frente, companheiro
Você é o guerrilheiro
Que a história nos deu.

Regamos o deserto da consciência
Um novo ser nasceu
É hora de ir em frente, companheira
Você é a guerrilheira
Que a história nos deu.

It's harvest time

Ademar Bogo

In history there are moments
When all victories
Seem to flee
But the one who never despairs
Wins, seeking in self-esteem
The unyielding strength to be.

By watering the desert of conscience
A new being has been born,
It's time to move on my friend
For you are the *guerrillero*
History gave to us.

We watered the desert of conscience
A new being has been born
It's time to move on my friend
For you are the *guerrillera*
History gave to us.

Nós todas

Pedro Tierra

Nós somos os sangues convocados dos rios que nutrem o Continente.
Nós somos o ventre que pare os filhos dos homens e sua ferocidade.
Nós somos moldadas em borro e fulgor: a matéria da vida.
Nós somos quem perdeu os filhos como o grito agudo devorado pela sombra do silêncio.
Nós somos aquelas que vigiam os risos da insônia.
Nós somos as mães de cobre e cinza dos povos indígenas exterminados, sobreviventes.
Nós somos quem palmilha o pó da América buscando fantasmas e só encontramos ossos.
Nós somos quem buscou com tanto amor e tal fúria e
dentes cerrados.
E esperança contra toda esperança que às vezes os encontramos um dia, ressuscitados como Abel, no Baixo Araguaia.[29]
Nós somos o grito que golpeia os janelas fechadas dos palácios.
Nós somos a mão que toca o manto da justiça que sempre nos escapa como miragem.
Com que nome batizamos nossa angústia?
Pureza, Isabel, Marta, Maria, Margarida, Roseli, Fátima, Adelaide…
Quem algum dia inquiriu as nascentes da dor?
Carregamos pedras como penitentes e aprendemos com os olhos que as nascentes da dor vertem rios de lágrimas:
Claras cordas de cristal e corte.
Não somos apenas mulheres que choram. Somos fecundas.
Somos as mulheres que vão parir a vida, quando a morte vos alcançar.
Nós somos a multiplicação das lutas como a Terra multiplica o cercal plantado.
Somos plantio e colheita.
Somos a raiz da esperança.

All we women

Pedro Tierra

We are the blood called upon from the rivers that feed the Continent.
We are the womb that bears the sons of men and their ferocity.
We are moulded in mud and its glow: the substance of life.
We are the ones that lost our sons like the sharp scream devoured by the shadow of silence.
We are the ones that watch over the laughter of sleeplessness.
We are the mother of copper and ashes of indigenous peoples exterminated, surviving.
We are the ones searching out phantoms through the dust of America only to find bones.
We are the ones that sought with so much love and with such fury, teeth clenched.
And hoping against hope that sometimes might we find them, come alive again, like Abel, in *Baixo Araguaia*.[29]
We are the shout that strikes against the closed windows of palaces.
We are the hand touching the mantle of justice that always escapes us like a mirage.
With what name shall we christen our anguish?
Pureza, Isabel, Marta, Maria, Margarida, Roseli, Fátima, Adelaide…
Who one day asked the sources of pain?
We carry stones like penitents and we learn with eyes that those born of sorrow weep in rivers of tears:
Clear cords of crystal and cuts.
We are not only women who cry, we are fertile.
We are the women who'll give birth to life, when death is reaching you.
We are the multipliers of struggle just as the land is the multiplier of the planted enclosure.
We are the sowing and the harvest.
We are the root of hope.

Constelações da luta

Charles Trocate

A Eli

As mãos abertas de uma mulher
Pedem um aceno de vida
Desafiam a gravidade do cruel
Põem nome no filho
E nas belezas

Os olhos vivos
Quase artesanais de uma mulher...
Põem luz nas bandeiras
Caçam uma pátria de terra
Por entre as tristezas anunciadas
E o primeiro arado

Os pés alvos de uma mulher
Conduzem a profundidade da cova
Corroem o fio elétrico da tortura
Geram o amor e as esperas,
Mãos polindo a flor
E o poema de combate.

The struggle's constellations

Charles Trocate

To Eli

The open hands of a woman
Ask for a sign of life
Challenge the gravity of the cruel
Give a name to the son
And to beauty

The eyes as lively
As a woman's handicraft…
Cast light in the banners
Hunting for a land that's home
Amidst the foretold griefs
And the first plough

The fair feet of a woman
Lead to the depth of the grave
Corrode the electric wire of torture
Generate love and hope,
Hands stroking the flower
And the poem of struggle.

Chegar ao mundo

Charles Trocate

Uma mulher voa
Milhares se ecoam no vinho e no pão
Abrindo o ventre
Nas terras plantadas
Menos cercadas...[30]
E tu caminhando chega
Serena e desobediente
Com o suor de tuas luzes
Chega nas sementes
No caule da vida!

Uma criança brinca
São canteiros e covas de trigo
Todas juntas
Nas escolas levantadas de alegria...
Sem ser prisão
E tu caminhando chega
Antes do mal
Viva e sem igual
Chega hoje flor matinal!

Uma bandeira inflamada
Feminina dentro do vermelho
Nua pelo vento
Juventude pelo amor
Nas mãos carregadas...
Sem ser ilusão industrial
E tu caminhando chega
Para ser filha
Chega ao mundo
No tempo da insurreição!

Coming into the world

Charles Trocate

A woman flies
Thousands echo each other in wine and bread
Opening their bellies
In planted fields
Without fencing…[30]
And you come marching
Serene and disobedient
With the sweat of your lights
Reaching the seeds
And the stem of life!

A child plays
There are flowerbeds and tombs of wheat
All together
Brought up in schools of joy…
Without being a prison
And you arrive marching
In the face of evil
Alive and without equal
Arrives today a morning flower!

A flag of flame
Feminine amidst the red
Naked in the wind
Youth through love
In burdened hands…
Without being an industry's illusions
And you marching come
To be a daughter
You arrive in the world
At a time of insurrection!

Por honra e por amor

José César Matesich Pinto

Quando escuto falar de paz e guerra
Ocupação, poder ou violência
Toco silêncio e fico em continência,
Por honra e por amor a Ana sem-terra.[31]

Fazendo a ronda de um acampamento
Conheci sua esperança e valentia
Ante a intenção de conhecer um dia
A terra própria para seu sustento.

Tinha tão arraigada em sua mente
A carência do chão que ela encerra,
Que a alusão popular de Ana sem-terra,
Tornara-se efetiva e condizente.

Muitas vezes a vi, junto a seu povo,
Em momentos difíceis e intranqüilos,
Eu no ingrato dever de reprimi-los,
E ela querendo não me ver de novo.

Talvez inda prossiga nessa lida,
Fazendo frentes criando filhos,
Com a fé que remove os empecilhos,
Nos caminhos da terra prometida.

Mas nunca mais a vi, desde o momento
Em que ficamos entre guerra ou paz,
E ela partiu, com todo o acampamento,
No rumo de Eldorado – Carajás.

For honour and for love

José César Matesich Pinto

When I hear them speak of peace or war
Of occupation, violence or of power
In curfew's silence I stay loyal,
In honour and love of Ana sem-terra.[31]

Doing the encampment rounds
I came to know her bravery, her hope
In her will to have one day
A land, a plot, of her own.

In her mind she'd kept so rooted
The lack of the land her name contained,
That the popular allusion to Ana sem-terra
Become effective and germane.

Many times I saw her, together with her own,
I in moments troubled and restless,
In my thankless duty of repression,
And she not wanting to see me again.

Perhaps she struggles on,
At the front, rearing children,
With that faith that moves mountains,
On the roads to her promised land.

But I never saw her again, since
We stood between war or peace,
And she left, with the rest of the camp,
For Eldorado – Carajás.

Primeira apresentação de *Retorno à Terra*, pelo Grupo de Teatro 'Vida em Arte', Assentamento Rondinha, Jóia, Rio Grande do Sul, 2000.
Foto de Solange Brum. Reprodução autorizada.

Opening performance of *Return to the Earth*, by 'Vida em Arte' (Life in Art) Theater Group, Rondinha Settlement, Jóia, state of Rio Grande do Sul, 2000.
Photo by Solange Brum. Reproduced by permission.

Resgate da tradição e da cultura do campo

Rehabilitation of tradition and country culture

Saudade no norte

Aracy Cachoeira

Velho Norte, antigo pouso de tropeiros,[32] rolando silenciosamente suas águas e o seu fardo de saudade.

Saudade dos tempos de fartura, da ingazeira onde em algazarra a meninada com seus frutos se fartava.

Saudade da sombra da gameleira,[33] que acolhia o retirante,[34] o 'rancador' de puaia[35] aventureiro das matas.

Hoje, suas margens descampadas, barrancos despencados pelos sulcos de erosão, é uma boca que quer gritar.

Quer saber onde estão as ramagens, e as raízes protetoras que seguravam barrancos e encostas.

Mas o grito está preso na garganta do rio, onde a poderosa piaba, baila soberana na areia, salpicada de cacos, desafiando o tempo, pois quase só ela restou.

E o Norte perguntando:

'Onde estão os tropeiros das pousadas, e os peixes que variavam o seu cardápio?

Cadê a meninada destemida que desafiava a nado as minhas águas na enchente de março?

Cadê as lavadeiras que jogavam versos, entoando cantigas ritmadas com o bater da roupa na pedra, e coravam roupas com sumo de S. Caetano[36] e sabão de decoada[37] nos verdes gramados?

Onde estão as árvores, proteção da terra, dos rios e do ar?'

É tudo lembrança nas margens do Velho Norte.

É tudo saudade, de tudo que protegia a qualidade de vida do homem.

Nostalgia in the North

Aracy Cachoeira

Old North, ancient repose of troopers,[32] silently rolling out its waters and its burden of nostalgia.
Nostalgia for the times of plenty, for creepers where, having a ball, the kids stuffed themselves with fruit.
Nostalgia for the shade of the *gameleira,*[33] that welcomed the *retirante,*[34] the adventurous puaia-picker[35] of the woods.
Today, its banks stripped, its sides collapsed by furrows of erosion, its mouth wanting to scream.
It wants to know where the foliage has gone, and the protective roots that shored up the sides and embankments.
But the scream is caught in the river's throat, where the powerful smelt dances sovereign in the sand, dotted with broken glass, defying time, since it alone is left.
And the North is asking:
'Where are the troopers in the inns, and the fresh-water fish that lent variety to their diet?
What became of the kids that dared to cross my waters in the floods of March?
What became of the washer-women that pour out their verses, intoning old songs to the rhythm of their clothes beating against stone, and coloured them with Saint Caetano juice[36] and washing soap[37] in the green fields?
Where are the trees that protected the land, the rivers and the air?'
All is but memory on the banks of the Old North.
All is but nostalgia for all that protected the quality of human life.

Lamentos e sonhos

Zé Pinto

Deixamos um dia as Gerais[38]
Em direção ao norte
Fomos tentar nossa sorte em outro lugar
Meu pai, minha mãe, meus irmãos,
Tudo o que possuíam
Era o sonho de um taco de terra pra poder plantar

Mamãe lamentando deixava pra trás
mês de Maria, a reza do terço
A coroação, a festa , o leilão
Rasgar outro chão voltar ao começo
Meu pai já ao longe olhava pra serra
Pros pés de café que um dia viu crescer
Num pau-de-arara buscava seu chão [39]
Pois nesse torrão nunca pode ter

A criançada só não reclamava
Porque menino é só festejar
Só lamentava meu irmão mais velho
Pois o canário não deu pra levar
E foi abrindo a porta da gaiola
Pro canarinho então poder voar
Mas como era tão acostumado
Deu um rasante e tornou voltar
Que pena, que pena, que pena

Adeus canário cantador
Adeus brincadeira de roda
Tomara que o sonho da terra
Não marque outra era
Realize agora

Foi nas marcas do cacai[40]
Que o nosso 'uai'[41] se perdeu
Foi depois de tanta briga
Que as espiga floresceu
Hoje inté tem cantoria
Festa do mês de Maria
Mas lá das Minas Gerais
A gente nunca esqueceu

Laments and dreams

Zé Pinto

One day we left Minas[38]
Heading north
We went to try our luck elsewhere
My father, mother, brothers, sisters,
All they had there
Was the dream of planting a little patch

Mamma, lamenting, left behind
Month of May, her rosary to say,
Coronation, feast, and auction
Another plot to dig from scratch
Father from afar now searched the slopes
For the coffee plants he'd once seen thrive
Now pining for his soil from the back of a truck[39]
For in this land he'd never more have such luck

Only the kids weren't complaining
'Cos for children only fun's at stake
Only my eldest brother lamenting
That his pet canary he couldn't take
And so the cage door he opened
For the little bird to fly through
But as it always used to do
First it swooped then back it flew
How sad, how sad, how sad

Farewell singing canary
Farewell ring o'roses
If only our dream of land
Won't have to wait for another era
Let it happen now

It was carrying our *cacai*[40]
That we lost our '*uai*'[41]
It was only after so much fighting
That we reaped our ears of corn
Today there's even singing
For the feast of the month of Mary
But we've never forgotten
Our Minas Gerai

Escola do Acampamento Oziel Alves Pereira na Fazenda Dissenha em Abelardo Luz, Santa Catarina.
Foto de Carlos Carvalho, Arquivos do MST de São Paulo Reprodução autorizada.

School in the Oziel Alves Pereira camp, on the Dissenha Farm in Abelardo Luz, Santa Catarina.
Photo by Carlos Carvalho, MST Archives São Paulo Reproduced by permission.

Educação

Education

Entrevista: reforma agrária e educação

Paulo Freire

O processo de Reforma Agrária inaugura uma nova história, uma nova cultura, a cultura que nasce de um processo de transformação do mundo. Por isso mesmo, ela implica em transformações sociais [...], por exemplo, a superação de uma cultura profundamente paternalista e fatalista em que o camponês se perdia [...], enquanto objeto quase puro excluído [...]. Por sua reincorporação ao processo da produção, ele ganha uma posição social que não tinha, uma história que ele não tinha [...]. Na verdade, ele descobre que o fatalismo já não explica coisa nenhuma e que, tendo sido capaz de transformar a terra, ele é capaz de transformar a história e a cultura. Da posição fatalista, ele renasce, numa posição de inserção, de presença na história, não mais como objeto, mas também como sujeito da história. Ora, isso tudo são tarefas educativas. Então, trabalhar no sentido de ajudar os homens e as mulheres brasileiras a exercer o direito de poder estar de pé no chão, cavando o chão, retificando o chão, fazendo com que o chão produza melhor é um direito e um dever nosso.

A educação é uma das chaves para abrir essas portas. Eu nunca me esqueço de uma frase linda que eu ouvi de um educador, de um alfabetizador camponês de um grupo de Sem Terra de um assentamento enorme no Rio Grande do Sul onde eu fui, quando ele disse: 'pela força do nosso trabalho, pela nossa luta, cortamos o arame farpado do latifúndio e entramos nele, mas quando nele chegamos, vimos que havia outros arames farpados, como o arame da nossa ignorância'. 'Então eu percebi melhor ainda naquele dia', disse ele, 'que quanto mais inocentes, tanto melhor somos para os donos do mundo'. [...] Eu acho que essa é uma tarefa que não é só política, que não é só ideológica, mas também pedagógica. Não há Reforma Agrária sem isso.

Eu vou mandar um recado para os jovens professores [...]: vivam por mim, já que eu não posso viver, com crianças e com adultos que, com sua luta, estão buscando ser eles mesmos e elas mesmas.[42]

Interview: agrarian reform and education

Paulo Freire

The process of Agrarian Reform begins a new history, a new culture, a culture born of a process of transforming the world. For this very reason, it implies social transformations [...], for example, the overcoming of a profoundly paternalist and fatalist culture in which the peasant got lost [...], as an almost totally excluded object [...]. Through his re-incorporation into the process of production, he acquires a social position he did not previously have, a history he did not have [...]. In truth, he discovers that fatalism no longer explains anything at all and that, having been able to transform the land, he is also capable of transforming history and culture. From out of that former fatalism, the peasant is reborn, inserted as a presence in history, no longer as an object, but as a subject of history. Now, this whole process involves the tasks of education. So, working in the sense of helping Brazilian men and women to exercise the right of standing erect on the ground, tilling the land, turning it around, making it produce more effectively, is our right and is our duty.

Education is one of the keys to open such doors. I never forgot that lovely phrase I heard from an educator, a peasant literacy worker from a group of Sem Terra in an enormous settlement in the state of Rio Grande do Sul where I once was, when he said: 'by the strength of our work, through our struggle, we cut through the barbed wire of the latifundium and we entered it, but when we got there, we saw that there were other barbed wires, like that of our ignorance'. 'Then I understood even better, on that day,' he said, 'that the more innocent we are, the better we are for the world's owners.' [...] I find that it is a task that is not only political, not only ideological, but also pedagogical. Without this there can be no Agrarian reform.

I send a message to young teachers [...]: live for me, now that I cannot live myself, with children and with adults who, in their struggle, seek to be themselves, men and women.[42]

Plantando ciranda

Aos sem-terrinhas

Zé Pinto

Antes não éramos nada
Pois sem saída ou chegada
Éramos coisas jogadas
Pelas pontes, viadutos
E, vivendo assim um ser
Não é possível ser nada.

Mais um dia ouviu-se um grito
Papai, mamãe se acordaram
E seguiram a multidão
E nós viramos semente
Semente de terra livre
Uma terra sem patrão

Ser livre é poder ser gente
Ser passarinho, ser flor
Ser criança, adolescente
Ser jovem, agricultor
Replantar cidadania
E colher um novo dia
Pelos canteiros do amor.

E nos caminhos da morte
Alguém semeou a vida
E nas mãos da consciência
Infância, pão e partilha.
Mas foi cantando ciranda[43]
Que resgatamos os sonhos
E viramos poesia.

Planting playground song

To the Little Landless

Zé Pinto

Before we were nothing
Neither leaving nor arriving
We were a mere something
Over bridges under viaducts thrown
And, living like that, a being
Can be no one.

But one day the shout was loud
Papa and Mamma rose
And followed the crowd
And we became a seed
The seed of free land
A land with no boss

To be free and be human
To be a little bird, a flower
To be a child, an adolescent
To be young, a peasant
Farmer, citizenship to replant
A new day to harvest
From the flowerbeds of love.

And on the trails of death
Someone sowed life
And in the hands of conscience
Childhood, bread and sharing
But it was in playground songs[43]
That we rescued our dreams
And became poetry.

Vai, meninada

Zé Pinto

Numa ciranda de roda vai a criançada
e a menina dos olhos desse caminhar
somos segredos da vida
numa flor desabrochar
numa flor desabrochar
Sementes de esperança no terra a brotar.

Quando crescer eu quero ser poeta
fazer poemas para liberdade
vou escrever em cada coração
uma canção para a felicidade
uma canção para a felicidade.

Vai meninada vai, vai
vem meninada vem
vem porque quem não ama criança, meu bem,
não pode amar mais ninguém
não pode amar mais ninguém.

Numa ciranda de roda vai a criançada
e a menina dos olhos desse caminhar
somos segredos da vida
numa flor desabrochar
numa flor desabrochar.
Sementes de esperança na terra a brotar.
Vamos cantar ao som dessa viola
brincar de roda à luz do luar
e aprender a ler nas entrelinhas
qual o segredo de saber amar.

Vai meninada vai, vai
vem meninada vem, vem
porque quem não ama criança,
meu bem não pode amar mais ninguém,
mais ninguém.

Go on, kids

Zé Pinto

In a ring-a-ring o' roses go the kids
and today's march's favourite girl
we're the secrets of life
in a flower unfolding
in a flower unfolding
Seeds of hope from the land in a twirl.

When I grow up I want to be a poet
to write poems of freedom
I shall write on every heart
a song of happiness
a song of happiness.

Go on kids, go on
come on kids, come on
come, 'cos if you don't love kids, my love,
you can't love anyone else
anyone else.

In a ring-a-ring o' roses go the kids
and today's march's favourite girl
we're the secrets of life
in a flower unfolding
in a flower unfolding.
Seeds of hope from the land in a twirl.
Let's sing to the sound of the guitar
play in a ring in the moonlight
and learn to read between the lines
the secret of how to love.

Go on kids, go on
come on kids, come on
come, 'cos if you don't love kids, my love,
you can't love anyone at all,
anyone at all.

Ciranda infantil

Zé Pinto

E um, é dois, é três,
Já aprendemos contar.
E quatro, é cinco, é seis,
agora nós vamos parar.
Um tempo pra gente brincar
antes de chegar a mil.

Em nome da Reforma Agrária ai, ai, ai
um viva à ciranda infantil[44]
um viva à ciranda infantil.

De ciranda em ciranda, aprender a cirandar
aprender a cirandar
Como o estatuto diz: estudar,
brincar feliz e aprender a cantar,
aprender a cantar.

E vamos lá.
Vamos plantar poesia, e vamos lá.
Vamos colher alegria, e vamos lá.
É hora de estudar.

E um, é dois, é três,
Já aprendemos a contar.
É quatro, é cinco, é seis,
Agora nós vamos parar.
Um tempo pra gente brincar
Antes de chegar a mil.

Em nome do Reforma Agrária ai, ai, ai
um viva à ciranda infantil.
Viva!

Children's playground songs

Zé Pinto

One, two, three,
Now we learn to add.
Four, five, six,
now we're going to fix.
Some time for us to play
before a thousand's had.

In the name of Agrarian Reform, ay, ay, ay.
Long live the children's *ciranda*.[44]
Long live the children's *ciranda*.

From one *ciranda* to another, learning to *ciranda*,
learning to *ciranda*,
as the rules say: study,
play happily, learning to sing,
learning to sing.

And so let's go.
Let's plant poetry, let's go.
Let's harvest joy, let's go.
It's time to study.

One, two, three,
Now we learn to add.
Four, five, six,
now we're going to fix.
Some time for us to play
before a thousand's had.

In the name of Agrarian Reform, ay, ay, ay,
long live the children's *ciranda*.
Viva!

O trabalho gera vida

Zé Pinto

Cinco horas da manhã
canta o galo 'garnizé'
meu pai levanta cedo
minha mãe já está de pé.
E a patinha no terreiro
faz quá, quá, quá, quá, quá, quá,
a galinha cacareja
pra dizer que vai botar.

Refrão
E eu também vou levantar
escovar os dentes, o rosto lavar
pegar a sacola, eu vou estudar
pra depois a outros poder ensinar.

No caminho da escola
aprendi a admirar
canto do passarinho
majestoso sabiá.[45]
Minha escola construída
com a força do mutirão
trabalho gera vida no valor da união.

Com os meninos e as meninas
não tem discriminação
pra na hora da merenda
aprender partir o pão.
Plantar horta na escola
pra chamar a atenção
como marca da vitória
que tivemos neste chão.

Work breeds life

Zé Pinto

Five o'clock in the morning
the bantam cockerel crows
father gets up early
mother already rose.
And the duckling in the yard goes
quack quack, quack quack, quack quack,
cluck cluck goes the hen
she is going to lay there and then.

Refrain
And I too am going to rise
brush my teeth, wash my face
take my school-bag, I'm going to study
so that one day I can teach others.

On the road to school
I learned to admire
the little bird's song
majestic *sabiá.* [45]
My school was built
from the strength of teamwork
work breeds life from acting in union.

Amongst the boys and girls
Discrimination's dead
when at break time
They learn to share their bread.
To plant a garden in the school
Calling everyone's attention
as a sign of the victory
that on this land we've won.

Pra soletrar a liberdade

Zé Pinto

Tem que estar fora de moda
criança fora da escola, pois há tempo
não vigora o direito de aprender
criança e adolescente numa educação
decente pra um novo jeito de ser
pra soletrar a liberdade na cartilha do ABC.

Ter uma escola em cada canto do Brasil
com um novo jeito de educar pra ser feliz
Tem tanta gente sem direito de estudar
É o que nos mostra a realidade do país.

Juntar as forças, segurar de mão em mão,
numa corrente em prol da educação
Se o aprendizado for além do Be A Bá,
todo menino vai poder ser cidadão.

Alternativa pra empregar conhecimento,
Movimento já mostrou para a nação
desafiando dentro dos assentamentos
Reforma Agrária também na Educação.

To spell out freedom

Zé Pinto

It must be uncool
for children to skip school
the right to learn has lapsed for some time now
for child and adolescent to have somehow
a decent education for a new way to be
to spell out freedom on the books of ABC.

On Brazil's every corner to set up a school
with a new way of teaching happiness for all
There are still so many without study as a right
that's what shows us this country's plight.

Joining forces, hand in hand,
in a headlong rush to learn
If apprenticeship goes beyond the ABC
every child as a citizen can be free.

Another way to use knowledge,
the Movement has shown the nation
taking up the challenge in the camps
Agrarian Reform, too, in Education

Vista geral do assentamento Alpina, em Teresópolis, Rio de Janeiro
Foto de Carlos Carvalho, Arquivos do MST de São Paulo Reprodução autorizada.

Panoramic view of the Alpina Settlement, in Teresópolis, state of Rio de Janeiro
Photo by Carlos Carvalho, MST Archives São Paulo Reproduced by permission.

Consciência ambiental

Environmental awareness

Martírio e redenção

Antonio Candido

Às vezes penso de que maneira pode ser lido hoje, cem anos depois, o clássico final da primeira Parte d'*Os sertões*, de Euclides da Cunha:

> O martírio do homem, ali, e o reflexo de tortura maior, mais ampla, abrangendo a economia geral da Vida. Nasce o martírio secular da Terra.

Em nossos dias o martírio da terra não é apenas a sêca do Nordeste. É a devastação predatória de todo o país e é a subordinação da posse do solo à sede imoderada de lucro. Se aquela agride a integridade da Natureza, fonte de vida, esta impede que o trabalhador rural tenha condições de manter com dignidade a sua família e de produzir de maneira compensadora para o mercado. Hoje, o martírio do homem rural é a espoliação que o sufoca.

Como consequência, tanto o martírio da terra (ecológico e econômico), quanto o martírio do homem (econômico e social) só podem ser remidos por meio de uma redefinição das relações do homem com a terra, objetivo real do MST. Por isso, ele é iniciativa de redenção humana e promessa de uma era nova, na qual o homem do campo possa desempenhar com plenitude e eficiência o grande papel que lhe cabe na vida social e econômica, porque as lides da lavoura são componente essencial de toda economia saudável em nosso país. Por se ter empenhado nessa grande luta com desprendimento, bravura e êxito, o MST merece todo o apoio e a gratidão de todos. Nele palpita o coração do Brasil.

Martyrdom and redemption

Antonio Candido

At times I think about the question of how today, a hundred years later, the classic finale of the first part of *Os Sertões/Rebellion in the Backlands*, by Euclides da Cunha, might be read:

> Man's martyrdom, there, reflects a greater, broader torture, embracing all of Life's economy. The age-old martyrdom of the land is born.

Nowadays the martyrdom of the land is not only the drought of the Northeast, it is the predatory devastation of the whole country and it is the subordination of possession of the soil to the uncontrolled thirst for profit. If that thirst attacks the integrity of nature, the fount of life, it prevents the rural worker from attaining the conditions necessary to keep his family in dignity and to produce for the market in a manner that will adequately repay him. Today, the martyrdom of rural man is the exploitation that suffocates him.

As a consequence, both the martyrdom of the land (ecological and economic) and the martyrdom of man (economic and social) can only be remedied through a re-definition of the relationship between man and land, the real objective of the MST. Thus, it is an initiative for human redemption and a promise of a new era, in which rural man might carry out fully and efficiently the great role that befits him in his social and economic life, because the toils of labour are an essential component of every healthy economy in our country. For having undertaken this great struggle with unselfishness, bravery and success the MST merits the total support and gratitude of all. Within the movement beats the heart of Brazil.

Marcas da erosão

Aracy Cachoeira

Numa tarde, sentado num cepo debaixo da goiabeira, meu zóio arregalô quando mirei o morro em frente a minha velha casa de enchimento.[46]

A terra nua da chapada, parecia ferida exposta sangrando silenciosa, a dor da marca da erosão.

Três dias se passaram!
A tarde agora era de temporal, de chuva grossa que chega de repente arrebentando tudo, jogando folhas para todo lado.
Eu, na janela da varanda, de novo me assustei olhando a chapada.
É que a enxurrada de terra vermelha que descia lá do morro, parecia um rio de sangue que descambava ladeira abaixo, levando nas suas águas, galhos, insetos, raízes, e junto com a lama e o mato, a dor da marca da erosão.

No terceiro dia a chuva se amainou e arredei de casa para ir ver a lavoura no boqueirão. [47]
Me instalei diante do que era minha roça! Agora quem sangrava era meu coração, partido pela dor da perda.
Não se via um pé de feijão, as hortas ou nem sabia o lugar, mandioca com as raízes para cima, abobreira e maxixeiro não sei onde foi parar.
Só via terra vermelha cobrindo as plantações.

Olhei lá pro morro, pro descampado da chapada. A cratera na ladeira, agora mais limpa, mais profunda, parecia garganta escancarada, boca aberta dando gargalhada, rindo do homem que inconseqüentemente semeia sua desgraça.
Se no morro tivesse árvore, se lá tivesse uma proteção, minha roça tinha se salvado, porque o mato segura o aguaceiro da chuva que se espalha umedecendo a terra por igual.
Mas quando o homem já acabou com o mato, a água passa direto pelas valetas e descé arregaçando, levando a cito tudo que topa pela frente, levando até o adubo natural do solo, deixando a terra cada vez mais seca.

Olhei de novo pro morro, me pareceu que ele parou de rir.
Eu também fiquei séria. Nos dias ali frente a frente, o morro desmatado e indefeso, e eu, pagando pelo alto preço da destruição da natureza, sentindo no peito dilacerado, a dor da marca da erosão.

Signs of erosion

Aracy Cachoeira

One afternoon, sitting on a stump under the guava tree, my eyes out on stalks when I looked at the hill in front of me at my old mud-block house.[46]

The bare land of the flat hilltop, seemed an open wound bleeding silently, the sorrow of the sign of erosion.

Three days went by!
Now the afternoon is stormy, with heavy rain that falls suddenly washing everything away, casting leaves on every side.
I, at the veranda windows, again felt panic as I looked at the flat hill-top
The torrent of red earth that poured down the hill seemed like a river of blood hurtling down, its waters bearing cockerels, insects, roots and, with the mud and the plants, the sorrow of the sign of erosion.

On the third day the rain abated, I got out of the house to see the plantation in the gully.[47]
I settled down in front of what used to be my plot. Now it was my heart that bled, broken by the pain of loss.
Not a stalk of beans to be seen, the orchards not a clue where they'd been, mandioc uprooted, I'd no idea where my pumpkin and squash patch was.
All I could see was red earth covering the plantations.

I looked over there at the hilltop stripped bare. The crater on the slope, now cleaner, deeper, seemed like a gaping throat, an open mouth guffawing, laughing at men for futilely sowing his own woes.
If there had been any trees on the hill, if there had been some protection, my plot would have been saved, for bushes hold back in the rain flood and spread the water evenly across the whole surface.
But when man has cut down woods forever, the water flows straight through the little furrows and breaks out, carrying before it everything in its path, even nature's loam of the soil, leaving the land ever drier.

I looked again at the hillside, it seemed to laugh no longer.
I too fell grave. For days face to face, the hill stripped naked and defenceless, and I paying a high price for the destruction of nature, feeling in my torn heart, the sorrow of the sign of erosion.

A natureza que eu aprendi a amar

Zé Pinto

Eu vi, eu vi, eu vi, eu vi
passarinho cantar
passarinho cantar.
Canta, canta passarinho,
que eu não vou te apedrejar.

Refrão
Tu és filho da mãe terra,
que eu aprendi amar
Tu és filho da mãe terra,
que eu aprendi a amar.

Tem papagaio, tem joão-de-barro,
tem beija-flor que é preciso preservar.

Refrão

Tem bem-te-vi, tem azulão,
tem canarinho que é preciso preservar

Refrão

Todos os pássaros
todos os bichos
todos as flores
que é preciso preservar

Refrão

Nossos peixes, nossos rios,
nossas vidas, nosso ar.
Nossos índios, nossas matas
a natureza que eu aprendi amar (bis)

Refrão

Nature that I've learned to love

Zé Pinto

I've seen, I've seen, I've seen, I've seen
a little bird a-singing
a little bird a-singing.
Sing, sing, little bird,
I promise I'll not throw a stone.

Refrain
You're a child of mother earth,
that I have come to love
You're a child of mother earth,
that I have come to love.

There's a parrot, there's a bower-bird,
there's a humming-bird, spare them all.

Refrain

There's a flycatcher, there's a bluebird
There's a small canary, spare them all.

Refrain

All the birds
All the beasts
all the flowers
spare them all.

Refrain

Our fish, our rivers,
our lives, our air.
Our Indians, our groves
Nature that I've learned to love (twice)

Refrain

Os deuses das matas

Eduardo Dias

As vozes dos deuses das matas
A ira dos anjos selvagens
Dirão sua voz
Maçaranduba[48] cai
Açaizeiro[49] cai
E o homem moto-serra ateia fogo
Macacaúba[50] cai
Samaumeira[51] cai
Sangria pelas mãos de outros valores
Tikuna, Kaiapó, Kamayurá,[52]
Bordunas[53] e flechadas no invasor
Tikuna, Kaiapó, Kamayurá,
Bordunas e flechadas no invasor
A fúria dos camponeses, pescadores
Num brado de vingança vou viver
Da seiva, que da terra há de crescer
Quintino[54] estará aqui
Batista[55] estará aqui
Fonteles,[56] Expeditos[57] vão brotar
E juntos com o Angelim[58]
Chico Mendes de Xapuri
Os anjos serão
Deuses e demônios em cada chão
Em cada árvore, com seu poder de dizer não

The woodland gods

Eduardo Dias

Voices of the woodland gods
Anger of the savage angels
With but one voice shall call
Maçaranduba[48], felled
Açaizeiro[49], felled
And the chain-saw man sets fire to all
Macacaúba[50], felled
Samaumeira[51], felled
Blood spilt at the hands of values that appal
Tikuna, Kaiapó, Kamayurá[52] tribes,
Slings[53] and arrows on the invader rain
Tikuna, Kaiapó, Kamayurá tribes
Slings and arrows on the invader rain
Country folk in fury, fishermen in pain
In a cry for vengeance shall I live
Off the sap that from the earth shall rise
Quintino[54] will be here
Batista[55] will be here
Fonteles,[56] Expeditos[57] will spring up again
And along with Angelim[58]
Chico Mendes of Xapuri
The angels soon will be
Gods and demons on every plot
With their power to say no, in every tree

A primeira ocupação do MST, Encruzilhada Natalino, Ronda Alta, estado do Rio Grande do Sul. Foto histórica de 1981, quando, ainda sob a vigência da ditadura militar, os sem-terra iniciavam o processo de formação do seu Movimento e de inclusão da reforma agrária na agenda política.
Juan Carlos Gomes. Foto reproduzida com a permissão do MST, São Paulo.

The first MST occupation, Encruzilhada Natalino, Ronda Alta, state of Rio Grande do Sul. Historic photo of 1981, when, still under the military dictatorship, the Landless Workers started the process of formation of the MST and of the inclusion of agrarian reform in the country's political agenda.
Juan Carlos Gomes. Photo reproduced with the permission of the MST, São Paulo.

Marchas, momentos decisivos, congressos

Marches, defining moments, congresses

Marchar e vencer

Ademar Bogo

Abriu-se para nós
Nesta fresta de tempo ao fim do século
A possibilidade de dizer:
Que fome, miséria e tirania não são heranças.

Heranças são as obras, sãos os feitos, são os sonhos
Desenhados pelos pés dos velhos caminhantes
Que plantaram na história sementes de esperança
E nos legaram a tarefa de fazer
Através da luta, o caminho de vencer.

Marchar é mais do que andar
É traçar com os passos
roteiro que nos leva à dignidade sem lamentos.

As fileiras como cordões humanos
Mostram os sinais dos rastros perfilados
Dizendo em seu silêncio
Que é preciso despertar
E colocar em movimento
Milhões de pés sofridos, humilhados em todo o tempo
Sem temer tecer a liberdade.

E nessas marcas de bravos lutadores
Iniciamos a edificação de novos seres construtores
De um projeto que nos levará à nova sociedade.

Marchamos por saber que em cada coração há uma esperança
Há uma chama despertada em cada peito
E a mesma luz é que nos faz seguir em frente
E tecer a história assim de nosso jeito.

A dor, a fome, a miséria e a opressão não são eternas
Eternos são os sonhos, a beleza e a solidariedade
Por estarem ao longo do caminho de quem anda
Em busca da utopia nas asas da liberdade.

To march and be victorious

Ademar Bogo

Opening up
In this chink of time at the century's end
Is our chance to cry:
Hunger, misery and tyranny are not legacies.

Our legacies are the work, achievements, dreams
Laid down by those that marched before
Planting seeds of hope in history
Bequeathing us the task of forging,
In our struggle, the path to victory.

To march is more than just to walk
It's tracing out in footprints
That route which leads to dignity without lament.

Processions, like the people hand-in-hand,
Signal in their profiled tracks
Proclaiming in their silence
That we must awaken
To set in motion
The suffering feet of millions, humbled through the ages,
Without the fear of weaving freedom.

And in the wake of these brave strugglers
We start to build ourselves anew, constructive
Of our aim to bear us to a new society.

We march to know that in each heart is hope
A flame afire in every breast
And that same light will make us march
To a history woven in our own way.

Pain, hunger, misery and oppression need not last
Eternal only are the dreams, the beauty and the solidarity
Forever on the road of those who walk
Towards utopia on the wings of freedom.

As marchas alimentam grandes ideais
Porque grande é o sonho de cada caminhante
Que faz nascer do pranto a alegria
Da ignorância a sabedoria
E das derrotas vitórias triunfantes.

Venham todos! – Dizem nossas bandeiras
Que se balançam como chamas nas fogueiras
E queimam as consciências de nossos inimigos
Que fazem da pátria galhos onde se aninham
Abutres que comem:
Das fábricas, os empregos,
Dos hospitais, os remédios e a saúde
Das escolas, as letras que educariam a juventude,
E da terra, o direito de viver a liberdade.

Assim a pátria passa ser de propriedade
Privada, escravizada e obrigada
A entregar aos filhos logo ao nascer
A incerteza de passar o dia e não ver o anoitecer.

Marchar se faz necessário
Para espantar os abutres desta estrada
E construir sem medo o amanhecer.
Pois, se eternos são os sonhos
Eterna também é a certeza de vencer.

The marches feed grand thoughts
For great is every walker's dream
As joy springs from our lamentation
Wisdom from our ignorance
From our defeats triumphant victory.

Come all of you! – So say our banners
Flickering like flames in the fire
And scorching the conscience of enemies
That make of our country branches for nesting
Vultures to feed on:
From our factories, the jobs,
From our hospitals, medicines and health,
From our schools, the lessons that would educate our youth,
And from the land the right to live in freedom.

So our country's come to be but a property
Private, enslaved and forced
To hand to its children at birth
The uncertainty of surviving the day, of seeing the night.

We must march
To scare the vultures from our roads
And construct a dawn without fear
For if dreams are everlasting
Eternal too is certain victory.

Poesia escrita durante a marcha realizada na Bahia – 1998

Ademar Bogo

Que diremos aos nossos filhos?
Quando acabar a comida,
Quando acabar o trabalho,
E a esperança de vida?
Que os governantes são bons?
Que os policiais são amigos do povo?
Que caixões de companheiros assassinados
São a vontade do Criador?

Se assim fizermos
Um dia faltará
Comida.
Já não terá esperança.
Nem nossos filhos com vida.
que diremos então?
Que tudo é dos senhores?
Que somos todos irmãos?
E só morrem sonhadores?
Não!

Já não podemos calar.
Chega o tempo de vencer,
Chega o dia de lutar,
Sem morrer.
A única forma de vencer a morte
É enfrentá-la.
único jeito de vencer é lutar,
único modo de fazer justiça,
É continuar lutando.
Assim viveremos eternamente.

Poem written on the march in Bahia – 1998

Ademar Bogo

What shall we tell our children?
When the food runs out,
When the jobs have gone,
What hope is there in life?
Are we to tell that governors are good?
That the police are the people's friends?
That the coffins of our murdered comrades
Are the will of the Creator?

If we do so
One day there'll be
No food
There'll be no hope
No life for our children.
What then shall we say to them?
That everything belongs to "Landlord"?
That we are all brothers?
And that only dreamers die?
No!

We can stay no longer quiet.
The time for victory is now,
The day has come to fight,
And not to die.
The only way to vanquish death
Is to confront it.
The only way to win is fight,
The only road to justice,
Is to struggle on.
And so we'll live forever.

E vamos indo

Zé Pinto

Se o que se canta também
Conta na construção da história,
Cantaremos juntos,
Se sabemos que sozinhos
Não vamos chegar lá,
Nos daremos as mãos pelo caminho,
Se o cansaço nos alcançar
Na estrada, socializaremos o sacrifício,
Pra aumentar a gana por justiça,
Em cada encruzilhada
Festejaremos uma vitória.
Assim nos educaremos,
Pra um novo jeito de ser gente.

And off we go

Zé Pinto

If also what is sung
Still counts in making history,
Then we shall sing together,
If we know we shan't arrive
If we stand alone,
Then we'll join hands as we go,
If tiredness affects us
On the way, we'll socialize the sacrifice,
To raise the thirst for justice
At every cross-road,
We'll celebrate a victory.
And so we'll learn
Anew to be ourselves.

A terra e seus guerreiros
(O dia da absolvição de Zé Rainha)

Ademar Bogo

A terra coloca-se frente a frente
Para dizer ao tribunal burguês
Que filho seu sempre é inocente.
No chão armas do crime, adormecidas
Foices, facões e enxadas apreendidas
Vão condenar a terra outra vez?
A mais 500 anos de xadrez?
De torturas, mortes e insensatez?
Vão condenar o que?
Nossa vontade de lutar?
Nosso destino de vencer?
Ou nosso direito de sonhar?

Que culpa podem ter as mãos de um povo
Que arma lonas para povoar a terra
Que usa a fome como arma de guerra
E faz da liberdade um canto novo?

Não! As sentenças não vêm de canetas douradas
Que dormem preguiçosas nos bolsos magistrados
Os passos dos Sem Terra escrevem as sentenças
E a eles a terra devolve recompensas

E o gosto de comer a liberdade.

Agora a terra em festa quer abraçar seu filho
Que marchará em busca da esperança

Libertaremos a terra e seus viventes
Este será o maior presente
Que ficará escrito na memória.
Vai Zé! Fazer mais luta e criar seus filhos
Vai Zé! Ajudar a colocar os trilhos
Por onde passará o trem da história.

E lá na frente na sombra das bandeiras
Renascerá a vida em uma só trincheira
E cantaremos o hino da vitória.

The land and its warriors
(The day of absolution of Zé Rainha)

Ademar Bogo

The land stands face to face
To tell the bourgeois court
Its child is always innocent.
On the ground lie weapons of crime, sleeping
Scythes, machetes and confiscated hoes
Shall they condemn the earth again?
To 500 more years of chess?
Of torture, death and senselessness?
What shall they condemn?
Our will to fight?
Our destiny of victory?
Our right to dream?

What guilt can rest in hands
That put up black plastic to people
That use hunger as a weapon of war
And turn freedom into a new song?

No! The sentences do not flow from the gold pens
That sleep lazily in the magistrates' pockets
The steps of the *Sem Terra* write the sentences
And the land gives them the recompenses

And the pleasure of eating freedom.

Now in celebration will the land embrace its child
Who will march in search of hope

We shall free the land and those who live there
That will be the greatest gift
To be inscribed in memory.
Go on Zé! Fight on and create more children
Go on Zé! Help to make rails
For the train of history.

And there in front under the banners
Life will be born again in a single trench
And we shall sing the anthem of victory.

145

O sonho e o tempo
(Pelos quinze anos do MST)

Ademar Bogo

Sonho se fez tempo
Plantado sobre a teimosia que se fez berço
Para dar vida ao guerreiro que decidiu nascer,
São quinze anos de tempo e mais de sonhos
Que a voz do povo buscou chamar a terra
E se fez força da paz fazendo a guerra.
Batalhas marcam os dias
Os livros marcam a história
Os hinos as alegrias.
pranto também faz parte deste longo caminhar
Cumpre o papel de regar o sonho tão valente
De quem acreditou que plantando sangue renasceria
E em cada passo que o povo daria...
Nas vitórias viveria eternamente.

E a terra feito um lençol macio se estende
Oferecendo seu colo umedecido
Ainda expondo os destroços da última batalha.
Com marcas de latifúndios entocaiados
Erguem-se: homens, mulheres e meninos
Riscando com um sopro a linha do destino
E marcam as próprias mãos
Com calos que lhes dão dignidade.

É a terra quem resgata o ser humano
Plantando na consciência
Coragem e resistência
Para fazer nascer a solidariedade.
E os mantos de lonas escaldantes
Se desenrolam para formar cidades
Sem muros nem dor de gente errante
Cada qual desenhando seu lugar
Deixando a porta aberta para a linha do horizonte
Onde está a bandeira envaidecida
Chamando com sua dança para seguir adiante.

Dream and time
(To fifteen years of the MST)

Ademar Bogo

The dream comes of age
Planted on a boldness cradling
Life for the determined warrior born,
Fifteen years ago in time and more in dreams
Since the people's voices sought to claim the land
And make of peace a force for making war.
Battles mark the days
Books mark the history
Anthems mark the joys.
Tears too are part of this long march
Ever watering the dream so valiant
Of those convinced that in sowing blood they'd be born again
That in every step the people made…
In its victories it would live forever.

And the land like a soft sheet spreads
Offering its moistened lap
Showing still the last battle's scars.
With marks of beleaguered latifundia
Arise: men, women and children
Tracing with a single sigh their line of fate
And marking their own hands
With callouses that dignify them.

It's the land that rescues human beings
In conscience planting
Courage and resistance
Sowing solidarity.
Mantles of scorching plastic unfurl
As they form their cities without walls
and without the woe of a wandering people
Each designing a place of one's own
Leaving ever-open a door to the horizon
Where stands their pride-filled banner
Calling in its dance for all to stride on.

Agora sobre a terra escreve-se com enxadas
Palavras que formam fartura e unidade
Não haverá mais fome nem tristeza
vale ressecado volta a ter beleza
E a voz entoa louvando a liberdade

Não haverá outras faces mais felizes
Do que estas penetradas de valores com raízes
Que nascem da alegria do coração
Do sonho e da paixão
Que cada um de nós
Planta em nosso peito.

Now on the land inscribed with hoes
Words forming fullness and unity
No more hunger no more sorrows
The dried up valley will recover its beauty
And its voice calls out in praise of freedom

There'll be no faces happier
Than those imbued with values rooted in
and springing from the joyous heart
Of dream and passion
That each of us
Bears planted in our breast.

1999: Feliz aniversário MST pelos 15 anos

Francisco Macilom Nunes Aquino

Nasci no ano de 1984
E não nasci do nada
Mas vou caminhando
Nesta longa estrada.

Na estrada da vida
Que não tem nada fácil
Temos que lutar
Não conheço o fracasso.

Já enfrentei várias barreiras
E nem por isso deixei de lutar
Nossos companheiros tombados na luta
Sempre vamos lembrar.

Neste tempo
Várias lutas
Muitas conquistas
Só consegue a vitória
Quem nela acredita.

Já lutei muito
Neste país, neste mundo
Em busca da terra
E contra o latifúndio.

Famílias desabrigadas
Já têm onde morar
Os trabalhadores no campo
Para o nosso Brasil mudar.

Não estou sozinho nesta luta
Canto com todos os cidadãos
Com a certeza na frente
E a história na mão.

1999: Many happy returns MST on your fifteenth birthday

Francisco Macilom Nunes Aquino

I was born in 'eighty-four
And not born from the void
But I'm forever marching
Down this long, long road.

On this road of life
It is no easy street
We must all face strife
I won't admit defeat.

Many barriers have I faced
Yet wouldn't give up at all
Companions fallen in the fight
We always will recall.

And all the time
Midst struggles
Many victories too
Yet those convinced of winning
Will finally come through.

Hard have I striven
In this country, in this world
In the constant search for land
Against the latifundium I stand.

Homeless families
Now have a place to dwell
Ever working in the fields
To change our Brazil.

In this struggle not alone
To sing with every citizen I stand
Conviction ahead
And history in hand.

Todos me conhecem
Neste país sem fim
De estado a estado
Sempre tem um lugar pra mim.

Sempre fui criticado
Mas sempre estou vencendo
Em quanto quem critica morre
Nós estamos só crescendo.

Meu nome todos tem que saber
Reforma Agrária
Uma luta de todos,
Sou o MST

Eu estou neste movimento
E também estou lutando
Esta é a minha homenagem
Parabéns MST, 15 anos!!!

In this endless country
Everyone knows me
From state to state forever
A special place for me.

I've always been criticized
But I've always won,
While our critics die
We can only grow.

My name is one that all must know
Agrarian Reform,
Everyone's fight to be free
I am the MST.

In this Movement, in this fight
Here's my homage, MST
Congratulations
You're fifteen!!!

Chegada à Brasília da histórica marcha nacional dos Sem Terra em 1997, em protesto contra a impunidade dos responsáveis pelo massacre de Eldorado de Carajás, um ano após o ocorrido.
Douglas Mansur. Foto reproduzida com a permissão do MST São Paulo.

Arrival in Brasília of the historic 1997 march, protesting against the impunity of the responsible for the Eldorado de Carajás massacre, one year after it took place.
Douglas Mansur. Photo reproduced with the permission of the MST São Paulo.

Massacres e mártires

Massacres and martys

Oziel está presente

Zé Pinto

Aquele menino era filho do vento
Por isso voava como as andorinhas
Aquele menino trilhou horizontes
Que nem um corisco talvez ousaria
Levava no rosto semblante de paz
E um riso de flores pro amanhecer
sol da estrada brilhou sua guerra
Mirou o seu povo com olhar de justiça
Pois tinha na alma um cheiro de terra
Tantas primaveras tinha pra viver
Pois tão poucas eras te viram nascer
Beijou a serpente da fome e do medo
Mas fez da coragem seu grande segredo,
Ergueu a bandeira vermelha encarnada
Riscou na reforma um 'a' de agrária
E assim prosseguiu.
Seguiu cada passo com uma fé ardente
A voz ecoando na linha de frente
Em tom de magia numa melodia de estar presente
E a marcha seguia, seguiam os homens,
Mulheres seguiam, crianças também caminhavam
Mas lá onde a curva fazia um 'S'
Que não se soletra com sonho ou com sorte[59]
Pras bandas do norte o velho demônio
Mostrou seu poder.
Ali o dragão urrou, o pelotão apontou,
As armas cuspiram fogo, e dezenove
Sem-terra, a morte fria abraçou.
Mas tremeu o inimigo com a dignidade do menino
Inda quase adolescente, pele morena, franzino
Sob coices de coturno, de carabina e fuzil
Gritou amor ao Brasil, num viva ao seu movimento,
E morreu!
Morreu pra quem não percebe
Tanto broto renascendo
Debaixo das lonas pretas, nos cursos de formação

Oziel is with us still

Zé Pinto

The boy was a child of the wind
So he flew like a swift
The boy reaped horizons
Not even a darting deer might risk
On his face forever peaceful
Was a flowering smile for the dawn
The highway sun reflected his war
He looked upon his people with justice's gaze
For his soul smelled of earth
So many springs he'd still to live
For so few eras saw your birth
He kissed the serpent of hunger and fear
But made of courage his secret dear,
He raised the banner scarlet red
An 'a' for agrarian he added to reform
And so marched on.
He took each step with burning faith
His voice echoed out at the front of the line
With a magical tone in an ever-present melody
And the march went on, as did the men,
And the women marched, as did the kids
But there where the bend was shaped like an 'S'
– not standing here for *sonho* or *sorte* [59] –
To the bands of the north the old demon
Showed its power.
There the dragon roared, the crowd pointed,
Weapons spat fire, and nineteen
sem-terra embraced chill death.
But the enemy trembled at the dignity of the boy
Still but an adolescent, dark-skinned, small
Under soldiers' kicks, carbine and rifle
He cried out his love for Brazil, *viva* to his movement,
And he died!
He died for those yet to grasp
how so many shoots are sprouting still
Under black bags, or in training,

Ou já nos assentamentos,
quando se canta uma canção,
ou num instante de silêncio
Oziel está presente,
Porque a gente até sente,
Pulsar o seu coração.

Or in the settlements, too,
Whenever a song is sung,
Or in a moment's silence,
Oziel is with us still,
Because people even feel
His pulsing heartbeat.

O nome da violência

Charles Trocate

A Eldorado dos Carajás

A oficina da violência
Está trabalhando,
Seus funcionários são algozes do povo
Um a um!

Os jornais noticiam
A indignação da lei
E nós dizemos nas ruas nesse 17 de abril
A efervescência da palavra
Justiça!
Tão escassa nos nossos dias...
A nossa paciência de esperar,
Não esperar mais
A voz primitiva da multidão ecoa
Nos tribunais tomando os seus dicionários
Abre o caminho com a justiça
De nossas bandeiras.

Os estranhos a isso, desconhecem!
A cor do nosso sangue, a memória
Dos hinos...
E a pauta de nossa utopia,
A fome engolindo decretos.

Olhamos...
A intransigência dos ditadores
Cavando covas em nossas manhãs
E dando suas sentenças,
Até quando existirá prisão
Aos condenados à miséria?
Carregamos pesados fardos de injúria
Mas nunca estamos mortos!

The name of violence

Charles Trocate

To Eldorado dos Carajás

The treadmill of violence
    Is at work,
Its apparatchiks bring death to the people
    One by one!

The newspapers announce
The indignation of the law
And we proclaim in the streets of the 17th of April
    The effervescent word
    Justice!
So rare in our time…
Our patient waiting,
    Waits no longer
The primitive voice of the crowd echoes
Through the courts, taking their dictionaries,
It opens up the roads with the justice
Of our banners.

Those unfamiliar with all this, don't know!
The colour of our blood, the memory
    Of our anthems…
And the aims of our utopia,
    Hunger swallowing decrees.

We look at…
The intransigence of the dictators
Digging graves in our mornings
And handing down their sentences,
How long will there be but prison
    For those condemned to misery?
We bear heavy burdens of insult
But we never die!

Não estamos deserdados
            Da terra,
Caminhamos com o seu fulgor,
Conhecemos a nossa legitimidade
Como também a justeza dos disparos
            E seus pesadelos!

Faremos da desigualdade da batalha
A beleza da vitória!
Do lugar de morrer,
            O lugar de sonhar
Do lugar de ceder,
            O passo de avançar.

We are not disinherited
      Of the land,
We march to its bursting forth
We know our legitimate rights
As we know too its certain gunshots
      And its nightmares!

We shall make from unequal battle
The beauty of victory!
From the place of dying,
      The place of dreaming
From the place of yielding,
The step ever forward.

Eldorado dos Carajás

MBGC[60]

1996
Quarta-feira, dezessete de abril,
Eldorado dos Carajás, Sul do Pará, Brasil,
Lá onde só Deus sabe o que acontece,
PA 150, Curva do S,
Por mais de um dia 1200 sem-terra
Bloqueiam a rodovia, reivindicam à sua maneira
A desapropriação da Fazenda Macaxeira.
40 mil hectares de um só dono
De uma terra entregue ao abandono
Grande propriedade, latifúndio improdutivo
Que só serve ao interesse especulativo
E o fazendeiro que não faz concessão
Está disposto a abrir mão
A 800 famílias que só sonham com um pedaço de chão.

E tentam a todo custo se manter de cabeça erguida
Mesmo famintos e lutando por comida
Gente simples, pobre sem muito recurso,
Cansados de esperar reforma agrária sair do discurso
Tudo que eles querem é a terra pra poder fazer uso
INCRA não dá crédito, não assenta, não cumpre prazo,
governo age com total descaso,
Insensibilidade diante do drama
E um profundo desprezo pela vida humana.
Planejam o que ninguém imagina
Enquanto a hora da matança se aproxima

Refrão
Sem justiça não existe paz
Não existe paz
Eldorado dos Carajás
Sem justiça não existe paz
Não existe paz
Eldorado dos Carajás.

Eldorado dos Carajás

MBGC[60]

1996
Wednesday, the seventeenth of April,
Eldorado dos Carajás, in the south of Pará, Brazil,
Where only God knows what's happening,
And on highway 150, at the S-bend,
1200 landless for more than a day
Block the road, claiming as best as they know
The disappropriation of Macaxeira.
Forty thousand hectares with a single owner
An estate left to weed
Fruitless latifundium, property vast
Serving speculators' interest first and last
Yet the unyielding owner
Is now disposed to cede
To 800 families for whom lands are but dreams.

They try at all costs to hold their heads high
Even when starving, struggling to eat
A people simple, poor, without means,
Of 'agrarian reform' talk they've grown so tired
The land put to use is all they desired
INCRA won't give credit, won't resettle and its deadlines will not keep,
And the government acts as if their lives were cheap,
Insensitive to their plight
And with a deep disdain for human life.
Planning the unthinkable
As the killing hour draws nigh

Refrain
No peace without justice
There'll be no peace
Eldorado dos Carajás
No peace without justice
There'll be no peace
Eldorado dos Carajás

De Paraupebas, de Marabá
Vieram dois destacamentos da Polícia Militar,
Coronel Mário Pantoja,
Com a sua corja,
Duzentos homens armados de forma ameaçadora,
Com revólver, escopeta, fuzil, metralhadora.
Chegaram na surdina, com sutileza
Prontos pra partir pra cima de gente indefesa
Sedentos de sangue e ao que tudo indica
Vão usar uma violência que não se justifica
São ossos do ofício, matar faz parte do serviço
A tensão aumenta, todo mundo se sente apreensivo,
Cada segundo conta, cada minuto é decisivo.
Mas der no que der
Os sem-terra não vão arredar o pé
Estão dispostos a resistir enquanto puder
Enquanto o Sr. Almir Gabriel
Só tá a fim de defender o latifúndio, o gado e o capim
A sua ordem tem tom de ameaça
Custe o que custar, de hoje não passa.

Refrão
Sem justiça não existe paz
Não existe paz
Eldorado dos Carajás
Sem justiça não existe paz
Não existe paz
Eldorado dos Carajás.

From Paraupebas, from Marabá
Come two squadrons of Military Police,
Colonel Mário Pantoja,
With his brigand band,
Two hundred men with menace armed,
With hand-guns, shot-guns, machine-guns, rifles.
Stealthily, furtive, arriving unseen
Ready to kill the defenceless it stifles
Thirsting for blood and, so it would seem,
Unjustified violence about to unleash
Hazards of office, killing's a job
All in dread, the tension mounts
Each second decisive, every minute counts.
But come what may
The landless won't budge
They'll resist to the utmost
While Senhor Almir Gabriel's only bother
Is to defend the latifundium, the herds and the fodder
His order has that tone of menace
Whatever the cost, today's the day.

Refrain
No peace without justice
There'll be no peace
Eldorado dos Carajás
No peace without justice
There'll be no peace
Eldorado dos Carajás.

E do ímpeto a polícia agiu do seu jeito,
Foi traiçoeira, sorrateira, covarde,
Às quatro e meia da tarde,
Tempo esgotado
cerco se fecha,
Os pau-mandados
Não deixaram brecha.
Reagir, bem que os sem-terra tentaram
Mas aí, é claro,
Este foi o pretexto usado
Para o primeiro disparo
Daí pra frente o que se viu
Foram execuções a sangue frio
Cenas de uma guerra civil.
A crueldade sem limite
Com todo seu requinte,
Porque contra força
Não existe argumentos
Ainda mais quando se trata
De um esquadrão de fuzilamento.

Foram quatorze minutos contados de fogo cerrado
Chumbo grosso, osso,
No meio daquele alvoroço se ouvia choro e grito
Das pessoas que tentavam fugir do conflito
Foi um corre-corre, um Deus-nos-acuda,
Pessoas desesperadas imploravam ajuda.
E o pior é que existe indícios
Que tudo foi premeditado
Desde o início
Todas as balas tinham endereço certo
E os tiros, foram todos dados de muito perto
Parecia coisa de grupo de extermínio seu menino
Não importava quem estivesse no caminho.

And all of a sudden the police have pounced,
Treacherous, cowardly, underhand,
At 4.15 in the afternoon,
The time's run out
Full siege is at hand
Hired heavies
Have left no room.
For resistance though the landless have tried
But it's oh so clear,
This was the excuse
To fire the first shot
And from then on, what?
Cold-blooded executions
Scenes from civil war.
Cruelty unlimited
Cruelty refined,
For against such force
No argument's aligned
Even less so when
From one firing squad alone.

Fourteen minutes' non-stop shooting
Hot lead… and bone,
Amidst the tumult rose crying and shouting
From those from the conflict attempting to flee
'Run, run!' was the shout, 'God help us!' the plea,
Desperate people help implored.
And worst of all the signs assured
It was all thought out
From the first
All the bullets had the right address
And the shots all fired at short range couldn't miss
So typical of an extermination squad, Oh boy,
It just didn't matter who stood in their way.

Homens, mulheres, crianças, dava tudo no mesmo
Porque os homens atiravam impunemente a esmo.
À torta e à direita, sem dar a mínima,
Sem escolher a vítima,
Lourival não conseguiu correr,
Ficou parado, confuso, levou um tiro de fuzil no peito,
Caiu morto de bruços.
Robson foi arrastado pelo cabelo
E não foi culpado.
Mesmo depois de já ter sido dominado
Oziel tinha sido jurado de morte pelos coronéis
Foi algemado, espancado com socos e pontapés,
Depois recebeu três tiros fatais
E teve o mesmo triste fim que os trabalhadores rurais.
Naquela batalha campal cujo resultado final
Foram dezenove mortos e sessenta e um feridos no total,
Todos vítimas da ação policial que foi brutal, violenta e sanguinária.
Promoveu execuções sumárias, uma tragédia parecida
Com a da Candelária, Carandiru, Vigário Geral, Corumbiara.

E Eldorado dos Carajás é um caso a mais
Que revela realmente do que ela é capaz
Julgou a opinião pública nacional
Causou repercussão internacional
Mas depois de um certo tempo
Caiu no esquecimento
Deve ser por isso que ninguém fica surpreso
Que até hoje nenhum dos acusados tenha sido preso.

Refrão
Sem justiça não existe paz
Não existe paz
Eldorado dos Carajás
Sem justiça não existe paz
Não existe paz
Eldorado dos Carajás.

Men, women, children, it was all the same
Because with impunity, at random, they shot.
They never choose the victim,
They never give a damn for human pain,
Lourival couldn't run, stood fixed,
Confused, he was hit in the chest,
Falling forward, dead.
Robson was dragged by the hair
Though guilty of nothing.
And even after he'd subdued
Oziel by the colonels was to death still sworn
Handcuffed, beaten, punched and kicked,
Then shot three times and left to die.
As the rural workers he met the same sad end
Whose final result in that battle for land
Was sixty-one wounded and nineteen dead,
Victims all of bloody violence and the brutal police
Whose summary executions made a tragedy to compare
With those of Carandiru, Candelária, Vigário Geral, Corumbiara.

And Eldorado dos Carajás is yet another show
Of just how far they're prepared to go
Public opinion, their judge, was, quickly, national
Causing ripples international
But after a while
All was forgotten
That must be the reason no one's surprised
No accused to this day arrested or tried.

Refrain
No peace without justice
There'll be no peace
Eldorado dos Carajás
No peace without justice
There'll be no peace
Eldorado dos Carajás.

A fronteira entre o espaço de luta e resistência e a base militar quando da ocupação da Fazenda Jangada. Getulina, São Paulo, 1993
Foto de Bernardo Mançano Fernandes, in *MST: Formação e territorialização*, São Paulo: Editora Hucitec, 1996. Reprodução autorizada.

The frontier between the Landless Workers' space of struggle and resistance and the military base during the invasion of the Jangada farm. Getulina, state of São Paulo, 1993
Photo by Bernardo Mançano Fernandes, in *MST: Formação e territorialização*, São Paulo: Editora Hucitec, 1996. Reproduced by permission.

A luta pela terra
Despossessão, viagens, ocupação, despejo

The struggle for land
Dispossession, journeys, occupation, eviction

Fantasia

Chico Buarque de Hollanda

E se de repente a gente não sentisse a dor que a gente finge e sente,
Se de repente a gente distraísse o ferro do suplício
Ao som de uma canção, então eu te convidaria
Prá uma fantasia do meu violão
Canta, canta uma esperança
Canta dando uma alegria, canta mais
Revirando a noite, revelando o dia, noite e dia, noite e dia
Canta a canção do homem, canta a canção da vida, canta mais
Trabalhando a terra, entornando o vinho, canta, canta, canta, canta
Canta a canção do gozo, canta a canção da graça, canta mais
Preparando a tinta, enfeitando a praça, canta, canta, canta, canta
Canta a canção de glória
Canta a santa melodia, canta mais
Revirando a noite, revelando o dia, noite e dia, noite e dia

Fantasy song

Chico Buarque de Hollanda

And if all of a sudden we shed the pain we feign and feel,
If all of a sudden we fled the iron rod of fear
For the sound of song, then I'd invite you in
To the fantasy of my guitar
Sing, sing, a song of hope
Sing, bring joy, sing on
Uplifting night, unveiling day, night and day, night and day
Sing the song of man, sing the song of life, sing on
Tilling land, spilling wine, sing song song sing
Sing the song of desire, sing the song of delight, sing on
Stirring colours, streets bedecked, song sing sing song
Sing the song of glory
Sing the sacred melody, sing on
Uplifting night, unveiling day, night and day, night and day

A história dos trabalhadores da Fazenda São João dos Carneiros

Irmã Teresa Cristina[61]

Numa pequena fazenda[62]
Depois de uma missão
Foi feito um primeiro encontro
Quando chegou o patrão
Dizendo não permitir
Que fizessem reunião.

Um dia saiu um boato
Que o patrão tinha vendido
A referida fazenda
A um médico desconhecido
Sem avisar aos posseiros[63]
Que já tinham preferido.

Do triste acontecimento
A turma foi informada
Todas as benfeitorias
Tinham entrado na enrolada
Suor de quarenta anos
Foi injustamente roubado.

Uma ação de preferência
Na justiça deu entrada
Começaram as agressões
A opressão organizada
Envenenaram animais
E a água foi trancada.

Assim passaram dez meses
De espera e tormento.
Com muita humilhação
Aguardavam o julgamento
mas pra justiça corrupta
Não importa sofrimento.

The story of the workers of the São João dos Carneiros Farm

Irmã Teresa Cristina[61]

On a little farm[62]
After a mission
Came a first encounter
When the owner came
Denying permission
For them to gather.

One day a rumour broke
That the owner had sold
That same little farm
To some doctor or other
Without telling the *posseiros*,[63]
Who had legal preference.

Of this sad event
The crowd was just told
That all their improvements
Were but part of the deal,
That their forty years' sweat
Had been unjustly robbed.

Their preference claim
Then went to court
Soon there was aggression
Organised oppression
Animals poisoned
The water shut off.

Ten months went by
In hope and in torment
With much humiliation
They awaited the judgement
But when justice is corrupt
Suffering doesn't count.

cerco foi apertando
Pra aquela gente sofrida
Só se falava em despejo
E ameaças de vida
Sem nenhuma garantia
A classe era perseguida.

Depois de muitos encontros
Chegaram a uma conclusão
Trinta famílias iriam
Fazer aquela ocupação
Era a única saída
Pra resolver a questão.

Dia e hora foi marcado
Ficou tudo combinado
Como se ia fazer
E quem seria informado
A divisão de tarefa
Tudo ficou programado.

Mas em toda terça-feira
Tinha muita apreensão
Com ameaças de despejo
Era aquela aflição
Mas Deus sempre protegeu
Nos livrou da humilhação.

Pra desapropriação
governo apressar
Fomos acampar no INCRA[64]
Três dias ficamos lá
Só voltamos com a certeza
Que iam nos apoiar.

Disfarçada de repórter
A UDR[65] foi lá
Verificar o ambiente
Para poder atacar
A turma inexperiente
Nem chegou a desconfiar.

The siege got ever tighter
For the people afflicted
Talk was only of being evicted
And of threats to their lives
Without guarantees
The class was persecuted.

After many a meeting
They came to one conclusion
Thirty families were to go
On the planned occupation
The only way out
To resolve the situation.

The day and time were fixed
All the details agreed
How it would be done
And who would be told
The tasks were allotted
Every plan put in place.

But each and every Tuesday
Brought such apprehension
With threats of eviction
Came so much affliction
Yet God protected always
And saved us from humiliation.

For the government to hasten
The disappropriation
We went to camp in INCRA[64]
Where for three days we stayed
We only came back
When certain of their aid.

Disguised as reporters
The UDR[65] came back
To check out the place
And prepare their attack.
Our group, so naïve,
Didn't even spot that.

Perto do acampamento
Uma senhora pegaram
Com um revólver na cabeça
Sua boca amordaçaram
Ameaçando matá-la
A roupa e bolsa rasgaram.

Vinte e quatro de outubro
Não podemos esquecer
Quando Sarney[66] viajou
E Paes[67] ficou no poder
A desapropriação
Ele procurou fazer.

Não foi feito o pagamento
dinheiro foi desviado
Foi mais uma decepção
Pra quem já estava cansado
De novo Sarney viaja
E Paes assume o reinado.

Agora o dinheiro sai
Disso nós tínhamos certeza
A ausência de Sarney
Pra nós era uma beleza
Realmente a verba veio
Pra amenizar a dureza.

Foi válida a experiência
E muita gente cresceu
Uma lição pro opressor
A nossa turminha deu
A força da organização
Muita gente percebeu.

Que nossa luta continue
Os companheiros se unir
Desafiando a UDR
Terra livre conseguir
E assim uma nova História
Bem depressa vai surgir.

Close to the camp
A woman they grabbed
Put a pistol to her head
And her mouth they gagged
They threatened to kill her
Tore her clothes and her bag.

We shan't forget
October twenty-four
When Sarney left[66]
And Paes came to power [67]
Disappropriation
He tried within that very hour.

Payment wasn't made
The money disappeared
One more disappointment
For those already drained
Again Sarney departs
And Paes takes the reins.

Now the money would be granted
Of that we were sure
Sarney's absence, for us,
Was good, so good,
The funding really came
To ease so much pain.

The experience was worth it
And many of us knew it
Our little group had given
Our oppressor a lesson
The power of organising
Was grasped by the people.

May our struggle go on
Let our comrades unite
Challenging the UDR
For free land to fight
And so a new History
Very soon will ignite.

Por uma nova realidade

Zé Pinto

Pra onde vai esta gente
Com um compromisso marcado
Amarelos de poeira
Em cima de um pau-de-arara[68]
Com um semblante sofrido
Uma canção revoltada
Jeito de quem descobriu
Onde vai dar a estrada,
Homens, mulheres e meninos,
Numa bandeira irmanados?
Este é um povo Sem Terra
Estão inscritos pra guerra
Vão implantar
Uma nova realidade fundiária.

For a new reality

Zé Pinto

Where are they headed
So clearly committed
Yellow with dust
On an open truck[68]
With long-suffering look
And a song of revolt
Like someone who's discovered
Where the road leads,
Men, women and children,
Joined as brothers under one flag?
This is a landless people
They've signed up for war
They'll sow the seeds
Of a new agrarian world.

Mãe, terra

Erlon Péricles

Terra,
Quero só um pedacinho
Pra plantar
futuro da nação,
Terra,
Pra quem é pequenininho,
E quer ver
esplendor da plantação.
Terra,
povo grita por ti,
Vai seguindo
Pela estrada em procissão,
Deus
Proteja a caminhada
Dessa gente
Nessa busca
Por um pedaço de chão.
Mãe Terra, perdoa
Tanta luta por teu nome
Tanto ódio, tanta fome,
Tanta dor no coração.
Mãe Terra, quem dera
Que vivêssemos em paz,
Pra dividir a colheita
Dos frutos que você dá.

Eu quero terra pra plantar.

Mother, land

Erlon Péricles

Land,
I only want a little plot
To plant
The future of the nation,
Land,
For whoever's oh so tiny,
And just wants to see
A splendid plantation.
Land,
The people clamours after you,
Ever onwards
In procession on the road,
God
Protect the trek
Of these folk
In their quest
For a plot of land.
Motherland, pardon
So much strife in your name
So much hatred, so much starving,
So much heart-felt pain.
Motherland, if only
We might live in peace,
To share the harvest
Of the fruits you reap.

I just want land to plant.

Pedacinho de chão

Ribamar Nava Alves

Ô pedacinho de chão
Trago tantas marcas
E o sonho nas mãos

Pra fugir da miséria
Caminhei muitas léguas
Por esse mundão
Foram dias cansados
Com os pés inchados
De tanto andar
Em fileiras marchamos
Por cidades passamos
Não esqueço jamais

Na beira de uma estrada
Sofremos lutamos
Mas não foi em vão
Mas não foi em vão

Ô pedacinho de chão
Trago tantas marcas
E o sonho nas mãos

Tenho os olhos voltados
Para um mundo novo
Que haverá de nascer

Das lutas do povo
Pra acabar de vez
Com a exclusão social

Com um projeto de vida
Tendo o ser humano
Em primeiro lugar

Na beira de uma estrada
Sofrendo, lutando
Mas não será em vão
Mas não será em vão.

Little plot of earth

Ribamar Nava Alves

Oh little plot of earth
I bear so many scars
And a dream in my hands

To flee from misery
I've travelled many leagues
Through this wide world
Tired, tired days
With swollen feet
From so much walking
In files we marched
Through cities passed
I'll never forget

At a road's edge
We suffer and fight
But it was never in vain
It was never in vain

Oh little plot of earth
I bear so many scars
And a dream in my hands

My eyes are turned
Towards a new world
Yet to be born

From the people's fight
To get rid forever
Of being left out

For a project for life
With human beings
First and foremost

At a road's edge
We still suffer and fight
But it will never be in vain
It will never be in vain.

Proteção com lonas pretas em Cruz no Rio Grande do Sul.
Foto de Carlos Carvalho, Arquivos do MST, São Paulo. Reprodução autorizada.

Shelter with black plastic in Cruz Alta the State of Rio Grande do Sul.
Photo by Carlos Carvalho, MST Archives, São Paulo. Reproduced by permission.

**Acampamentos e resistência:
as casas de lona preta**

**Encampments and resistance:
the houses of black plastic**

Uma segunda abolição

Haroldo de Campos

Considero o Movimento dos Sem Terra um segundo (e, espero, definitivo) momento do longo e difícil processo de liberação do Brasil da escravidão: o primeiro e juridicamente formal ocorreu em 13 de maio de 1888, quando a escravidão foi abolida pela Princesa Isabel. A propósito, o Brasil foi o último país das Américas a abolir o crime contra a humanidade que já fora objeto de amarga condenação pelo grande cientista alemão Alexander von Humboldt (*Essai Politique sur l' Île de Cuba*, Paris 1826). Depois de declarados livres, os ex-escravos foram abandonados ao seu destino e reduzidos a uma condição miserável, sendo esta uma das razões mais fortes para a discriminação social e iníqua distribuição de renda no país. Em nossos dias, independentemente da cor ou procedência social, uma grande massa de brasileiros, reduzidos à miserabilidade, está lutando por uma efetiva REFORMA AGRÁRIA, contra os grandes latifundiários, uma minoria de pessoas muito ricas que menosprezam a sorte da parcela miserável de nossa população. Essa luta – na minha opinião – corresponde à luta pela liberdade e conquista da cidadania, devendo ser apoiada pelos intelectuais brasileiros politicamente conscientes, a exemplo da campanha abolicionista do Romantismo brasileiro, que foi apoiada por escritores como Luís Gama (poeta e jornalista, ex-escravo) ou Castro Alves (poeta, autor do célebre poema contra a escravidão, 'Vozes de África', 1868).

A second abolition

Haroldo de Campos

I consider the *Sem Terra* Movement a second (and I hope definitive) moment of the long and difficult process of liberating Brazil from slavery (the first official one was on May 13 1888, when slavery was abolished by Princess Isabel). Incidentally, Brazil was the last country in the Americas to abolish that crime against humanity that was already bitterly condemned by the great German scientist Alexander von Humboldt (*Essai Politique sur l'Île de Cuba*, Paris 1826). After being pronounced free, the ex-slaves were abandoned to their own fate and reduced to a miserable condition, one of the strongest reasons for social discrimination and the iniquitous distribution of wealth. Nowadays, independently of colour and of racial origin, a great mass of Brazilians, reduced to misery, are struggling for a true AGRARIAN REFORM against owners of great uncultivated latifundia, a minority of very rich people that despises the fate of that miserable stratum of the Brazilian population. This struggle, in my opinion, corresponds to a struggle for freedom and a conquest of citizenship and ought to be supported by politically aware Brazilian intellectuals, as was the case with the campaign for abolitionism and against slavery of our Romantic era supported by such as Luís Gama (poet, journalist and ex-slave) or Castro Alves (poet and author of the celebrated anti-slavery poem 'African Voices' of 1868).

E daí?

Zé Pinto

Alan? Alan, quem será?
Parece um nome importante...
Qual é qual nada senhor!
Claro, não deixa de ser!
Mas pra quem vive na estrada com um outro parecer.
Alan, é um companheiro com três anos de idade
Apesar dos teus cabelos com um belo brilho de sol
A face forçando a cor,
Tal qual flor de girassol
Vive debaixo de lona,
Negando o falso comando
Que insiste em repetir
Vá roceiro, vai embora,
Vai morrer lá na cidade,
Ora, ora meu irmão!
Se o Paulo fosse mais santo,
No Pontal não tinha pranto [69]
Pois no Paranapanema, [70]
justo seria a teima
De arrancar pela raiz
que faz tão infeliz
Uma criança pequena.
Mas nos barracos da vida
Alan inda é maioria.
E DAÍ?

What next?

Zé Pinto

Alan, Alan, is that you?
It sounds such an important name...
Nay, not I sir!
Of course, it's still you!
But for those that live on the road it has another meaning.
Alan, you're a comrade three years old
Despite your hair of lovely sunshine
Your face aflush with colour,
Like a sunflower blossom
You live beneath black plastic,
Denying false commands
Insistent on repeating
Plod on ploughman, plod away,
Trek and perish in the city,
Now, now my brother!
If Paulo were more of a saint,
In Pontal there'd be less complaint [69]
In Paranapanema, you see, [70]
Daring justice would be
Tearing out by the roots
What makes a little child
Grow up so sad.
But in the shacks of life
Alans abound... a majority.
WHAT NEXT?

Nos lugares onde andei

Ana Cláudia

Nos lugares onde andei
Havia risos supressos
Havia corpos franzinos
E a beleza de meninos
Que corriam pelados.
Onde andei haviam fardos
Carregados por guerreiros
Flores rubras nos terreiros
Sementes e esperanças.
Andei por casas pretas
Feitas na condição
De lagartas que mexem
Antes da transformação
Podia ser simplesmente
Um lugar comum,
Onde gente e guaiamum
Quer dizer a mesma coisa...
Mas mesmo quando chovia
povo todo sorria
Da sua espera ensopada.
Nos lugares onde andei
Tive uma intuição
Foi a de mexer na terra
Me misturar com sua mão
E nela encontrei ouro
Cálcio, ferro e pão.
E senti uma alegria
Enquanto lhe revolvia
Com enxada e paixão
Senti cheiro de moça
Que preparava festiva
No fim da separação.
Nos lugares onde andei
Me perdi na imensidão
De tantas palavras não ditas
E me encontrei broto
Onde impõe-se o aborto das vidas.

In the places where I walked

Ana Cláudia

In the places where I walked
Was laughter suppressed
Were puny bodies
And the beauty of children
Running naked.
Where I walked were burdens
Borne by fighters
In the yards were red flowers
Seeds and hope.
Through black houses I walked
Made in the manner
Of caterpillars creeping
Before their transformation
It could be simply
A common place,
Of people and pumpkins
That's to say the same things...
But even when it was raining
The people were still laughing
At their sodden hopes.
In the places where I walked
I had an intuition
It was to touch the land
To mix myself up with its hand
And in it I found gold
Calcium, iron and bread.
And I felt a joy
As with passion and pick
I turned it over
I felt the smell of the young girl
Preparing to party
When the separation's over.
In the place where I walked
I lost myself in the vastness
Of so many words unspoken
And I found myself budding with life
Where lives are forced to be aborted.

Procurando o jeito

Zé Pinto

Era verão nesta lua
Sol escaldante no ar
E pra colher alegria o sonho de ocupar,
Toda terra improdutiva e produtiva também,
Pois pensando com justiça
A terra pertence aos pobres
Porque assim, será nobre o jeito de produzir

Que emperra esta luta?

E quando a melhor proposta
For fruto da discussão,
Se levanta e vai pra prática
Palpitando o coração
Sonhando com a vitória
De ver plantado este chão
Para depois repartir,
Quando este campo florir,
E esta flor virar grão!

In search of the knack

Zé Pinto

Under that moon it was summer
Scorching sun still in the air
And to harvest happiness the dream of occupation,
All unproductive and productive land too,
For thinking of justice
The land belongs to the poor
For this way the knack of production will be noble

What delays this struggle?

And when the best proposal
Is the fruit of our discussion,
We rise up and act as one
Our hearts thumping
Dreaming of the victory
Of seeing this ground planted
Only to share again,
When this countryside flowers,
And the flowers turn to grain!

Floriô

Zé Pinto

Arroz deu cacho e o feijão floriô,[71]
milho na palha, coração cheio de amor.

Povo sem-terra fez a guerra por justiça
visto que não tem preguiça este povo de pegar
cabo de foice, também cabo de enxada
pra poder fazer roçado e o Brasil se alimentar.

Com sacrifício debaixo da lona preta
inimigo fez careta mas o povo atravessou
rompendo cercas que cercam a filosofia
de ter paz e harmonia para quem planta o amor.

Erguendo a fala gritando Reforma Agrária,
porque a luta não
para quando se conquista o chão
fazendo estudo, juntando a companheirada
criando cooperativa pra avançar a produção.

Flowerings

Zé Pinto

Rice in sheaves and beans in blossom[71]
Corn on the husk, hearts brimming with love.

A landless people for justice went to war
never lazy are they, it's clearer still,
to take up handles of sickle and hoe,
so their plots can feed themselves and Brazil.

At their sacrifice beneath black plastic
the enemy scoffed: but still the people crossed
smashing fences offensive to their philosophy:
for whoever plants love there'll be peace and harmony.

Raising the voice of Agrarian Reform,
for the struggle does not weaken
when the ground is taken,
making schools, bringing comrades together,
creating a co-operative for production to grow.

Tributo ao trabalhador sem-terra

Eduardo Silva Amaro

Debaixo de uma lona preta
Existe um ser angustiado
Com fome de vencer
Com sede frio
suor enconde o rosto
Numa longa caminhada
Nas mãos calejadas
A foice e a enxada
E a esperança de sobreviver
Muitas vezes vivendo
Em condições bem precárias
Se desenvolvendo sem
a paz necessária
Assistem a perda
De um companheiro e irmão
Que dá sua vida por um
pedaço de chão
Vendo seus filhos crescerem
Sem perpectivas
De freqüentar uma escola
Boa saúde e comida
Só a conquista da terra
Não é suficiente
Quem é que se preocupa com
com o futuro desta gente
E os poderosos
Ainda querem que tenhamos paciência
Nada fazem
assistindo o sofrimento
Do trabalhador na miséria
Vendo o sangue desta gente
Misturar com a terra
A luta continua com
a mesma intensidade
A reforma é lenta

Tribute to the landless worker

Eduardo Silva Amaro

Under black plastic
There's an anguished soul
Hungry to conquer
And with thirst cold
Sweat hides his face
On a long march
In his calloused hands
The sickle and the hoe
And the hope of surviving
Often living
So precariously
Developing without
A needed peace
They witness the loss
Of companion and brother
Giving his life for a
Piece of ground
Seeing his children grow
Without prospects
Of attending school
Good health and food
The conquest of the land alone
Is not enough
Who is there to care
About the future of these people
And the powerful
Still want us to be patient
They do nothing
As they witness the suffering
Of the worker in his misery
Seeing the blood of these people
Mixed with the soil of the land
The struggle goes on with
The same intensity
Reform is slow

Aumentando a ansiedade
desta gente
Por liberdade, igualdade e
justiça competente
E você meu irmão
que faz para contribuir?
Creio que nada.
Preferem assistir
Nossa gente sendo massacrada,
Banida
E assim como você
Ser explorada
Precisamos lutar
De cabeça erguida
De mãos dadas e com os
pés no chão
Nossa maior arma e
ferramenta
É a cooperação
Reforma Agrária
Uma luta de todos
Reforma Agrária
Uma luta de todos
Quando muitos não se mexem
E os que lutam são poucos.

Increasing the anxiety
Of these people
For liberty, equality and
Competent justice
And you my brother
What are you doing to contribute?
Nothing I believe.
You all prefer to witness
Our people being massacred,
Banished
And just like you
Being exploited
We need to fight
Head held high
Hand in hand and with us
Feet on the ground
Our greatest weapon,
The tools we use
Are co-operation
Agrarian reform
A fight we all share
Agrarian Reform
A fight we all share
When many won't get involved
And the ones that fight are but few.

História de uma criança sem-terra

Rosane de Souza

Há 15 anos muitas pessoas começaram uma linda história em busca de dignidade, contra a fome e a miséria, mulheres se fizeram mães, eu nasci, eis minha trajetória:

Era uma casa muito engraçada
Era de lona e não de tábua
Esta casinha chama barraco
Quem mora nela é quem não tem terra.

Quem tem uma casa no assentamento
Morou primeiro no acampamento
Hoje tem horta pro seu sustento
Porque produz o seu alimento.

Eu sou criança e quero escola
Nela aprender e brincar de bola
Sou Sem Terrinha já sei lutar
Quero o direito de estudar.

Na minha escola vou aprender
A contar as histórias do meu povo
Semear as sementes do amanhã
E também colher.

Eu sou colona, eu sou criança
Tenho orgulho e esperança
Que todo mundo tenha saúde
Cuide da vida e da natureza
Cuidar da vida e cuidar da terra
Porque a terra é nossa riqueza...

Feliz Aniversário MST!

Story of a landless child

Rosane de Souza

Fifteen years ago, lots of people began a beautiful story, they sought dignity, they fought against hunger and poverty, women became mothers, I was born. This is my part in it:

There was a funny house
Made of plastic, not of planks
This little house they call a hut
And in it live the landless.

Those housed now in the settlement
Lived first in the encampment,
Today there's a garden to feed them
Because it gives them nourishment.

I'm a child and I love school
There I can learn and then play ball
As a Little Landless child I can fight
Now I want to go to class by right.

In my school I'll learn to tell
Stories of how my people sow
The seeds of tomorrow
And reap them as well.

I'm a *colona* I'm a child
With the hope and pride
That all will share good health
Will care for life and nature
Care for life and for the land,
Because the land's our wealth...

Happy Anniversary MST!

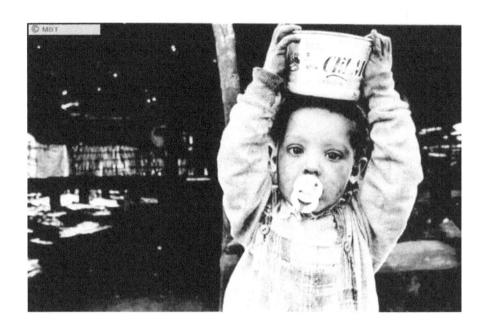

Criança carregando água no acampamento Oziel Alves Pereira, na Fazenda Dissenha, em Abelardo Luz, Santa Catarina.
Foto de Carlos Carvalho, Arquivos do MST de São Paulo.
Reprodução autorizada.

Small child carrying water in the Oziel Alves Pereira camp, on the Dissenha farm, in Abelardo Luz, Santa Catarina.
Photo by Carlos Carvalho, MST Archives, São Paulo. Reproduced by permission.

Assentamentos: o afago da terra

Settlements: the caress of the land

Assentamento

Chico Buarque de Hollanda

> Quando eu morrer
> que me enterrem na
> beira do chapadão
> contente com minha terra
> cansado de tanta guerra
> crescido de coração
> Tôo
>   Guimarães Rosa

Zanza daqui
Zanza pra acolá
Fim da feira, periferia afora
A cidade não mora mais em mim
Francisco, Serafim
Vamos embora
Ver o capim
Ver o baobá
Vamos ver a campina quando flora
A piracema, rios contravim
Binho, Bel, Bia, Quim
Vamos embora
Quando eu morrer
Cansado de guerra
Morro de bem
Com a minha terra:
Cana, caqui
Inhame, abóbora
Onde só o vento semeava outrora
Amplidão, nação, sertão sem fim
Oh Manuel, Miguilim
Vamos embora

Settlement

Chico Buarque de Hollanda

> When I die may
> I be buried
> at the clearing's edge
> happy with my land
> weary of warring
> with swollen heart
> I lie
>
> Guimarães Rosa

Ramble here
Ramble there
End of fair, beyond the city's rim
The city dwells no more in me
Francisco, Serafim
Let's get away
See the grass
See the baobab
Let's go and see the blossoming fields
And spawning shoals leaping upstream
Binho, Bel, Bia, Quim
Let's get away
When I die
Weary of war
I die at one
With my land:
Sugar-cane and persimmon
Yam and pumpkin
Where once the wind sewed
Only open nation, backlands without end
Oh Manuel, Miguilim
Let's get away

Assim vou continuar

Zé Pinto

A flor que mais me marcou
Na luz do meu recitar
Foi uma jovem em movimento
Que um dia ousou sonhar
E isso te fez tão bela
Quanto uma deusa do mar

Sei que estou acampada
Tô aqui com muita gente
Sei que a luta segue em frente
Vou ter terra para plantar
Mas vou ser sempre Sem Terra
Assim vou continuar

Vamos ter cooperativa
Como tem noutros lugares
Construiremos escola para a meninada estudar
Também posto de saúde
Ter um posto telefônico

Energia, e a poesia de uma casa pra morar
Mas vou ser sempre Sem Terra
Assim vou continuar
Realmente se essa força chamada MST
For crescendo deste jeito
Na luta por terra e pão
Construindo educação
Ensinando e aprendendo
Nessa briga por direito
No amanhã muito próximo
Muita coisa vai mudar

A liberdade virá
Os canhões se apagarão
E agora é só canção
Melodia de amar
E se tu me perguntar
Agora não será mais sem-terra?
Respondo: claro que sim
Pois uma coisa é ser sem-terra
Outra coisa é ser Sem Terra
Assim vou continuar.

So I shall continue

Zé Pinto

The flower that touched me most
In the light of my singing
Was a young girl in motion
Who one day dared to dream
And it made you as lovely
As a goddess of the sea

I know that I'm in this camp too
With such a crowd I'm here
I know the struggle still goes on
I know I'll soon have land to seed
But I'll always be *Sem Terra*
That's what I'll always be

We'll soon have our co-operative
As others elsewhere do
We'll build a school for the kids to learn
Our own health centre
And a telephone, too

Electricity, and the poetry of a house to dwell in
But I'll always be *Sem Terra*
That's what I'll always be
If the force called MST
Really goes on growing
In the fight for land and bread
Building education
Teaching and learning
In this battle for our rights
In a tomorrow so close
So much will change

Freedom will come
The cannons will be silenced
And now we'll just hear song
A melody of love
And if you ask me
Will you no longer be *sem- terra*?
I'll reply: but of course I shall
For it's one thing to be landless
Another to be a *Sem Terra*
Forever, that is what I'll be.

Nova cultura

Ana Cláudia

Que nas trilhas da liberdade,
Não falte as marcas do sonho
De quem ousou levantar-se
Não falte o brilho, a partilha
Do pão e da certeza,
E a alegria da estrada
Jogue sementes à margem.
Que no sangue corra sempre
Riso frouxo de criança
Pra alimentar a esperança
De quem faz caminho
E aprendamos que sozinhos
Nunca iremos chegar.
Que nessa construção
Tenha estampado
A conquista da descoberta,
E a porta entreaberta
Do nosso querer
Fique livre e curiosa
Pra descobrir
Na cultura do povo,
Um novo jeito de ser.
PODER SER.

New culture

Ana Cláudia

On the long trails of freedom
May the trace of dreams not fail
For those who dared to protest.
May the light never pale
In sharing bread and in certainty,
May the joy of the highroad
Sow seeds along the way.
May the children's brittle laughter
Flow ever in our blood
To nourish strong the hope
Of all who take to the road.
And may we learn that alone
We never shall arrive.
That in this enterprise
May forever be stamped
The conquest of discovery,
And may the half-open door
Of our desire
Be free and eager
To discover,
In the culture of the people,
A new way of being.
OF BEING AT ALL.

Conspiração

Ana Cláudia

Cheguem conheçam...
Conspirem os oprimidos desta terra
Que só o lixo restou,
Olhem no espelho do tempo
que a miséria bordou.
Eis que da folha seca
Brotou vida, brotou luz!
Quem acredita, busca, permeia
Traz outros pra ver
Pra sentir, se emocionar, viver!
E a terra fértil, da esperança plantada
A terra-mãe agradecida
Nos fornece em seus braços
Doce guarita.

Estamos atentos, vigilantes...
E as correntes que cultivamos
São de solidariedade,
Não se quebram na primeira grade.
Nossa garganta tem uma multidão
Que grita e que canta
E que reconquista
A terra, o nome, e a liberdade
Que ecoa no campo e na cidade
E joga semente
Onde quer que haja gente,
Onde quer que haja fome,
E a esperança tenha nome de liberdade.

Conspiracy

Ana Cláudia

Let them come let them know…
Let the oppressed of this land conspire
For only the garbage is left,
Let them look in the mirror of time
At what wretchedness broached.
See how dry leaves
Spawned life, spawned light!
Those who believe, look, filter
After others to see
To feel, to share emotion, to live!
And fertile land, planted in hope
Mother earth gratefully
Gives us, in her arms,
Sweet shelter.

Alert we are, vigilant…
And the currents we breed
Are of solidarity,
Unbroken at the first fence.
In our throats is a throng
That screams and sings,
Reconquers
The land, a name, and freedom
That echoes over field and town
And spreads seeds
Wherever people are found
Wherever hunger breeds,
And hope assumes the name of freedom.

Antes do sol se cobrir

Zé Pinto

Quando voltares pra terra
Procure logo um canteiro
Plante um pezinho de sonho
Mas não o deixe sozinho
Chame a comadre, o compadre
Chame os parentes mais próximos
Também os desconhecidos
Crianças, jovens, adultos, idosos
Operários, camponeses, um jardineiro amigo

Que estejam todos presentes
Antes do sol se cobrir
Porque o tempo é sagrado
Quando o fardo é prosseguir

Antes de pegar a estrada explique com atenção
Quero pedir a vocês que cuidem bem deste sonho
Porque as ervas daninhas não gostam da plantação
Não deixem faltar adubo nem água e nem carinho
Pois quem caminha sozinho não sabe pra onde ir
Mas se vamos de mãos dadas na arte de replantar
Vamos descobrindo já: todo fruto que brotar
Tem que ser pra repartir

Before the sun goes down

Zé Pinto

When back to the land you come
Then look for a bed of flowers
Plant a little dream
But leave it not alone
Call your sister, call your brother
Call your closest kin
Even those not known to you
Call children, youths, adults, aged
Workers, peasants, gardener friends

Let all be here
Before the sun goes down
For time is sacred
When our burden is to march

Before taking to the road explain it well
I'm asking you to tend this dream
For weeds detest it when we plant
Manure never spare, nor water, nor care
Who journeys alone never knows where to go
But if hand in hand we artfully resow
We learn and learn: every fruit that's borne
Is for all to share

Um convite para se repartir a produção
Foto de Carlos Carvalho, Arquivos do MST de São Paulo Reprodução autorizada.

An invitation to share the production
Photo by Carlos Carvalho, MST Archives, São Paulo Reproduced by permission.

Diversidade de gênero: canções e poemas

Gender diversity: lyrics and poems

Preconceito: um problemão

Nas escolas, nas famílias,
Na sociedade e na vida,
O preconceito é um problemão
Para o futuro da nação.
Que cultura é essa? (bis)

A cultura está errada,
A de sermos diferentes:
Amor é normal,
Independente de se o sexo é igual.
Que cultura é essa? (bis)

Os problemas têm solução
Se partirmos para a ação,
Mas o Brasil vai evoluindo:
Vamos fazer revolução
Se acabarmos com o preconceito
E a discriminação.
Que cultura é essa? (bis)

Preconceito? Aqui, não, meu irmão!

**Música composta pelos(as) estudantes do Ensino Médio – noite.
Colégio Estadual do Campo Contestado – Lapa – Paraná.
Workshop: 26 de abril de 2016.**

Prejudice: a huge problem

In schools, in families,
In society, in life,
Prejudice is a huge problem
For the nation's future.
What culture is this? (repeat)

A culture that's wrong
That makes us different
'Cos love is normal,
Whether same-sex or not.
What culture is this? (repeat)

The huge problem may be solved
If we get out there for action
But Brazil is progress:
So why not start a revolution?
Get rid of prejudice
End discrimination.
What culture is *that*? (repeat)

Prejudice? No, brother, not here, not now!

Lyrics composed by secondary school students – evening.
Contestado Rural State School – Lapa – Paraná.
Workshop: 26 April 2016.

Quero ser livre para escolher

Eu prefiro ser livre para escolher
Do que ter aquele velho preconceito sobre tudo. (2x)
Eu preciso viver, não mais me esconder,
E não ter aquela velha opinião sobre tudo, (2x)
Sobre o que é o amor, porque eu já sei quem sou.

Eu prefiro ser livre para escolher
Do que ter aquele velho preconceito sobre tudo.

Eu quero viver onde a sociedade me respeite e me aceite.
Eu quero dizer para todo mundo o que eu não disse antes.
Eu preciso viver, não mais me esconder
E não ter aquela velha opinião sobre tudo,
Sobre o que é o amor, porque eu já sei quem sou.

**Música composta pelos(as) estudantes do Ensino Médio – tarde.
Colégio Estadual do Campo Iraci Salete Strosak – Assentamento
Marcos Freire – Paraná.
Workshop: 28 de abril de 2016.**

I want to be free... to choose
I'd rather be free to choose now
Than to have that old prejudice weigh me down. (2x)
I need to live now, no longer hide,
Without the weight of that old opinion (2x)
About what love is. I know who I am.

I'd rather be free to choose now
Than to have that old prejudice weigh me down.

I want to live where society respects and accepts me.
I want to tell everyone what I didn't say before.
I need to live now, no longer hide,
Without the weight of that old opinion,
About what love is, for I know who I am.

Lyrics composed by secondary school students – afternoon.
Iraci Salete Strosak Rural State School – Marcos Freire Settlement –
Paraná.
Workshop: 28 April 2016.

Sou assim por mim

Homossexualidade:
Sou assim não pelos outros,
Mas por mim.
O rap é legal;
Consigo assim,
Assim, assim.

Do meu corpo cuido eu
E o meu gosto quem decide sou eu.
Não teria preconceito
Se eu não fosse
Assim, assim, assim,

Mas gostaria de respeito
Não só para mim,
Mas para todas que rimam
Assim, assim, assim.

Rap composto pelos(as) estudantes do 8º e 9º anos do Ensino
Fundamental – tarde.
Colégio Estadual do Campo Contestado – Lapa – Paraná.
Workshop: 18 de março de 2016.

I'm like this for me

Homosexuality:
I'm like this not for others,
But for me.
Rap is cool;
I can be, you see,
Like that, like this.

Of my body I take care
My taste decides who's me.
There'd be no prejudice
If I weren't
Like that, like this, like me.

But, please, respect me.
Not just for me,
But for all who rhyme
Like that, like this, like me.

Rap composed by students of the 8th and 9th grades of Primary School – afternoon.
Contestado Rural State School – Lapa – Paraná.
Workshop: 18 March 2016.

.

O preconceito morreu

Na linha do quadro a professora escreveu
Com letra emendada:
O preconceito morreu.

Com amor e compreensão
E paz no coração,
Duas mulheres unidas:
Uma nova geração.

Vou lhe dizer
Que, com amor,
Nós podemos destruir o preconceito
Que hoje mora aqui.

Não importa se é homem com homem
Ou mulher com mulher;
O que importa é ser reconhecido
E ser como se é.

**Música composta pelos(as) estudantes do Ensino Médio – tarde.
Colégio Estadual do Campo Iraci Salete Strosak – Assentamento
Marcos Freire – Paraná.**
Workshop: **28 de abril de 2016.**

Prejudice is dead

On the board the teacher wrote
With amended words:
Prejudice is dead.

With love and understanding
And peace in the heart,
Two women together:
A new generation.

I'll tell you
That, with love,
We can destroy the prejudice
That lives here today.

Who cares if it's man with man
Woman with woman;
What matters is to be seen
And to be as you are.

Lyrics composed by secondary school students – afternoon.
Iraci Salete Strosak Rural State School – Marcos Freire Settlement –
Paraná.
Workshop: 28 April 2016.

Progredir sem mudanças?

É impossível progredir
sem mudança
E aqueles que não mudam
suas mentes
Não podem mudar nada.
Nosso céu tem mais estrelas –
O meu, o seu, o céu de todos.
Aliás, quantos céus existem?
Quantos seres diferentes existem?
Há céus e seres diferentes. (bis)

As pessoas fecham os olhos
Para a realidade –
O princípio das coisas
São átomos e espaços vazios;
O resto é só questão de opinião.

Há céus e seres diferentes. (bis)
As pessoas fecham os olhos
Para as mudanças da realidade —

**Poema composto pelos(as) estudantes do Ensino Médio – manhã.
Colégio Estadual do Campo Iraci Salete Strosak – Assentamento
Marcos Freire – Paraná.**
Workshop: **28 de abril de 2016.**

Progress without change?

It's impossible to progress
without change
And those who don't change
their minds
Change nothing at all.
Our sky has more stars –
Mine, yours, the celestial sky of all,
Yes how many skies are there?
How many different beings?
Different skies and beings, too. (repeat)

People close their eyes
To changed realities –
The basic principles
Are atoms and emptiness;
The rest just a matter of opinion.

There are different skies and beings, too. (repeat)
People close their eyes
To changed realities —

Poem composed by secondary school students – morning.
Iraci Salete Strosak Rural State School – Marcos Freire Settlement –
Paraná.
Workshop: 28 April 2016.

Brasília amarela

Brasil, um país tão da honra,
Não tem aceitação.
Ninguém respeita os outros,
A diferença de todos.

Queremos a igualdade,
Respeito na sociedade
E liberdade de expressão:
Amar é a solução.

Lalalalalalá.

**Música composta pelos(as) estudantes do Ensino Médio – manhã.
Colégio Estadual do Campo Iraci Salete Strosak – Assentamento
Marcos Freire – Paraná.**
Workshop: **28 de abril de 2016.**

Yellow Brasília

Brazil, such an honourable country,
Will not accept,
Will not respect others,
Nor the difference in us all.

We want equality,
Respect in society
Freedom of expression:
Loving's the answer.

Lalalalalalá.

Lyrics composed by secondary school students – morning.
Iraci Salete Strosak Rural State School – Marcos Freire Settlement –
Paraná.
Workshop: 28 April 2016.

Somos todos humanos

Ninguém é perfeito
Como ninguém é imperfeito
Somos todos humanos,
Somos todos do mesmo jeito.

Vamos pensar diferente
Se quisermos que o mundo
vá para frente.
Temos caráter, sem preconceito;
Só queremos respeito.

Diversidade de gênero é legal,
É ideal, é ideal.
Vamos pensar assim, assim, assim:
Nem todo mundo é
Igual a mim!

Música composta pelos(as) estudantes do 8º e 9º anos do Ensino Fundamental – tarde.
Colégio Estadual do Campo Contestado – Lapa – Paraná.
Workshop: **26 de abril de 2016.**

We're all human

Nobody's perfect,
No one's imperfect.
We're all human,
Made from the same clay.

Let's think in a different way.
We want the world order
to move with a sway.
We have our will, so prejudice… no more;
Respect is what we're waiting for.

Gender diversity's cool,
Let be it, let it be.
Let's think like this, like this:
There will be an answer
Just as there was for me!

Lyrics composed by students of the 8th and 9th grades of Primary School – afternoon.
Contestado Rural State School – Lapa – Paraná.
Workshop: 26 April 2016.

Quero me casar também!

Respeite, respeite o que sou.
Quero casar, como você se casou,
Quero amar, como você amou.
Respeite, pois sou o que sou.

Precisamos depressa
Aceitar a homoafetividade
Em nossa sociedade,
Respeitar a diversidade.
Amor é motivo de felicidade.

**Poema composto pelos(as) estudantes do Ensino Médio – tarde.
Colégio Estadual do Campo Iraci Salete Strosak – Assentamento
Marcos Freire – Paraná.**
Workshop: **28 de abril de 2016.**

I want to get married too!

Respect, respect what I am.
I want to get married, the way you can,
I want to love, just as you can,
Respect, 'cos this is who I am.

Quick! We need to embrace
Same-sex relations
In our society,
So, respect diversity.
Love puts a smile on our face.

Poem composed by secondary school students – afternoon.
Iraci Salete Strosak Rural State School – Marcos Freire Settlement –
Paraná.
Workshop: 28 April 2016.

O direito de amar e de se divertir

O preconceito é grande,
Mas se pararmos pra pensar
O quanto eles são felizes
com o amor que sentem
Mulheres com mulheres
E homens com homens
Têm também o direito de amar
Dançar

Poema composto pelos(as) estudantes do 8º e 9º anos do Ensino Fundamental – tarde.
Colégio Estadual do Campo Contestado – Lapa – Paraná.
***Workshop*: 15 de junho de 2016.**

The right to love and have fun

Prejudice is huge,
But if we stop and sing
They've got
that lovin' feelin'
Woman with woman
And man with man
They also have the right
To love… dancing.

**Poem composed by students of the 8th and 9th grades of Primary School
– afternoon.
Contestado Rural State School – Lapa – Paraná.
Workshop: 15 June 2016.**

Por que eu nasci errada?

Nasci numa família numerosa:
Nove mulheres e dois homens.
Família humilde, com muito amor maternal.
Fui crescendo, vendo, percebendo
Eu era diferente, não era igual.
Minhas irmãs, femininas, meigas.
Fora do normal.
Elas brincavam de bonecas e casinhas
Eu era um piá infernal.

O tempo foi passando e eu só analisando.
Estudei, brinquei, namorei, tudo parecia normal.
De repente percebi que eu era diferente.
Aquela vida não era pra mim,
Não foi para isso que eu nasci.

Infeliz, agoniada, fora do prumo.
Difícil aceitar, mas eu não era normal.
Restava pensar e pensar…
Restava pensar e pensar.
Impossível acreditar;
No meio de oito irmãs
Eu me percebia desigual.

Ainda hoje sofro, sonho, analiso
E ainda não encontrei a resposta.
Só queria, do fundo do coração
Ter nascido, crescido,
vivido, amado,
Como uma mulher normal.

Anseios, desejos, encontros e desencontros,
Um sonho desigual.
Por mais que o tempo passe,
Eu vejo, leio, aprendo,
Mas ainda não me aceito
Como uma pessoa normal.

Why was I born wrong?

I was born into a big family:
Nine women, two men.
A humble family, lots of motherly love.
As I grew up, I felt
I was different, not the same.
My sisters, feminine, gentle.
Me, sturdy, awkward,
Out of step.
They played little dolls' houses,
While I was an infernal boy.

Time passed with me just thinking,
I studied, played, dated; all seemed normal.
Suddenly I realized I was different.
That life was not for me,
That was not what I was born to be.

Sad, in pain, out of the way.
Hard to accept I wasn't normal.
Thinking over and over again,
Ever shutting myself off.
It's impossible to believe,
But amongst eight sisters
I saw myself as the odd one out.

Still I suffer, dream, ponder
And haven't an answer.
I only wanted, in my heart,
To have been born, grown,
lived, loved,
As a normal woman.

I long, desire, date, sometimes I disagree.
Unequal dreams…
No matter how much time passes by,
I see, I read, I learn,
But still don't accept myself as I,
As me, as a normal me.

E essa é a pergunta que eu mesma me faço:
Por que eu nasci errada?
Por mais que eu tente,
Eu não consigo ser o que sou,
Fora do armário.

Depoimento de uma estudante, colocado sob forma de cordel pela educadora Ione Sereia.
Colégio Estadual do Campo Estrela do Oeste – Santa Maria do Oeste – Paraná.
Seminário: 24 a 26 de novembro de 2016.

And here's what I ask myself,
Why was I born wrong?
As hard as I try,
I can't be what I am,
Out of the closet.

A student's testimonial cast in *cordel* form by the teacher Ione Sereia.
Estrela do Oeste Rural State School – Santa Maria do Oeste – Paraná.
Seminar: 24-26 November 2016.

Mais oxigênio para mim

Bom se fosse fácil
Alguém passar pela gente
Sem nos julgar.
Sem nos colocar dentro das caixas,
Dos padrões pré-estabelecidos
Pela sociedade monocromática,
Em que o arco-íris,
Com todas as suas cores e brilho, é ofuscado,
É escondido pela fumaça
Pela poluição do preconceito, da discriminação.

Assim como os CFC's, CO2, metano
Corroem a camada de ozônio
Que protege toda a vida terrestre
E toda a sua diversidade,
O preconceito, o racismo, as fobias do mal
Destroem todas as cores,
As vidas coloridas e a diversidade humana;
Sobrevive então a monocromia.

Viva!
Sinta!
Brilhe!
Grite todas as formas de amor,
Todas as formas de cor!

Poema composto pelo educador Edenilson Prestes Mendes, Drag Queen Priscilla Stefany.
Colégio Estadual do Campo Aprendendo com a Terra e com a Vida – Cascavel – Paraná.
Seminário: 24 a 26 de novembro de 2016.

More oxygen for me

It would be so nice
If someone could just pass by
Without judging
Without putting us in boxes,
Patterns pre-conceived
By a black-and-white society
Which cover up the rainbow,
Bright colours hidden
By the smoke of prejudice
By the pollution of discrimination.

Just as gasses, carbon, methane
Corrode the ozone layer
That saves all life on earth
In its diversity.
Prejudice, racism, and all the phobias
Wipe away the colours,
Bright lives, diversity.
Yet monochrome prevails.

Live!
Feel!
Shine!
Shout out all the forms of love,
All the colours of the rainbow!

Poem composed by the teacher Edenilson Prestes Mendes, Drag Queen Priscilla Stefany.
Rural State School Aprendendo com a Terra e com a Vida – Cascavel – Paraná.
Seminar: 24-26 November 2016.

As cores de 'Edi'

Branco,
Rosa,
Azul,
Preto.

Criança,
Mulher,
Homem,
Negro.

Cada um com sua cor
Cada um com seu jeito.
Mas tem cor que é dor
E a sua dor me condena.

Usar azul eu não quero
Rosa pra mim não combina.
Usava o branco e o preto
Viver assim era minha sina.

Igualdade, respeito
Direito de ser quem sou.
Usar a cor que eu quero
E ser por todos aceito.

Venho clamar a você
Que me desrespeita,
Não aceita,
Posso ser sangue de seu sangue
Mas a igreja me rejeita

Fui o desvalorizado
Homossexual, travesti.
Sou igual a você
A morte, eu já senti.

The colours of 'Edi'

White,
Pink,
Blue,
Black.

Child,
Woman,
Man,
Black.

Each one with their colour
Each one their own way.
But there's colour that's sorrow
And sorrow kills me.

To wear blue's not for me,
Pink, I think, is not my way.
I wore black and white
Life like that was my fate.

Equality, respect
The right to be who I am.
To use the colour I want
And be accepted by them.

I come to beseech you
If you disrespect me
You don't accept me,
I may be blood of your blood.
But the church rejects me.

I've been devalued,
Homosexual, transvestite.
I'm just like you
Death, already felt.

Grito, clamo por respeito
Que todos me aceitem assim.
Eu sou ser humano,
Eu tenho sentimento.
Não sintam pena de mim.

Poema composto pela educadora Roseli Lemonie
Colégio Estadual do Campo Chico Mendes – Quedas do Iguaçu –
Paraná.
Seminário: 24 a 26 de novembro de 2016.
© Vozes Sem Terra

I shout, cry out for respect
Let all accept me as I am.
I'm a human being,
I too have feeling.
Do not feel sorry for me.

Poem composed by educator Roseli Lemonie
Chico Mendes Rural State School – Quedas do Iguaçu – Paraná.
Seminar: 24-26 November 2016.

Conflito: pai/filho

Filho – Pai, eu sou gay.
Pai – O que isso quer dizer, garoto?
Filho – Eu gosto de homem e não de mulher.
Pai – Não criei você para ser assim. Você é homem, não mulher. Gostar de homem?
Filho – Eu sei, pai, mas não há nada que possa mudar isso.
Pai – Você já sabe, eu não aceito essa escolha.
Filho – Isso não tem nada a ver, pai, eu posso sim gostar de homem, não vai mudar nada.
Pai – Nao te considero mais meu filho, some daqui. E esqueça, esqueça que tem pai.

Filho – Calma, pai. Você está nervoso, não sabe o que está dizendo. Vou sair, sim, mas quando você aceitar, pode me procurar, eu o perdoo pelo que está dizendo. Eu amo você. Desculpa por te fazer passar por isso.

Mãe – Cadê meu filho? O que você fez? Você não tem o direito de expulsá-lo, ele é seu filho.
Pai – Expulsei-o de casa porque ele virou gay. Não aceito isso, nunca vou aceitar!

Mãe – Cadê nosso filho?
Pai – Estou arrependido, vou atrás dele.

Diálogo teatral elaborado pelos(as) estudantes do 8º e 9º anos do Ensino Fundamental – tarde.
Colégio Estadual do Campo Contestado – Lapa – Paraná.
***Workshop*: 15 de junho de 2016.**

Conflict: father/son

Son – Dad, I'm gay.
Father – What does that mean, boy?
Son – I like men not women.
Father – I didn't bring you up like this. You're a man, not a woman. To like a man?
Son – I know, dad, but nothing can change all that.
Father – But you already know, I do not accept that choice.
Son – That's got nothing to do with it, father, I really can like men, that won't change.
Father – You're not my son anymore. Get out of here! Forget that I'm your father.

Son – Easy, dad! You're angry. You don't know what you're saying. I'm leaving home, but when you accept it, come and get me. I forgive what you've said. I love you. I'm sorry for putting you through all this.

Mother – Where's my son? What have you done? You've not right to kick him out, he's your son.
Father – I've kicked him out 'cos he's turned gay. I won't accept it, I'll never accept it!

Mother – Where is our son?
Father – I'm sorry, I'm going after him.

Theatre dialogue composed by students of the 8th and 9th grades of Primary School – afternoon.
Colégio Estadual do Campo Contestado – Lapa – Paraná.
Workshop: 15 July 2016.

Performance da Drag Queen Priscilla Stefany como Malévola, no Pré-Assentamento Resistência Camponesa, em 2016.
Foto de Edieni Rodrigues. Reprodução autorizada.

Drag Queen Priscilla Stefany's performance as Maleficent in the Pre-Settlement Resistência Camponesa/Peasant Resistence in 2016.
Photo by Edieni Rodrigues. Reproduced with permission.

Notas

Notes

Notas

[1] 'Cerca' se refere a arame farpado, importante simbologia dos Sem Terra.

[2] Poema comemorativo escrito por ocasião do décimo aniversário do Jornal *Sem Terra*. Fonte: *Calendário Histórico dos Trabalhadores*, 3a edição, 1999, p.58. Reprodução autorizada.

[3] *Favelas:* Formações urbanas onde pessoas de baixíssima ou nehuma renda constroem, sobretudo nas encostas dos morros, suas casas ou barracões improvisados; esses aglomerados são geralmente desprovidos de condições mínimas de conforto, higiene, privacidade e segurança, sendo as vias de acesso extremamente precárias.

[4] O chão onde pisava o boi: é comum os latifundiários colocarem algumas cabeças de gado nas fazendas para que elas não sejam classificadas como improdutivas e não correrem o risco da desapropriação.

[5] Movimento dos Trabalhadores Rurais Sem Terra (MST).

[6] Cerca: Ver nota 1.

[7] Ordem e progresso: O lema da bandeira do Brasil, criada ao final do século XIX, cujas cores são o verde, o amarelo, o azul e o branco; as estrelas representam o número de estados.

[8] Poema originalmente publicado na coletânea *Crisantempo*, de autoria de Haroldo de Campos (São Paulo: Editora Perspectiva, 1998). Reprodução autorizada pelo autor.

[9] 'Região pouco povoada do interior [do Brasil], em especial, a zona mais seca que é a caatinga, ligada ao ciclo do gado e onde permanecem tradições e costumes antigos (*Dicionário Houaiss da Língua Portuguesa,* Rio de Janeiro: Editora Objetiva, 2001).

[10] Neruda (Pablo Neruda): poeta e embaixador chileno, nascido em 1904, recebedor do Prêmio Nobel de Literatura em 1971, vindo a falecer em 1973, poucos dias após a morte do Presidente Salvador Allende. Sua poesia inicial, marcada por uma temática amorosa e uma grande sensualidade, a exemplo de *Vinte poemas de amor e uma canção desesperada* (1924), transforma-se após sua vivência da Guerra Civil Espanhola, o que ele relata na coleção *Espanha no coração* (1938). A partir desse divisor de águas, ele abraça o marxismo, como se evidencia em *Canto em Estalingrado* (1942).

[11] Drummond: (Carlos Drummond de Andrade), poeta nascido em Minas Gerais em 1902. De sua longa, diversa e profícua carreira literária, cita-se *Brejo das almas* (1934) e *Sentimento do mundo* (1940) onde se evidencia um desejo de solidariedade com os homens.

Notes

[1] 'Fence' relates to the Landless's symbology of barbed wire.

[2] Commemorative poem written on the occasion of the tenth anniversary of the *Sem Terra* newspaper (Source: *Calendário Histórico dos Trabalhadores*, 3a edição, 1999, p.58. Authorized reproduction).

[3] *Favelas*: urban areas where people of low income, or none at all, build their improvised houses or huts, especially on the sides of hills. These agglomerations are generally lacking in minimum comfort, hygiene, privacy, and safety, with extremely precarious accesses.

[4] The ground where the ox trod: it is common for landowners to put a few head of cattle on farms so that they will not be classified as unproductive and so run the risk of disappropriation.

[5] Movement: i.e. *Movimento dos Trabalhadores Rurais Sem Terra* – MST (Movement of the Landless Rural Workers).

[6] Fences: see note 1.

[7] Order and Progress: slogan printed on the Brazilian flag, created at the end of the nineteenth century. The colours of the flag are green, yellow, blue, and white. The stars represent the number of states.

[8] Poem originally published in the collection *Crisantempo*, authorship of Haroldo de Campos (São Paulo: Editora Perspectiva, 1998). Reprinted with the author's permission.

[9] *Sertão*/Backlands: 'A sparsely populated region of the interior [of Brazil], especially the driest area, the *caatinga* [brushwood area], connected to the cattle cycle, where old customs and traditions persist' (from the *Dicionário Houaiss da Língua Portuguesa,* Rio de Janeiro: Editora Objetiva, 2001).

[10] Pablo Neruda: poet, Chilean ambassador, born in 1904, Nobel Prize for Literature, 1971, died 1973, a few days after the death of President Salvador Allende. His early poetry, noted for its sensuality and love themes, like *Veinte poemas de amor y una canción desesperada* (*Twenty Poems of Love and a Song of Despair*), 1924, changed after his experience in the Spanish Civil War, which he tells of in the collection *España en el corazón* (Spain in the Heart), 1938. After this major departure, he embraced Marxism, as can be seen in *Canto en Estalingrado* (*Song in Stalingrad*), 1942.

[11] Drummond (Carlos Drummond de Andrade): poet born in Minas Gerais in 1902. From his long, diverse, and prolific literary career, one may cite *Brejo das almas* (*Swamp of Souls*), 1934, and *Sentimento do mundo* (*Feeling of the World*), 1940, in which the wish for solidarity with human beings is evident.

253

[12] João Cabral de Melo Neto: Poeta e diplomata, nascido em Recife, Pernambuco, em 1920. Seu poema narrativo *Morte e vida severina*, tendo como subtítulo *Auto de Natal pernambucano*, escrito entre 1954 e 1955, constitui um dos marcos na literatura brasileira no tratamento do problema da terra.

[13] Marighella (Carlos Marighella, 1911-1969) foi um revolucionário brasileiro, destacado líder da luta armada contra a ditadura militar. Seus quarenta anos de militância tiveram início no Partido Comunista Brasileiro (PCB), com o qual rompe em 1968. Foi o fundador e dirigente nacional da Ação Libertadora Nacional (ALN), organização disposta a iniciar a luta armada, cujo nome ecoa o espírito revolucionário da Aliança Nacional Libertadora (ANL), comandada por Luís Carlos Prestes. Aos 57 anos, foi assassinado pela ditadura (1969).

[14] Casaldáliga (D. Pedro Maria Casaldáliga): Bispo, de origem espanhola, da prelazia de São Félix do Araguaia, no Mato Grosso. Testemunhou de perto o número crescente de posseiros pobres num contexto de conflitos e assassinatos pela terra. Sua *Antologia retirante* (bilíngüe), foi publicada em plena ditadura (1978) pela Editora Civilização Brasileira. Suas poesias expressam seu compromisso com os oprimidos.

[15] As canções aqui transcritas, com autorização do autor, foram gravadas por ele para acompanhar a exposição *Terra* de Sebastião Salgado. A canção 'Assentamento' é também trilha sonora do filme *O sonho de Rose*, de Tetê Morais.

[16] Os mendigos que moram nos espaços públicos debaixo dos viadutos utilizam caixas de papelão para improvisarem uma casa ou erguerem o equivalente a uma parede que lhes assegure uma certa privacidade.

[17] Regionalismo do Vale do Mucuri para trapo, molambo.

[18] Expressão da solidariedade dos Sem-Terra com outros destituídos e excluídos, os mendigos Sem-Teto que residem debaixo do Viaduto do Chá, no centro da cidade de São Paulo. O poema, escrito em 1988, integra a coletânea (inédita) de autoria de Aracy Cachoeira intitulada *Poemas de São Paulo*. A autora relata que se encontrava nessa cidade, numa noite de intenso frio, quando viu o mendigo expirando seus últimos suspiros. Por ele, nada mais havia a fazer. Movida de um intenso sentimento de fraternidade, ela interrompe seu trajeto para escrever para ele esse réquiem.

[12] João Cabral de Melo Neto: poet and diplomat, born in Recife, Pernambuco, in 1920. His narrative poem *Morte e vida severina* (*Death and Life of Severino*), is sub-titled *Auto de Natal pernambucano*. Written in 1954-55, it is one of the foremost works in Brazilian literature to treat the land problem.

[13] Marighella (Carlos Marighella, 1911-1969): Brazilian revolutionary, the important leader of the armed struggle against the military dictatorship. His forty years of militancy began with the Brazilian Communist Party (PCB), with which he broke in 1968. He was the national founder and director of the *Ação Libertadora Nacional* – ALN (National Liberation Action), an armed organization whose name echoes the revolutionary spirit of the *Aliança Nacional Libertadora* – ANL (National Liberation Alliance) commanded by Luís Carlos Prestes. Marighella was assassinated at 57 by the dictatorship.

[14] Casaldáliga (D. Pedro Maria Casaldáliga): Bishop of Spanish origin, prelate of São Félix do Araguaia, in Mato Grosso, a witness of the growing number of poor squatters in a context of conflict and killing for land. His bilingual *Antologia retirante* (*Migrant Anthology*) was published during the dictatorship (1978) by the Editora Civilização Brasileira. His poems express his commitment to the oppressed.

[15] The song translated here, with the author's permission, was recorded by Chico to accompany the exhibition *Terra*, by Sebastião Salgado.The song 'Settlement' is also the soundtrack of the film *O sonho de Rose/Rose's Dream*, by Tetê Morais.

[16] Cardboard: the beggars who live in the public spaces underneath the viaducts use cardboard boxes as improvised shelters or put up the equivalent of a wall to gain some privacy.

[17] In the original poem, the word *estilangado,* a regionalism of the Mucuri River Valley for rags, tattered dress, is used.

[18] Viaduct or Overpass: an expression of solidarity of the *Sem-Terra* with other destitute and excluded people, the *Sem-Teto* (Roofless) beggars who live under the Chá Overpass in the centre of São Paulo. The poem, written in 1988, is part of the (unpublished) collection by Aracy Cachoeira, with the title *Poemas de São Paulo* (*Poems of São Paulo*). The author says that she found herself in that city one very cold night, when she saw the beggar breathe his last breath. For him, nothing more could be done. Moved by a deep feeling of solidarity, she interrupted her journey to write this requiem.

[19] Galdino Jesus dos Santos era um indígena Pataxó Hã-Hã-Hã, 44 anos, conselheiro em sua comunidade localizada no sul da Bahia. Ele chegou em Brasília, juntamente com uma delegação de mais oito líderes do seu povo, no dia 17 de abril de 1997, para uma série de reuniões relativas ao direito de posse e propriedade de área de cinco fazendas localizadas na terra indígena. Na madrugada do dia 20 de abril de 1997, Galdino dormia sob um abrigo de usuários de ônibus na via W-3 Sul, quando acordou completamente em chamas. Cinco rapazes de classe média alta, entre 17 e 19 anos, haviam usado dois litros de álcool combustível para a 'brincadeira' de atear fogo às suas vestes. Com queimaduras em 95% do corpo, ele veio a falecer na madrugada de 21 de abril. O resultado do julgamento – a condenação dos réus pelo Tribunal do Júri, por se tratar de homicídio por motivo torpe, praticado por meio cruel e sem permitir a defesa da vítima – é visto pelo Conselho Indigenista Missionário como a recuperação de um espaço de esperança e um desestímulo à impunidade.

[20] Pataxó, Maxacali, Ianomâmi, Kaiowá, Ticuna, Guajajara, Guarani and Xacriabá são povos nativos que habita(va)m o Brasil e países vizinhos.

[21] Referência aos 500 anos do descobrimento do Brasil pelos portugueses em 1500. O momento propiciou um grande questionamento, sobretudo pelos despossuídos, não só da 'invasão' e da colonização portuguesa que representou para eles a exclusão e a despossessão. Inúmeros foram também os protestos contra o próprio clima de comemoração.

[22] Tribo do Vale do Jequitinhonha que conseguiu, com a ajuda da Comissão Pastoral da Terra (CPT), receber de volta a terra que havia sido perdida para os fazendeiros da região. O poema foi escrito em 15/04/2000, quando da saída da caravana indígena de Belo Horizonte para participar da Conferência dos Povos Indígenas em Porto Seguro, estado da Bahia. O poema se transformou em hino dos Aranãs.

[23] Rio importante do norte de Minas Gerais.

[24] Vide nota 1.

[25] GETAT: Grupo Executivo das Terras do Araguaia-Tocantins: criado pelo goveno brasileiro pelo Decreto-lei nº 1.767, de 1º de fevereiro de 1980, subordinado à Secretaria-Geral do Conselho de Segurança Nacional, tendo como Presidente um representante da referida Secretaria, com a finalidade de coordenar, promover e executar as medidas necessárias à regularização fundiária na área de atuação da Coordenadoria Especial do Araguaia-Tocantins, criada em fevereiro de 1977 (**http://www.planalto.gov. br/ccivil_03/decreto-lei/Del1799.htm**). Segundo o autor do poema, o GETAT se afastou das funções de organismo de regularização fundiária e

[19] Galdino Jesus dos Santos, 44 years old, of the indigenous tribe Pataxó Hã-Hã-Hã, was a counselor in his community, located in the south of Bahia. He arrived in Brasília with a delegation of more than eight leaders of his people, on April 17, 1997, for a series of meetings relating to the ownership rights of a property with an area of five farms located on native lands. In the early hours of April 20, 1997, Galdino was sleeping at a bus-stop in W-3 south, when he woke up on fire. Five young men of the upper middle-class, aged 17 to 19, had doused him with two litres of inflammable alcohol for the 'joke' of setting fire to his clothes. With burns on 95% of his body, he died the next day. The result of the trial – the jury's conviction of the defendants for homicide for base motives and cruelty to a defenceless victim – was seen by the Indigenous Missionary Council as a recovery of hope and a discouragement to impunity.

[20] Pataxó, Maxacali, Ianomâmi, Kaiowá, Ticuna, Guajajara, Guarani and Xacriabá are native peoples who inhabit(ed) Brazil and neighbouring countries.

[21] A reference to the 500 years of the Discovery of Brazil by the Portuguese in 1500. The commemorative year brought a good deal of questioning, especially by the dispossessed, not only of the Portuguese 'invasion' and colonization, which represented for them exclusion and dispossession, but also a great number of protests against the commemoration itself.

[22] The Aranãs are a tribe of the Valley of the Jequitinhonha River, which, with the help of the Pastoral Land Commission (CPT), succeeded in recovering the land that had been lost to the farmers of the region. The poem was written on April 15, 2000, on the departure of the indigenous caravan from Belo Horizonte to take part in the Conference of Indigenous Peoples in Porto Seguro, Bahia. The poem has become the anthem of the Aranãs.

[23] Jequitinhonha is an important river in the north of Minas Gerais.

[24] See note 1.

[25] GETAT, or *Grupo Executivo das Terras do Araguaia-Tocantins* (Executive Group of the Araguaia-Tocantins Lands) was created by the Brazilian government, Decree-law No. 1.767 of February 1, 1980. Subordinate to the General Secretary of the National Security Council, its president is a representative of the Secretary, its purpose is to coordinate, promote, and execute the laws necessary for land regulation in the working area of the *Coordenadoria Especial do Araguaia-Tocantins* (Special Coordinator of Araguaia-Tocantins), created in February, 1977. (**http: //www. planalto.gov.br/ccivil_03/decreto-lei/Del1799.htm**). According to the

acabou se tornando um aparato de repressão às lutas dos trabalhadores rurais durante a ditadura militar.

[26] Vide nota 1.

[27] Teixeirinha: líder sem-terra morto por policiais militares do estado do Paraná, dentro do próprio acampamento. Há os que entendem ter sido o assassinato uma retaliação à morte de outros policiais militares.

[28] Vide nota 21.

[29] Baixo Araguaia: Região junto à nascente do Rio Araguaia, que corta a maior parte das terras indígenas do país e onde ocorreu a Guerrilha do Araguaia. Em 1969, um grupo de guerrilheiros do PC do B (Partido Comunista do Brasil), de linha maoísta, passou a viver da agricultura e a estabelecer relações com os camponeses da região, conscientizando-os da necessidade da luta contra os latifundiários e o governo. Os 70 guerrilheiros, acuados pelas tropas enviadas pelo governo para combatê-los, resistiram nas matas por mais de dois anos, sendo, todavia, derrotados, por uma expedição de 6000 soldados em 1975 (Morisawa, Mitsue. *A história da luta pela terra e o MST.* São Paulo: Expressão Popular, 2001. p. 101). Por ordem do Exército, seus corpos foram incinerados para que não restassem vestígios da Guerrilha na história. Dois guerrilheiros conseguiram escapar ao cerco. Todavia, um dirigente que sobreviveu foi posteriormente assassinado no que ficou conhecido como 'A Chacina da Lapa'. O outro sobrevivente é atualmente Deputado Federal pelo PT.

[30] Vide nota 1.

[31] Ana *sem-terra:* alusão à personagem Ana Terra, do primeiro livro, *O continente,* da trilogia *O tempo e o vento,* de autoria de Érico Verísimo. Emblema da mulher corajosa que, tendo perdido todos os familiares, exceto seu filho Pedro Terra, defende a terra quando dos conflitos no sul do país pela pela demarcação de fronteiras.

[32] Tropeiros: No extenso e montanhoso estado de Minas Gerais, os tropeiros eram condutores de tropas de mulas, bestas e cavalos que transportavam, em grandes balaios, os produtos oriundos das fazendas agro-pecuárias para as cidades grandes e a capital. Sua importância na história cultural do estado se faz sentir na culinária, sendo eles os responsáveis pelo tradicional feijão tropeiro de Minas, no qual se misturam os produtos que eles transportavam, como o próprio feijão, carnes, torresmos, lingüiças e a farinha de mandioca.

[33] Gameleira: árvore frondosa que cresce nas margens dos rios e cujas raízes fortes protegem as margens contra a erosão. No norte de Minas, era também um local de encontro para as lavadeiras e os tropeiros.

author of the poem, the GETAT withdrew from the function of land regulation and ended up becoming part of the apparatus for the repression of the rural workers' struggle during the dictatorship.

[26] See note 1.

[27] Teixeirinha: *Sem Terra* leader killed by military policemen of the State of Paraná in his own encampment. There are those who see the murder as a retaliation for the death of other military policemen.

[28] See note 21.

[29] Baixo Araguaia: a region near the source of the Araguaia River, which goes through most of the indigenous lands of the country, where the Araguaia Guerrilla War took place. In 1969, a group of guerrillas of the PC do B (Communist Party of Brazil), a Maoist group, began to farm and establish relations with the peasants of the region, teaching them the need to fight against the landowners and the government. The seventy guerillas, attacked by government troops, held out in the bush for more than two years, but were defeated by an expedition of 6000 soldiers in 1975 (Morisawa, Mitsue. *A história da luta pela terra e o MST*. São Paulo: Expressão Popular, 2001, p. 101). By order of the army, their bodies were burned so that nothing would remain of the war in history. Two guerrillas managed to escape, but one leader who survived was later murdered in what became known as the *A Chacina da Lapa* (The Lapa Massacre). The other survivor is currently a federal representative for the Labour Party.

[30] Fencing: see note 1.

[31] Ana *sem-terra*/Landless Anna: an allusion to the character Ana Terra, from the first novel, *O continente* (*The Continent*) of Érico Veríssimo's trilogy *O tempo e o vento* (*Time and the Wind*). She is the symbol of the courageous woman who, after losing all the members of her family but her son Pedro Terra, defends the land during the conflicts in the south of the country over the demarcation of borders.

[32] Troopers or caravan-drivers: in the large, mountainous state of Minas Gerais, these people drove trains of mules and horses that carried in large panniers the products coming from the farms for the capital and other large cities. Their importance in the cultural history of the state is seen in the cuisine, as they were the ones responsible for the traditional *feijão tropeiro* (trooper's beans) of Minas, in which they mixed the products they carried, such as beans, meat, *linguiça*, dried fat, manioc flour.

[33] *Gameleira*: a leafy tree that grows on river-banks, whose strong roots protect the banks from erosion. In the north of Minas, it was also a meeting-place for washerwomen and the *tropeiros*.

[34] Retirante: os sertanejos da região árida do Nordeste brasileiro que emigravam para outros estados do Brasil, sobretudo os do Sul, passavam por Minas, estado geograficamente situado entre o Nordeste e São Paulo, para onde, em geral, eles se dirigiam.

[35] *Puaia:* raiz medicinal muito usada no Vale do Mucuri e do Jequitinhonha (norte de Minas Gerais) por seus efeitos depurativos do sangue. Sendo a puaia para exportação uma grande fonte de renda, a sua obtenção, na virada do século XIX, provocou um grande desmatamento na região.

[36] Sumo de São Caetano: planta que se enrama nas cercas e nas moitas; usada como alvejante natural pelas lavadeiras, ao invés de cloro ou anil.

[37] Sabão de decoada: produto natural retirado das cinzas de algumas árvores ou da palhada do feijão, em substituição à soda cáustica na lavagem de roupas. A cinza é colocada numa cesta de taquara e, sobre ela, derrama-se água quente; o que é filtrado é a decoada.

[38] A canção descreve uma família de retirantes deixando o estado de Minas Gerais em direção à região amazônica. Tradicionalmente, o termo retirante é usado no contexto dos nordestinos que deixam o sertão em direção ao litoral e ao sul, sobretudo São Paulo, em decorrência de secas prolongadas. Ele registra, assim, novos fluxos de migração interna decorrentes não das condições climáticas inóspitas mas do problema da falta da terra. No poema, os regionalismos do estado de Minas, notadamente o *uai*, começam a mesclar-se com os do Norte, como *cacai* (V. nota 40). O autor resgata a fala caipira do homem do campo brasileiro. Gerais refere-se a Minas Gerais, um estado central, cujas atividades predominantes são a agropecuária e a mineração. Os mineiros são considerados arraigados às suas tradições culturais, e leais aos laços afetivos e de amizade. O passado colonial do estado deixou fortes marcas de religiosidade na cultura, como se evidencia na canção.

[39] Pau-de-arara: Caminhões cobertos com lonas, com bancadas de madeiras rústicas que muito incomodavam os passageiros, usados com freqüência para o transporte dos retirantes do Nordeste. As penosas e desumanas viagens nos pau-de-arara da Paraíba ou de Pernambuco ao Rio de Janeiro ou São Paulo duravam em torno de 20 dias. A famosa Feira de São Cristóvão surgiu como ponto de encontro e despedida dos que se valiam desse meio de transporte. O termo pau-de-arara é usado nos estados sulinos como referência pejorativa aos nordestinos (**http://www.feiradesaocristovao.art. br/historia.htm**).

[34] *retirante*/migrant: the people of the arid *sertão* region in the Brazilian northeast, who migrated to other states in Brazil, especially those in the south, passing through Minas, the state geographically located between the Northeast and São Paulo, where they were usually going.

[35] *Puaia*: a medicinal root much used in the Mucuri and Jequitinhonha river valleys (in the north of Minas Gerais) for its blood-purifying effects. As the *puaia* for exportation was a large source of income, its gathering caused great deforestation at the turn of the last century.

[36] Sap of São Caetano: a plant that coils around the fences and the brush, used as a natural bleach by washerwomen in the place of chlorine or indigo.

[37] Strained-soap: natural product taken from the ashes of certain trees or bean-husks as a substitute for caustic soda in the washing of clothes. The ash is put in a bamboo basket and hot water is poured over it: what is strained is the soap.

[38] The song describes a family of migrants leaving the state of Minas Gerais, heading toward the Amazon region. Traditionally, the term *retirante* (migrant) is used in the context of those people from the northeast who leave the *sertão* for the coast or the south, especially São Paulo, because of the prolonged droughts. In the song, *retirante* thus points to new waves of internal migration resulting not from climactic conditions but from the problem of landlessness. The regionalisms of the state of Minas, notably the *uai*, begin to mix with those of the north, like *cacai* (see note 40). The author attempts to record the speech of rural people in Brazil. Minas [Gerais] is a central state in Brazil, whose predominant economic activities are farming, stockraising, and mining. The *mineiros* (miners), or people from Minas, are considered attached to their cultural traditions and loyal in their affective relationships and friendships. The state's colonial past has left strong influences of religion in the culture, as can be seen in the song.

[39] Back of a truck: the term 'pau-de-arara', literally a stick for macaws to perch on, metaphorically describes the trucks used for the transportation mostly of the *retirantes*/migrants from the North-East, with its very uncomfortable wooden seats and a canvas covering. The inhumane journeys on the *pau-de-arara* from the states of Paraíba or Pernambuco to Rio de Janeiro or São Paulo could be twenty days long. The famous São Cristóvão fair emerged as a meeting point and farewell for those using this means of transportation. The term *Pau-de-arara* is also used in the southern states as a pejorative reference to those who migrated from the North-East (**http:// www.feiradesaocristovao. art.br/historia.htm**).

261

[40] Cacai: no Norte do Brasil, é um saco que se amarra às costas para carregar comida quando se vai para a mata.

[41] *Uai/uai:* Um regionalismo sobretudo de Minas Gerais. O *uai* constitui uma expressão de surpresa, espanto ou admiração.

[42] Reprodução da entrevista autorizada pelo MST de São Paulo. A gravação do depoimento foi apresentada durante o I Encontro Nacional de Educadores de Reforma Agrária (ENERA): Movimento Sem Terra: Com Escola, Terra e Dignidade, realizado em Brasília, UNB, 28 a 31 de Julho de 1997. Em 1997, aos 76 anos, morre o Professor Paulo Freire.

[43] Ciranda: cantiga de roda rimada, muito comum no Brasil; também dança de roda. A música e a letra das cirandas, em sua maioria, de origem portuguesa, permanecem na literatura oral brasileira.

[44] Vide nota 43.

[45] *Sabiá:* palavra de origem tupi que designa um pássaro muito admirado pela beleza do seu canto.

[46] Casa de enchimento ou de barro batido: tipo de construção comum no norte de Minas Gerais; é feito um travamento de varas, como uma peneira, no qual o barro é batido.

[47] Boqueirão: local preferido para plantio, geralmente uma encosta de montanha onde os morros formam uma meia lua.

[48] *Maçaranduba:* árvore nativa do Brasil, que fornece madeira de lei vermelha com tom de chocolate, de grande uso na marcenaria.

[49] *Açaizeiro:* O açaí é uma palmeira das margens dos rios e dos terrenos pantanosos da região Amazônica.

[50] *Macacaúba:* Árvore da região do Amazonas, cuja madeira é usada em mobiliário de luxo.

[51] *Samaumeira:* Árvore de grande tronco e flores vistosas

[52] *Tikuna, Kaiapó, Kamayurá:* Os Tikuna são um povo indígena da região do Amazonas; os Kaiapó, são outro povo indígena, hoje muito reduzido, que habita as margens do Rio Xingu, nos estados do Mato Grosso e no sul do estado do Pará; os Kamayurá são também indígenas, de língua tupi-guarani, que vivem no Mato Grosso, ao sul do Parque Indígena do Xingu.

[53] Borduna: O termo borduna refere-se a uma arma indígena, longa, feita de madeira dura, para ataque, defesa e caça (*Dicionário Houaiss da Língua Portuguesa,* Rio de Janeiro: Editora Objetiva, 2001). Entre os sertanejos do Rio Araguaia, borduna é o cacete indígena (*Dicionário Aurélio Eletrônico*).

[40] *Cacai*: in the north of Brazil, a bundle tied to one's back to carry food into the bush.

[41] *Uai*/why!: regionalism, especially in Minas Gerais, expressing surprise, astonishment, or wonder.

[42] Reprint of extracts from the interview authorized by MST, São Paulo. The recording of the statement was presented during the National Meeting of the Educator of Agrarian Reform (ENERA): With School, Land and Dignity, held at the University of Brasília (UnB), 28 to 31 July 1997. In 1997, at the age of 76, not long after the recording of this interview, Professor Paulo Freire died.

[43] *Ciranda*: a round or rhymed song, common in Brazil; also a dance round. The music and lyrics of *cirandas*, mostly of Portuguese origin, remain in Brazilian oral literature.

[44] See note 43.

[45] *Sabiá*: a word of Tupi origin designating a bird much admired for the beauty of its song.

[46] mud-block hut: a type of dwelling common in the north of Minas Gerais, built with a lattice-work of sticks on which mud is packed.

[47] hollow: a preferred locale for planting, generally on the side of a mountain where the hills form a half-moon.

[48] *Maçaranduba*: tree native to Brazil, which has a red wood with a dark brown hue that is very useful in cabinet-making.

[49] *Açaizeiro*: the *açaí* is a palm from the Amazon region found on the banks of rivers and swampy lands.

[50] *Macacaúba*: a tree from the Amazon region whose wood is used in expensive furniture.

[51] *Samaumeira*: a tree with large trunk and attractive flowers.

[52] *Tikuna, Kaiapó, Kamayurá*: indigenous peoples. The Tikuna are found in the Amazon region; The Kaiapó, today greatly reduced, live along the banks of the Xingu River, in the state of Mato Grosso and in the south of the state of Pará; the Kamayurá are of the Tupi-Guarani linguistic group and live in the state of Mato Grosso, in the south of the Xingu Indigenous Reserve.

[53] *Borduna*/Cudgel: a long indigenous weapon for attack, defence, and hunting, which is made of hard wood (*Dicionário Houaiss da Língua Portuguesa,* Rio de Janeiro: Editora Objetiva, 2001). Among the country people of the Araguaia River, *borduna* is the indigenous cudgel (*Dicionário Aurélio Eletrônico*).

[54] Quintino: Quintino Lira foi um líder dos camponeses no nordeste do Pará, assassinado em setembro de 1984 pelos latifundiários da região. Dotado de uma personalidade muito forte, revoltou-se quando suas terras foram tomadas. Ficou famoso por suas fugas da polícia. Virou lenda na região.

[55] Batista: [João] Batista foi um advogado combativo em defesa da classe trabalhadora, também deputado pelo PC do B. Foi assassinado em frente à mulher e filhos.

[56] Fonteles: nome por que é conhecido na região Paulo Fonteles, advogado e deputado pelo PC do B. Também foi assassinado.

[57] Expeditos: Expedito Ribeiro e Souza foi poeta, lavrador e presidente do Sindicato de Trabalhadores Rurais no sul e sudeste paraense; foi a sétima pessoa assassinada em Rio Maria por sua liderança ou ligação com o movimento sindicalista rural. Depois de sua morte, foi fundado, em 1991, pelo Padre Ricardo Rezende, o Comitê Rio Maria, que é uma rede internacional de solidariedade que visa acabar com os assassinatos de lavradores e sindicalistas por pistoleiros contratados pelos grandes fazendeiros no Sul do Pará (**http://www.riomaria.org/por_o_ que_e.htm**). A forma plural do nome, Expeditos, indica ser ele representativo de um sem número de líderes rurais assassinados na região.

[58] Angelim: O terceiro presidente cabano, aos 21 anos de idade, ocasião em que o Movimento entrou na sua fase nais radical. Cabano, nesse contexto, refere-se à República dos Cabanos, proclamada durante a terceira fase da Cabanagem, uma revolução na província do Grão Pará, que corresponde hoje aos Estados do Pará e do Amazonas (1833-36). O nome provém de cabana, habitação pobre, montada sobre estacas. Inicialmente uma expressão da insatisfação dos grandes proprietários e políticos locais contra o poder central no Rio de Janeiro, transformou-se depois em uma revolta das populações mestiças e indígenas vivendo em péssimas condições. Foram 40.000 as vítimas das lutas (*Enciclopédia Delta Universal*).

[59] 'S', 'sonho ou sorte': perde-se a aliteração em inglês ('dream or fate').

[60] As iniciais MBGC se referem a 'Manos da Baixada de Grosso Calibre', um grupo de favelados em Belém, capital do estado do Pará, que integra o movimento *hip hop* da favela.

[61] Irmã Teresa Cristina: uma religiosa ligada à Comissão Pastoral da Terra (CPT), que teve um papel importante na genealogia do MST.

[54] Quintino: Quintino Lira was a peasant leader in the northeast of Pará, murdered in September 1984 by the landowners of the region. Possessed of a strong personality, he rebelled when his land was taken. He became famous for his escapes from the police and became a legend in the region.

[55] Batista: João Batista was a lawyer who fought to defend the working-class, and a representative of the Communist Party of Brazil. He was murdered in front of his wife and children.

[56] Fonteles: the name by which Paulo Fonteles is known in the region, a lawyer and representative of the Communist Party of Brazil, also murdered.

[57] Expeditos: Expedito Ribeiro e Souza was a poet, farmworker, and president of the Union of Rural Workers in the south and southeast of Pará. He was the seventh person murdered at Rio Maria owing to his leadership and connection with the rural union movement. After his death, the *Comitê Rio Maria* (Rio Maria Committee) was founded, in 1991, by Father Ricardo Rezende. It is an international solidarity network that aims at ending the murders of farmworkers and union-members by gunmen under contract to the large landowners in the south of Pará (**http: //www.riomaria.org/por_o_que_e.htm**).The plural form of his name, Expeditos, indicates that he is the representative of a great number of rural leaders murdered in the region.

[58] Angelim: Third Cabano President, at 21 years of age, on the occasion of which the Movement entered its most radical phase. *Cabano*, in this context, refers to the Republic of Cabanos, proclaimed during the third phase of the Cabanagem, a revolution (1833-36) in the province of Grão Pará, which corresponds today to the states of Pará and Amazonas. The name comes from *cabana* (hut, cabin), a poor dwelling built on stakes. Initially an expression of the dissatisfaction of the large landowners and local politicians against the central power of Rio de Janeiro, it changed its meaning after a revolt of the mixed indigenous populations, living in terrible conditions.The fighting resulted in 40,000 victims (*Enciclopédia Delta Universal*).

[59] *sonho ou sorte*: dream or fate.

[60] The initials MBGC refer to the *Manos da Baixada de Grosso Calibre* (Large Calibre Brothers of the Baixada), a *favela* hip-hop group in Belém, capital of the State of Pará.

[61] Sister Teresa Cristina: a nun connected to the Pastoral Land Commission (CPT), which had an important role in the genealogy of the MST.

265

[62] Poema narrativo dentro da tradição do cordel, literatura popular em versos, típica do Nordeste brasileiro. Originalmente, as histórias eram muitas vezes notícias narradas em versos, disseminadas pelos cantadores nas feiras de diversos lugares. Esse poema registra o processo de expropriação e ocupação como forma de acesso à terra. A Fazenda São João dos Carneiros está relacionada com uma grande vitória da luta pela terra em 1989. O ocorrido foi em Quixadá, no estado nordestino do Ceará, uma região historicamente associada a grandes conflitos agrários e constantemente assolada por problemas de seca.

[63] É o camponês que, tendo a posse da terra, não é proprietário. Para ser proprietário é preciso ter a posse e o domínio, por meio de uma certidão de propriedade que no Brasil é denominada escritura (Fernandes, Bernardo Mançano. *Gênese e Desenvolvimento do MST*. São Paulo: MST,1998, p.56).

[64] INCRA – Instituto Nacional de Colonização e Reforma Agrária. Foi criado em 1970, no governo militar do general Emílio Garrastazu Médici, para ser o órgão executor da reforma agrária. Foi extinto em 1987, no primeiro governo da Nova República – José Sarney, e recriado em 1989, pelo mesmo governo. Hoje está vinculado ao Ministério do Desenvolvimento Agrário – MDA. Desde sua fundação tem executado projetos de colonização e de assentamentos rurais (Fernandes, Bernardo Mançano. *Pequeno Vocabulário da Luta pela Terra*. Inédito).

[65] UDR: União Democrática Ruralista. Fundada em 1985 por fazendeiros [...] do setor pecuarista e contrários à reforma agrária. No início atuou mais em Goiás, sul do Pará, Pontal do Paranapanema (São Paulo) e Triângulo Mineiro; depois espalhou-se por vários estados. Atuava de diversas formas, organizando os fazendeiros, articulando milícias armadas, pressionando o governo e os parlamentares. Teve destacada atuação contra a reforma agrária durante a Constituinte. Seu declínio começou no final de 1988, quando foi assassinado, no Acre, Chico Mendes, dirigente sindical e lutador a favor da reforma agrária. Sua morte foi executada por fazendeiros da UDR. A mesma acusação pesa contra eles no assasinato do padre Josimo Tavares, em 1986, em Imperatriz (Maranhão). Seu ocaso completou-se em 1989, quando lançou seu principal dirigente (Ronaldo Caiado) como candidato à Presidência da República, isolando-se dos demais partidos conservadores. A partir de 1990, encerrou suas atividades. Foi reaberta em 1996, mas somente na região do Pontal do Paranapanema, com uma insignificante participação de fazendeiros retrógrados (Fernandes, Bernardo Mançano e Stedile, João Pedro. *Brava gente: a trajetória do MST e a luta pela terra no Brasil*. São Paulo: Editora Fundação Perseu Abramo, 1999, nota 8, p. 93).

[66] Sarney (José Sarney): Presidente do Brasil (1985-1990).

[62] Narrative poem in the *cordel* tradition, popular narrative verse typical of the Brazilian northeast. Originally, the stories were often news narrated in verse and disseminated by the singers in local fairs. This poem tells of the process of expropriation and occupation as a form of access to the land. The São João dos Carneiros Farm is associated with a great victory in the land struggle in 1989, which took place in Quixadá, in the northeastern state of Ceará, a region historically associated with great agrarian conflicts and constantly devastated by drought.

[63] The rural worker, one who has possession of the land without being the owner. To be the owner, it is necessary to have possession and legal right, through a property deed that in Brazil is called an *escritura* (Fernandes, Bernardo Mançano. *Gênese e Desenvolvimento do MST*. São Paulo: MST, 1998, p.56).

[64] INCRA – National Institute of Colonization and Agrarian Reform. Created in 1970 during the military government of General Emílio Garrastazu Médici, to be the executive organ of agrarian reform. It was extinguished in 1987, during the first government of the New Republic – of José Sarney – and recreated in 1989, by the same administration. Today, it is a part of the Ministry of Agrarian Development (MDA). From its foundation, it has undertaken projects of rural colonization and settlement (Fernandes, Bernardo Mançano. *Pequeno Vocabulário da Luta pela Terra*. Unpublished).

[65] UDR: Rural Democratic Union. Founded in 1985 by farmers of the stockraising sector and those who were opposed to agrarian reform. In the beginning, the organization was more active in Goiás, the south of Pará, Pontal do Paranapanema (São Paulo) and the Triângulo Mineiro; later, it spread through several states. It acted in several ways: organizing farmers, forming armed militias, pressuring the government and congressmen. It had notable action against agrarian reform during the Constitutional Convention. Its decline began at the end of 1988, when Chico Mendes, union leader and fighter for agrarian reform, was murdered in Acre, his death being the work of UDR farmers. The same accusation has been made against them for the death of Father Josimo Tavares, in 1986, in Imperatriz, Maranhão. The UDR's decline was complete in 1989, when its main leader, Ronaldo Caiado, became a candidate for the presidency and the party was isolated from the other conservative parties. It terminated its activities in 1990, recommenced in 1996, but only in the region of the Pontal do Paranapanema, with an insignificant number of reactionary farmers (Fernandes, Bernardo Mançano and Stedile, João Pedro. *Brava gente: a trajetória do MST e a luta pela terra no Brasil*. São Paulo: Editora Fundação Perseu Abramo, 1999, p. 93, n. 8).

[66] Sarney (José Sarney): President of Brazil (1985-1990).

[67] Paes (Antônio Paes de Almeida) Presidente da Câmara dos Deputados que exerceu a Presidência da República, por motivo de viagem do Presidente da República.

[68] Ver nota 39.

[69] Pontal: Pontal do Paranapanema.

[70] Paranapanema, Pontal do.

[71] Floriô: jeito caipira de dizer floresceu, deu flor. O caipira é o habitante do campo ou da roça, caracterizado por um modo peculiar de falar, resultante de uma cultura predominantemente oral e da permanência de arcaismos.

[67] Paes (Antônio Paes de Almeida): President of the Chamber of Deputies, who served as acting President of the Republic when the President was abroad.

[68] For open truck or *pau-de-arara* see note 39.

[69] *Pontal*: Pontal do Paranapanema

[70] *Paranapanema*, Pontal do

[71] *Floriô*: country-like or *caipira* way of saying blossoming. The *caipira* is one who lives in the rural areas and has a peculiar way of talking as the result of a predominantly oral culture and the permanence of archaisms.

NOTAS SOBRE OS AUTORES

INTELECTUAIS E ARTISTAS BRASILEIROS

Frei Betto: Frade dominicano e escritor, é figura de proa nas comunidades eclesiais de base que anteciparam a Teologia da Libertação. Militante contra a ditadura militar, esteve muitos anos preso. Assessor de diversos movimentos sociais brasileiros dentre os quais a Pastoral Operária e a Central de Movimentos Populares. Consultor do MST. Ex-assessor do Presidente Lula. Tem 45 livros publicados, dentre os quais *O que é comunidade eclesial de base* (várias edições); *Fidel e a religião* (1.300.00 exemplares vendidos só em Cuba); *Das catacumbas*, cartas da prisão, escritas quando ele estava encarcerado pela ditadura militar (1969-1973), traduzido em 9 idiomas; seu livro em parceria com Emir Sader ressalta a civilização e a barbárie na virada do século (publicado pela Boitempo).

Haroldo de Campos: Nasceu em 1929 e faleceu em 2003, São Paulo, formou-se em Direito e doutorou-se em literatura pela Universidade de São Paulo. Um dos fundadores do Movimento Concretista em São Paulo na década de 50. É também ensaísta, tradutor, e teórico internacionalmente conhecido. Uma das figuras mais ativas nos movimentos mundiais de poesia experimental e visual por mais de três décadas. Doutor Honorário pela Universidade de Montréal; várias outras premiações, dentre as quais a Lumière UNUPADEC (Roma, 1998), da Fundação Octavio Paz (México, 1999), o Prêmio Roger Caillois (França, 1999) e o Prêmio Jabuti (Brasil, 1991, 92, 93, 94, 99). Professor Emérito de Semiótica da PUC de São Paulo, Professor Visitante junto às Universidades deYale (1978) e do Texas em Austin (1971 e 1981). Tournées de magistério e palestras na Alemanha, Espanha, França, Itália, Canadá e outros países. Sua carreira inclui em torno de 12 livros de poesia, 18 de estudos literários, 14 de transcriações, bem como projetos para o teatro, cinema e artes plásticas.

Antonio Candido: Escritor, sociólogo. Renomado crítico literário e cultural. Destacada contribuição para a historiagrafia literária brasileira, notadamente através de sua *Formação da Literatura Brasileira*. Inspirou um importante segmento da crítica social no Brasil. Suas atividades incluíram a cátedra de Teoria Literária e de Literatura Comparada na Universidade de São Paulo, o magistério como Professor Associado da Universidade de Paris e como Visitante na Universidade de Yale.

NOTES ON CONTRIBUTORS

BRAZILIAN INTELLECTUALS AND ARTISTS

Frei Betto: Dominican friar and writer; leading name in the Base Ecclesial Communities that anticipated Liberation Theology. A militant against dictatorship, he was for several years a political detainee. Assessor to several social movements in Brazil, amongst which the Pastoral of the Workers and the Central Popular Movements. Consultant to the MST. He is a former advisor to President Lula. He has published forty five books, amongst which *O que é comunidade eclesial de base/What are Base Ecclesial Communities* (reprinted many times); *Fidel e a religião/Fidel and Religion* (1,300,000 volumes sold only in Cuba); *Das catacumbas/From the Catacombs,* letters which he wrote in prison during the military dictatorship (1969-1973), translated into nine languages; his co-authored book with Emir Sader foregrounds civilization and barbarism at the turn of the century (published by Boitempo).

Haroldo de Campos: Born 1929, died in 2003, in São Paulo; graduated in law and later completed a doctorate in literature from the Universidade de São Paulo. One of the founders of the movement of Concrete Poetry in São Paulo in the 1950s. He is also an internationally known essayist, translator, and theorist. He was one of the most active figures in world movements of experimental and visual poetry for over three decades. He was awarded an honorary doctorate from the University of Montréal and several important prizes, among which are the Lumière UNUPADEC (Rome, 1998), the Octavio Paz Foundation prize (Mexico, 1999), the Roger Caillois prize (France, 1999), the Jabuti prize five times (Brazil, 1991, 92, 93, 94, 99). Emeritus professor of semiotics at the Catholic University of São Paulo, visiting professorships at Yale University (1978) and the University of Texas at Austin (1791 e 1981). Teaching and lecture tours in Germany, Spain, France, Italy, Canada, and others. His career includes some twelve books of poetry, eighteen of literary studies, fourteen of 'transcreations', as well as projects for the theatre, cinema, and plastic arts.

Antonio Candido: A writer, sociologist and cultural theorist. A renowned literary critic and foremost historian of Brazilian Literature, particularly for his *Formation of Brazilian Literature*. He inspired an important strain of socio-criticism in Brazil. Formerly a Professor of Literary Theory and Comparative Literature at the University of São Paulo, Associate Professor of the University of Paris and Visiting Professor at the University of Yale.

Paulo Freire: Educador de adultos brasileiro, autor da célebre *Pedagogia do oprimido*, dentre outras contribuições para uma educação crítica. Exilado durante a ditadura militar, ele deu continuidade a sua pedagogia fora do Brasil, em especial no Chile. Ele exerceu o magistério também na Universidade de Harvard. De volta ao Brasil, ele assumiu a Secreataria da Educação de São Paulo. Morreu em 2 de maio de 1997.

Chico Buarque de Hollanda: Compositor, intérprete e escritor. Carreira de sucesso ininterrupto há mais de três décadas. Expoente da linha crítica da música popular brasileira. Filho do historiador e sociólogo Francisco Buarque de Hollanda, ele nasceu no Rio em 1944 e iniciou sua carreira na década de 60. Foi escolhido o Músico do Século no Brasil pela revista *Isto É*. Durante a ditadura militar, ele ficou em exílio voluntário por dois anos na Itália. Como romancista, ele é mais conhecido por *Fazenda Modelo – Novela Pecuária, Estorvo* e *Benjamim*. Suas peças de teatro mais conhecidas são *Roda Viva, Calabar, Gota D'água* e *Ópera do Malandro*.

CANTADORES/COMPOSITORES DO MST

Ademar Bogo: Militante do MST, ex-seminarista, que atua no Setor de Formação do Movimento. Sistematiza em livros e Cadernos de Formação diversos aspectos da cultura do Movimento, como a mística, a educação e a música. É também conhecido como poeta e pela autoria de músicas do Movimento, notadamente o 'Hino do MST'.

Aracy Cachoeira (Aracy Maria dos Santos): Nasceu em em 1953 no estado de Minas Gerais, em Água Formosa (Vale do Mucuri), onde se encontra a Cachoeira da Beleza que dá origem ao seu cognome. Herdou de seu pai a arte da poesia e o dom da narrativa caipira, ligados à infância no meio rural. Preocupada com a questão indígena no Brasil, em 1995 criou a personagem *Jacira Maxacali*, uma índia que faz protestos em defesa dos índios e da natureza. A escrita passou a ser a arma de combate de Aracy Cachoeira na esperança de transformação de uma nova sociedade.

Zé Pinto: Nasceu em Minas Gerais. Sua família emigrou, quando ele era criança, para Rondônia, no norte do Brasil. Seu trabalho artístico em acampamentos e assentamentos se iniciou aos 13 anos. Um dos coordenadores do primeiro CD do MST, *Arte em Movimento,* no qual assina nove canções. Participou também do *Primeiro Festival Nacional de Canções da Reforma Agrária,* do qual originou-se o segundo CD do MST. Produtor do CD de músicas infantis do MST para o qual contribui com 11 canções. *Uma Prosa Sobre Nós* é seu CD individual. Autor de livros de poesia, como *Poesia que brota da luta*. Fez trabalhos de divulgação da cultura do MST, em Portugal e na Alemanha, Bélgica e Espanha.

Paulo Freire: Brazilian educator of adults, the author of the celebrated *Pedagogia do oprimido/Pedagogy of the Oppressed*, amongst other contributions towards the development of a critical dimension in education. Exiled during the military dictatorship, he continued his pedagogy outside Brazil, particularly in Chile. He also taught at Harvard University. Back in Brazil, he became Minister of Education for São Paulo. He died on 2 May 1997.

Chico Buarque de Hollanda: Composer, singer and writer. Unbroken career of success for over three decades. An exponent of the politically-committed strain of Brazilian Popular Music. The son of the historian and sociologist Francisco Buarque de Hollanda, he was born in 1944 in Rio and started his career in the 1960s. He was chosen Brazil's Musician of the Century in a competition sponsored by *Isto É*, a prominent weekly news magazine. During the military dictatorship, he went into a self-imposed exile for two years in Italy. As a novelist, he is better known for *Fazenda Modelo – Novela Pecuária/Model Farm – A Cattle-Raising Story, Estorvo/Turbulence* and *Benjamim*. His most famous plays are *Roda Viva, Calabar, Gota D'água/Last Straw*, and *Ópera do Malandro/The Trickster's Opera*.

CANTADORES/POET-SINGERS OF THE MST

Ademar Bogo: Ex-seminarian; a militant in the MST who works in the Sector of Training of the Movement; he has systematized in books and booklets diverse aspects of the Movement's culture, such as the *Mística*, education, and music. He is also known as a poet and composer of the Movement's music, notably the 'MST Anthem'.

Aracy Cachoeira (Aracy Maria dos Santos): Born in 1953 in the state of Minas Gerais, in Água Formosa (Valley of the Mucuri River), where the Cachoeira da Beleza/Waterfall of Beauty gives rise to her name. She inherited from her father the art of poetry and the gift for the *caipira* narrative, associated with her childhood in the rural area. Her concern with the plight of the natives in Brazil led to the creation of the character *Jacira Maxacali*, an Indian who claims the rights of the natives and the preservation of nature. Writing is for Aracy Cachoeira a weapon to transform society.

Zé Pinto: Born in the state of Minas Gerais. When he was a child, his family migrated to Rondônia, in the north of Brazil. He started his artistic work in encampments and settlements at the age of thirteen. One of the producers of the first CD of the MST, *Arte em Movimento/Art in Movement,* to which he also contributes with nine songs. He also joined the *Primeiro Festival Nacional de Canções da Reforma Agrária/First Agrarian Reform Festival,* which gave rise to the second CD. He produced the CD of children's songs of the MST, to which he also contributed with eleven songs. *Uma Prosa Sobre Nós/A Chat About Us* is his individual CD. Author of poetry books as *Poesia que brota da luta/Poetry that Sprouts from the Struggle*. He disseminated the MST culture in Portugal, Germany, Belgium and Spain.

273

Pedro Tierra (Hamilton Pereira): Militante informal do MST; participou da Comissão Pastoral da Terra (CPT) com João Pedro Stedile. Utiliza o pseudônimo de Pedro Tierra em suas poesias. Define-se como um companheiro dos sem-terra pela identidade de objetivos políticos e por ser filho de retirantes. Começou a escrever versos enquanto preso político durante a ditadura militar. Libertado, contribuiu para fundar Sindicatos de Trabalhadores Rurais em alguns estados do país. Longa trajetória de luta política. Foi secretário agrário do Diretório Nacional do PT. Convidado em 1997 para dirigir a Secretaria de Cultura de Brasília. Diretor da Fundação Perseu Abramo. Oito livros publicados. *Dies Irae* aborda a violência no Brasil, em particular no campo.

Charles Trocate: Nasceu em Castanhal, nordeste do Pará em 1977. Em 1983 sua família migrou para o sul do estado. Mora atualmente em Marabá. Entrou para o MST em 1993, aos 15 anos de idade, quando participou de um curso para jovens filhos de acampados. Em 1995 começou a escrever seus primeiros poemas. Sua literatura engajada nasceu nos acampamentos e assentamentos e reivindica a reforma agrária e mais dignidade humana.

CRIANÇAS E JOVENS SEM-TERRA

Francisco Macilom Nunes Aquino: 17 anos, Magistério PB, Assentamento Safra, Santa Maria da Boa Vista, estado de Pernambuco.

Fábio Junior de Lima: 10 anos, estudante da Escola Municipal Ouro Verde, Assentamento Ouro Verde, em Lagoa Grande, estado de Pernambuco.

Rosane de Souza: 14 anos, sétima série, Escola Estadual de Primeiro Grau 25 de Maio, Assentamento Chico Mendes, Fraiburgo, estado de Santa Catarina.

Pedro Tierra (Hamilton Pereira): Informal militant of the MST; he participated in the *Pastoral Land Commission* (CPT) with João Pedro Stedile. Pseudonym of Pedro Tierra in his poetry. He defines himself as a comrade of the *sem-terra* by virtue of the shared political identity and as the son of migrants. He started writing verses when a political prisoner of the military dictatorship. When free, he contributed for the founding of unions of rural workers in many Brazilian states. A lifetime trajectory of political struggle. Agrarian secretary to the National Directorate of the PT/Workers's Party. Invited in 1997 to direct the Department of Culture of Brasília. Director of the Perseu Abramo Foundation. Eight published books. *Dies Irae* focuses on violence in Brazil, particularly in the rural areas.

Charles Trocate: He was born in 1977 in Castanhal, in the north-east of the state of Pará (Amazon region). In 1983 his family migrated to the south of Pará. He now lives in Marabá. He joined the MST in 1993, at the age of fifteen, when he took a course for the children in the encampments. In 1995 he started writing poetry. His engaged literature, born out of the encampments and settlements, demands agrarian reform and dignity for men.

LANDLESS CHILDREN AND YOUTHS
Francisco Macilom Nunes Aquino: seventeen years old, Magistério PB, Safra Settlement, Santa Maria da Boa Vista, Pernambuco.
Fábio Junior de Lima: ten years old, a student at the Ouro Verde Municipal School, in the Ouro Verde Settlement, in Lagoa Grande, Pernambuco.

Rosane de Souza: Landless child, fourteen years old, seventh grade, 25 de Maio State School, Chico Mendes Settlement, Fraiburgo, Santa Catarina.

ORGANIZADORES

Else R. P. Vieira: Professora Titular de Estudos Brasileiros e Comparados Latino-Americanos e Coordenadora de Estudos Lusófonos do Queen Mary, University of London. Ex-pesquisadora visitante senior em Estudos Latino-Americanos na Universidade de Nottingham; ex-professora visitante de Estudos Brasileiros da Universidade de Oxford (Centre for Brazilian Studies) e da Universidade Federal de Juiz de Fora. *Visiting Fellow in Brazilian Studies*, Universidade de Oxford (*Centre for Brazilian Studies*). Outras filiações: Universidade de Oxford, Wadham College; Universidade de Harvard, David Rockefeller Center for Latin American Studies; Universidade da Califórnia em Berkeley, Center for Latin American Studies; UMIST. Carreira anterior no Brasil; Coordenadora do Programa de Pós-Graduação em Literatura Comparada e Lingüística Aplicada da UFMG. Coordenadora do Projeto e editora do banco de dados *As Imagens e as Vozes da Despossessão: A Luta pela Terra e a Cultura Emergente do MST* (*Movimento dos Trabalhadores Rurais Sem-Terra do Brasil)* (**www.landless-voices.org**). Coordenadora dos Projetos *Screening Exclusion: The Boom of Brazilian and Argentine Documentary Film-Making 2001-2005; Escritores Brasileiros no Exterior* e *The Feminization of Brazilian Diaspora Literature.* Cocoordenadora do Projeto de Impacto 'Gender and Education in Brazil's Rural Areas (**http://landless-voices2.org/**). Vários livros, capítulos de livros e artigos publicados internacionalmente e no Brasil, dentre os quais o best-seller *City of God in Several Voices: Brazilian Social Cinema as Action* (Nottingham: Critical, Cultural and Communications Press , 2005).

Bernard McGuirk: Professor Emérito de Literaturas das Línguas Românicas e Teoria Literária, ex-diretor do Curso de Pós-Graduação em Teorias Críticas e Estudos Culturais, recebedor da premiação Lord Dearing Inaugural Award for Distinction in Learning and Teaching, Universidade de Nottingham. De 1996 a 1998 atuou como Presidente da Associação de Hispanistas da Grã-Bretanha e da Irlanda; em 2002 foi agraciado com a Comanda da Ordem do Mérito, Portugal, sendo também Presidente do Consórcio Internacional para o Estudo de Sociedades Pós-Conflito e Membro Honorário do Institute of Modern Languages Research, Universidade de Londres. Lecionou em diversas universidades na Europa, América Latina e Estados Unidos, incluindo a École Normale Supérieure em Paris e a Universidade de Oxford, na qualidade de Laming Research Fellow do Queen's College. Suas últimas monografias são *Erasing Fernando Pessoa* (2017), *Latin American Literature and Post-structuralism* (2018), and *Is there a Latin American Text in this Class?* (2020).

EDITORS

Else R. P. Vieira: Professor of Brazilian and Comparative Latin American Studies and Chair of Lusophone Studies at Queen Mary, University of London. Previously Visiting Senior Research Fellow in Latin American Studies at the University of Nottingham; Visiting Fellow in Brazilian Studies at the University of Oxford (Centre for Brazilian Studies); Visiting Professor at the Federal University of Juiz de Fora, Brazil. Other affiliations include: University of Oxford, Wadham College; University of Harvard, David Rockefeller Center for Latin American Studies; University of California at Berkeley, Center for Latin American Studies; UMIST. Her previous career in Brazil includes the Directorship of Postgraduate Studies in Comparative Literature and Applied Linguistics at UFMG. Director of the project and Academic Editor of the database *The Sights and Images of Dispossession: The Fight for the Land and the Emerging Culture of the MST* (www.landless-voices.org). Director of the projects *Screening Exclusion: The Boom of Brazilian and Argentine Documentary Film-Making 2001-2005*; *Brazilian Writers Abroad*; *The Feminization of Brazilian Diaspora Literature*. Co-Director of the Impact Project *Gender and Education in Brazil's Rural Areas* (**http://landless-voices2.org/**). She has published several books, chapters, and articles, internationally and in Brazil, amongst which the best-seller *City of God in Several Voices: Brazilian Social Cinema as Action* (Nottingham: Critical, Cultural and Communications Press , 2005).

Bernard McGuirk: Emeritus Professor of Romance Literatures and Literary Theory, formerly Director of the Postgraduate School of Critical Theory and Cultural Studies, recipient of the Inaugural Lord Dearing Award for Distinction in Learning and Teaching, University of Nottingham. From 1996 to 1998 President of the Association of Hispanists of Great Britain and Ireland, in 2002 he was created Commander of the Order of Merit, Portugal, is President of the International Consortium for the Study of Post-Conflict Societies and Honorary Fellow of the Institute of Modern Languages Research, University of London. He has taught at universities throughout Europe, Latin America and the United States, including the École Normale Supérieure in Paris and at the University of Oxford where he was Laming Research Fellow of The Queen's College. His latest monographs are *Erasing Fernando Pessoa* (2017), *Latin American Literature and Post-structuralism* (2018), and *Is there a Latin American Text in this Class?* (2020).

Made in the USA
Las Vegas, NV
22 May 2024

90228938R00229